CIVIL WAR

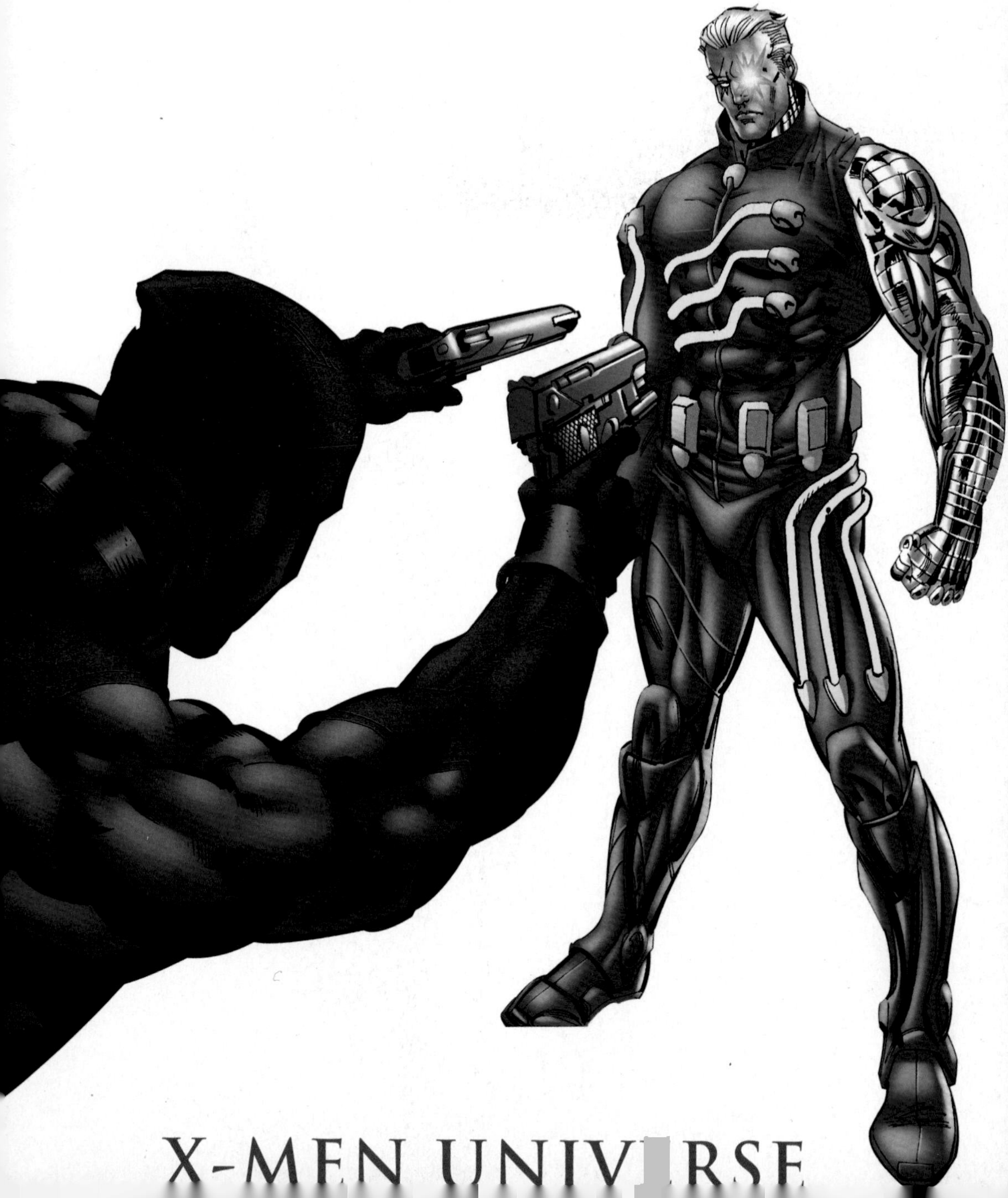

X-MEN UNIVERSE

A

MARVEL COMICS

PRESENTATION

CIVIL
X-

X-FACTOR
#8-9

WRITER
PETER DAVID

ART
DENNIS CALERO

COLOR ART
JOSE VILLARRUBIA

LETTERER
VIRTUAL CALLIGRAPHY'S
CORY PETIT

COVER ART
RYAN SOOK
WITH JOSE VILLARRUBIA

ASSISTANT EDITORS
MOLLY LAZER &
AUBREY SITTERSON

EDITOR
ANDY SCHMIDT

CABLE & DEADPOOL
#30-32

WRITER
FABIAN NICIEZA

PENCILER
STAZ JOHNSON

INKERS
KLAUS JANSON
WITH JOHN STANISCI

COLORIST
GOTHAM

LETTERER
DAVE SHARPE

COVER ART
AMANDA CONNER

EDITOR
NICOLE BOOSE

COLLECTION EDITOR
JENNIFER GRÜNWALD

ASSISTANT EDITORS
MICHAEL SHORT &
CORY LEVINE

ASSOCIATE EDITOR
MARK D. BEAZLEY

SENIOR EDITOR,
SPECIAL PROJECTS
JEFF YOUNGQUIST

SENIOR VICE PRESIDENT
OF SALES
DAVID GABRIEL

PRODUCTION
JERRY KALINOWSKI

BOOK DESIGNER
DAYLE CHESLER

VICE PRESIDENT OF CREATIVE
TOM MARVELLI

EDITOR IN CHIEF
JOE QUESADA

PUBLISHER
DAN BUCKLEY

WAR
MEN UNIVERSE

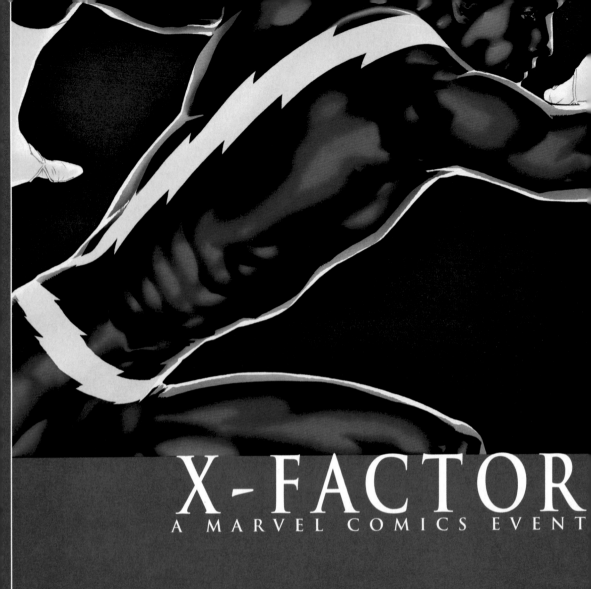

X-FACTOR

A MARVEL COMICS EVENT

CIVIL
WAR

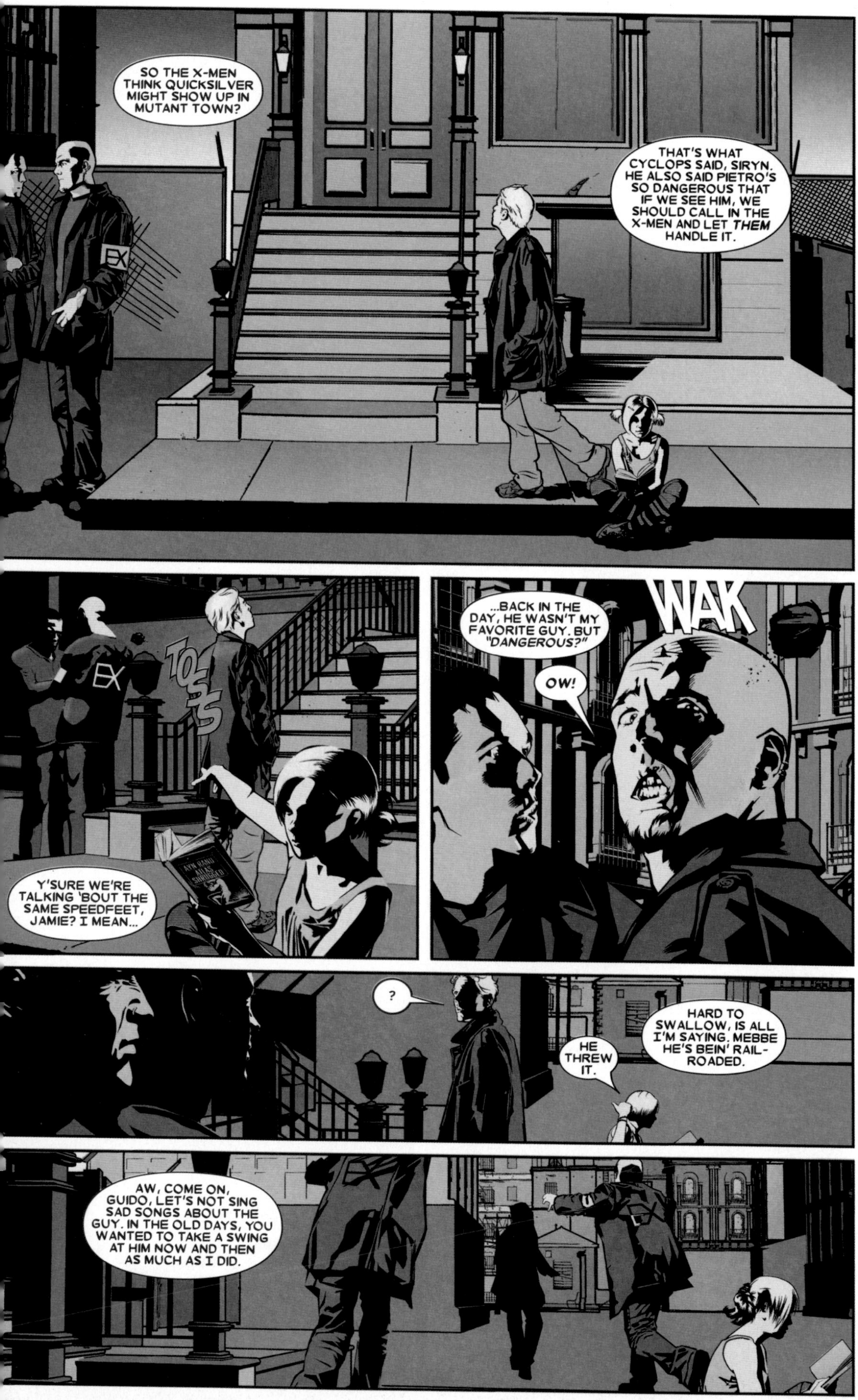
SO THE X-MEN THINK QUICKSILVER MIGHT SHOW UP IN MUTANT TOWN?
THAT'S WHAT CYCLOPS SAID, SIRYN. HE ALSO SAID PIETRO'S SO DANGEROUS THAT IF WE SEE HIM, WE SHOULD CALL IN THE X-MEN AND LET THEM HANDLE IT.
TOSS
Y'SURE WE'RE TALKING 'BOUT THE SAME SPEEDFEET, JAMIE? I MEAN...
...BACK IN THE DAY, HE WASN'T MY FAVORITE GUY. BUT "DANGEROUS?"
WAK
OW!
?
HE THREW IT.
HARD TO SWALLOW, IS ALL I'M SAYING. MEBBE HE'S BEIN' RAIL-ROADED.
AW, COME ON, GUIDO, LET'S NOT SING SAD SONGS ABOUT THE GUY. IN THE OLD DAYS, YOU WANTED TO TAKE A SWING AT HIM NOW AND THEN AS MUCH AS I DID.

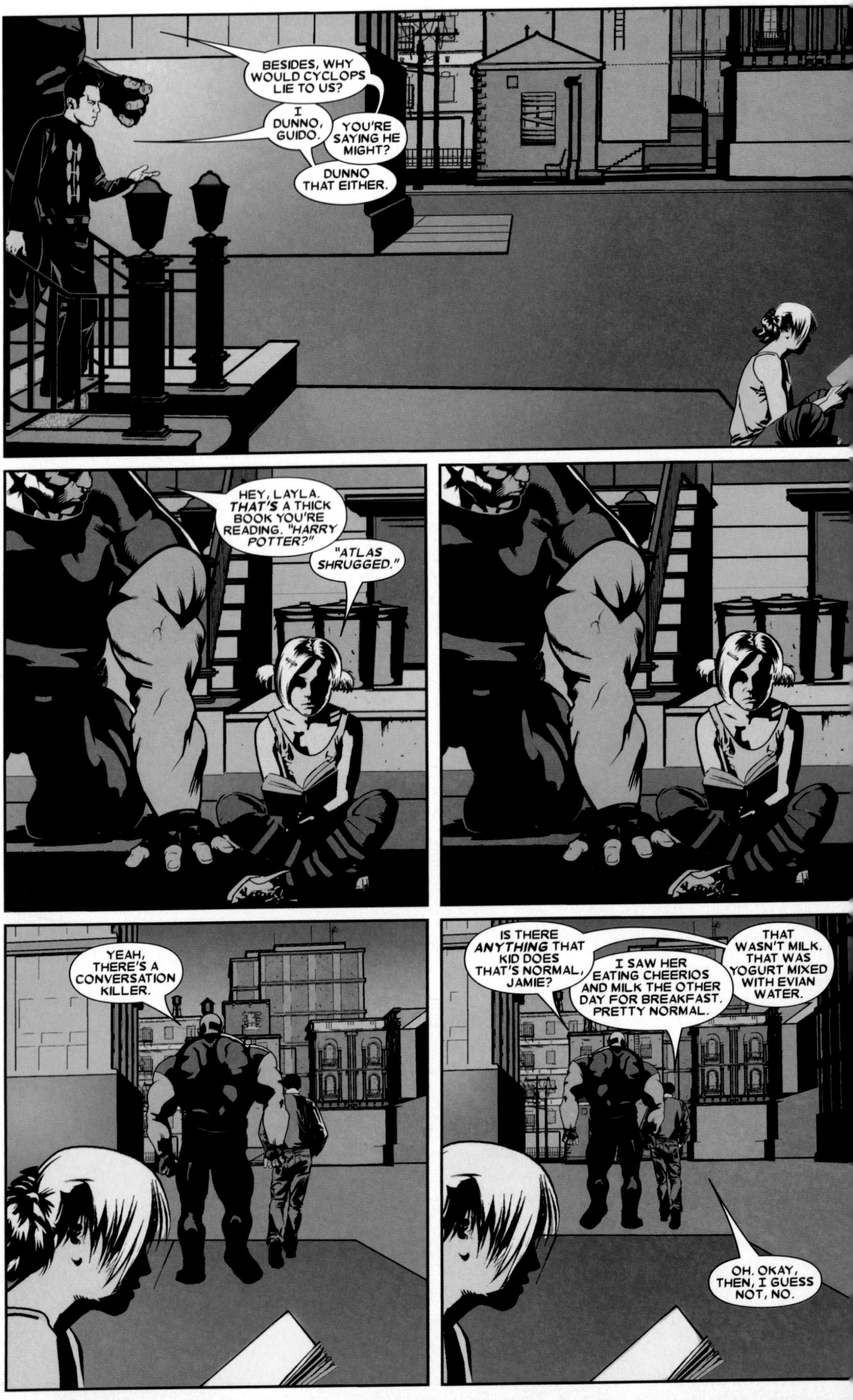
BESIDES, WHY WOULD CYCLOPS LIE TO US?
I DUNNO, GUIDO.
YOU'RE SAYING HE MIGHT?
DUNNO THAT EITHER.
HEY, LAYLA. *THAT'S* A THICK BOOK YOU'RE READING. "HARRY POTTER?"
"ATLAS SHRUGGED."
YEAH, THERE'S A CONVERSATION KILLER.
IS THERE *ANYTHING* THAT KID DOES THAT'S NORMAL, JAMIE?
I SAW HER EATING CHEERIOS AND MILK THE OTHER DAY FOR BREAKFAST. PRETTY NORMAL.
THAT WASN'T MILK. THAT WAS YOGURT MIXED WITH EVIAN WATER.
OH. OKAY, THEN, I GUESS NOT, NO.

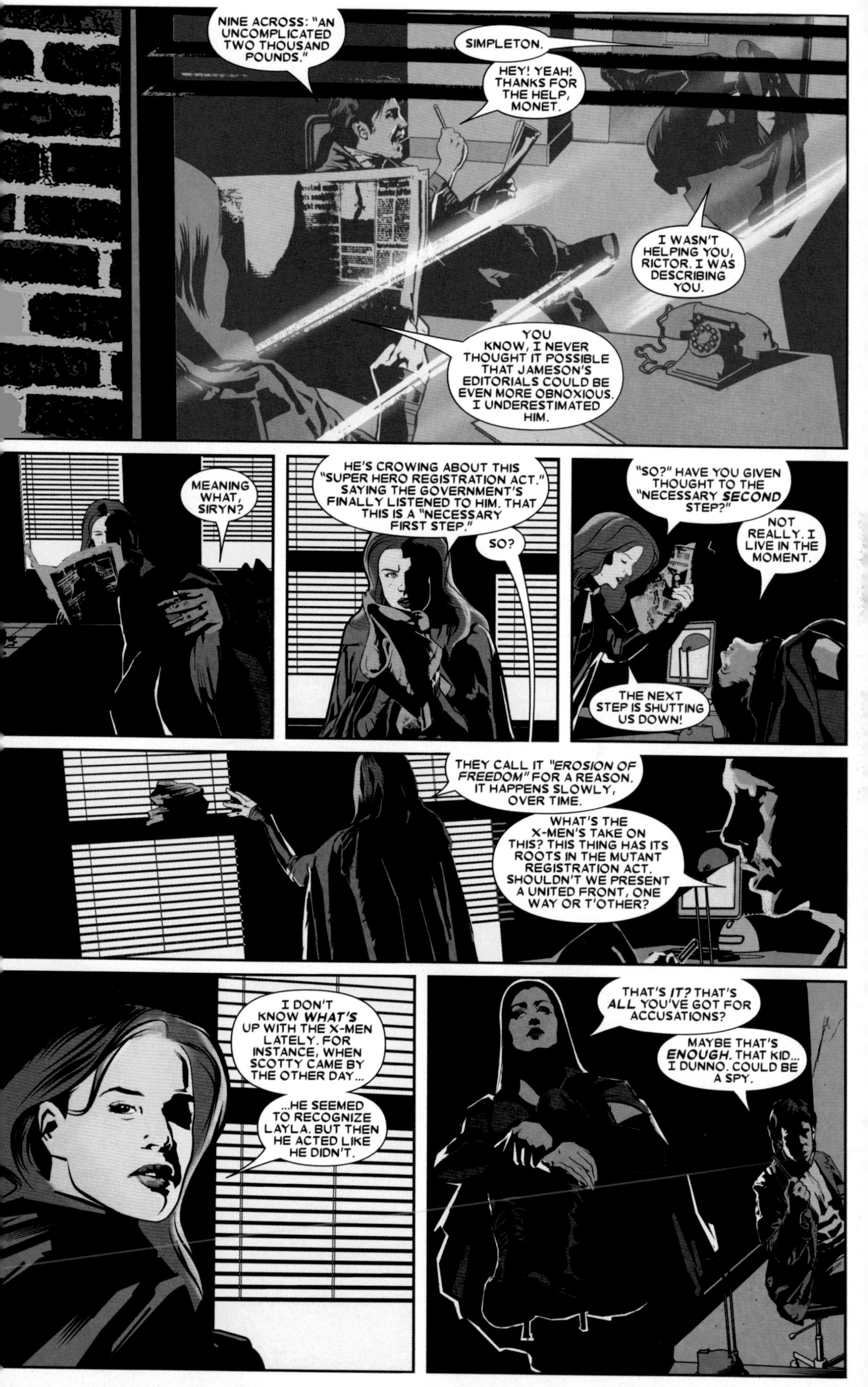
NINE ACROSS: "AN UNCOMPLICATED TWO THOUSAND POUNDS."
SIMPLETON.
HEY! YEAH! THANKS FOR THE HELP, MONET.
I WASN'T HELPING YOU, RICTOR. I WAS DESCRIBING YOU.
YOU KNOW, I NEVER THOUGHT IT POSSIBLE THAT JAMESON'S EDITORIALS COULD BE EVEN MORE OBNOXIOUS. I UNDERESTIMATED HIM.
MEANING WHAT, SIRYN?
HE'S CROWING ABOUT THIS "SUPER HERO REGISTRATION ACT." SAYING THE GOVERNMENT'S FINALLY LISTENED TO HIM. THAT THIS IS A "NECESSARY FIRST STEP."
SO?
"SO?" HAVE YOU GIVEN THOUGHT TO THE "NECESSARY *SECOND* STEP?"
NOT REALLY. I LIVE IN THE MOMENT.
THE NEXT STEP IS SHUTTING US DOWN!
THEY CALL IT *"EROSION OF FREEDOM"* FOR A REASON. IT HAPPENS SLOWLY, OVER TIME.
WHAT'S THE X-MEN'S TAKE ON THIS? THIS THING HAS ITS ROOTS IN THE MUTANT REGISTRATION ACT. SHOULDN'T WE PRESENT A UNITED FRONT, ONE WAY OR T'OTHER?
I DON'T KNOW ***WHAT'S*** UP WITH THE X-MEN LATELY. FOR INSTANCE, WHEN SCOTTY CAME BY THE OTHER DAY...
...HE SEEMED TO RECOGNIZE LAYLA. BUT THEN HE ACTED LIKE HE DIDN'T.
THAT'S *IT?* THAT'S ***ALL*** YOU'VE GOT FOR ACCUSATIONS?
MAYBE THAT'S ***ENOUGH.*** THAT KID... I DUNNO. COULD BE A SPY.

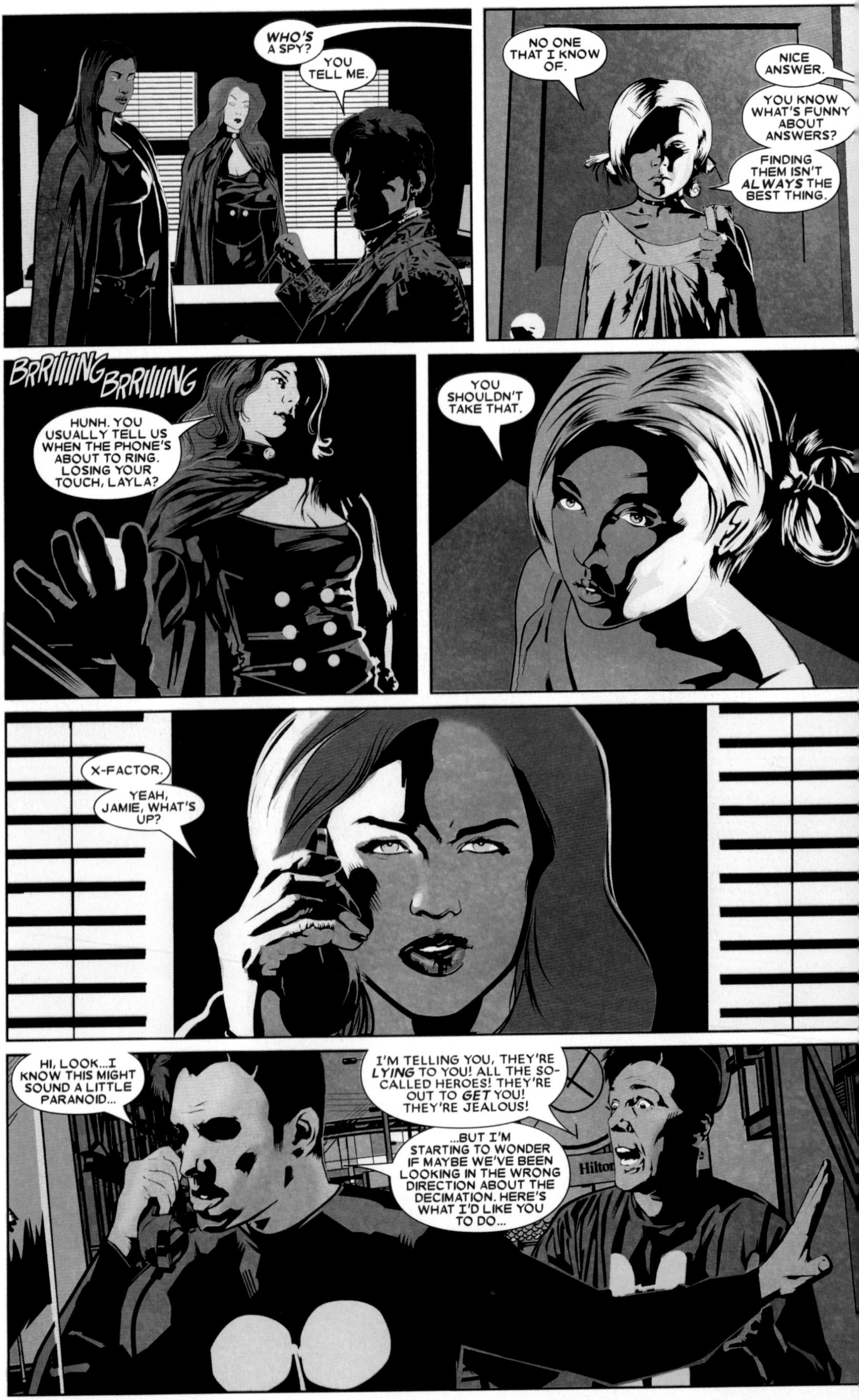
WHO'S A SPY?
YOU TELL ME.
NO ONE THAT I KNOW OF.
NICE ANSWER.
YOU KNOW WHAT'S FUNNY ABOUT ANSWERS?
FINDING THEM ISN'T ALWAYS THE BEST THING.
BRRIIIIING BRRIIIIING
HUNH. YOU USUALLY TELL US WHEN THE PHONE'S ABOUT TO RING. LOSING YOUR TOUCH, LAYLA?
YOU SHOULDN'T TAKE THAT.
X-FACTOR.
YEAH, JAMIE, WHAT'S UP?
HI, LOOK...I KNOW THIS MIGHT SOUND A LITTLE PARANOID...
I'M TELLING YOU, THEY'RE LYING TO YOU! ALL THE SO-CALLED HEROES! THEY'RE OUT TO GET YOU! THEY'RE JEALOUS!
...BUT I'M STARTING TO WONDER IF MAYBE WE'VE BEEN LOOKING IN THE WRONG DIRECTION ABOUT THE DECIMATION. HERE'S WHAT I'D LIKE YOU TO DO...

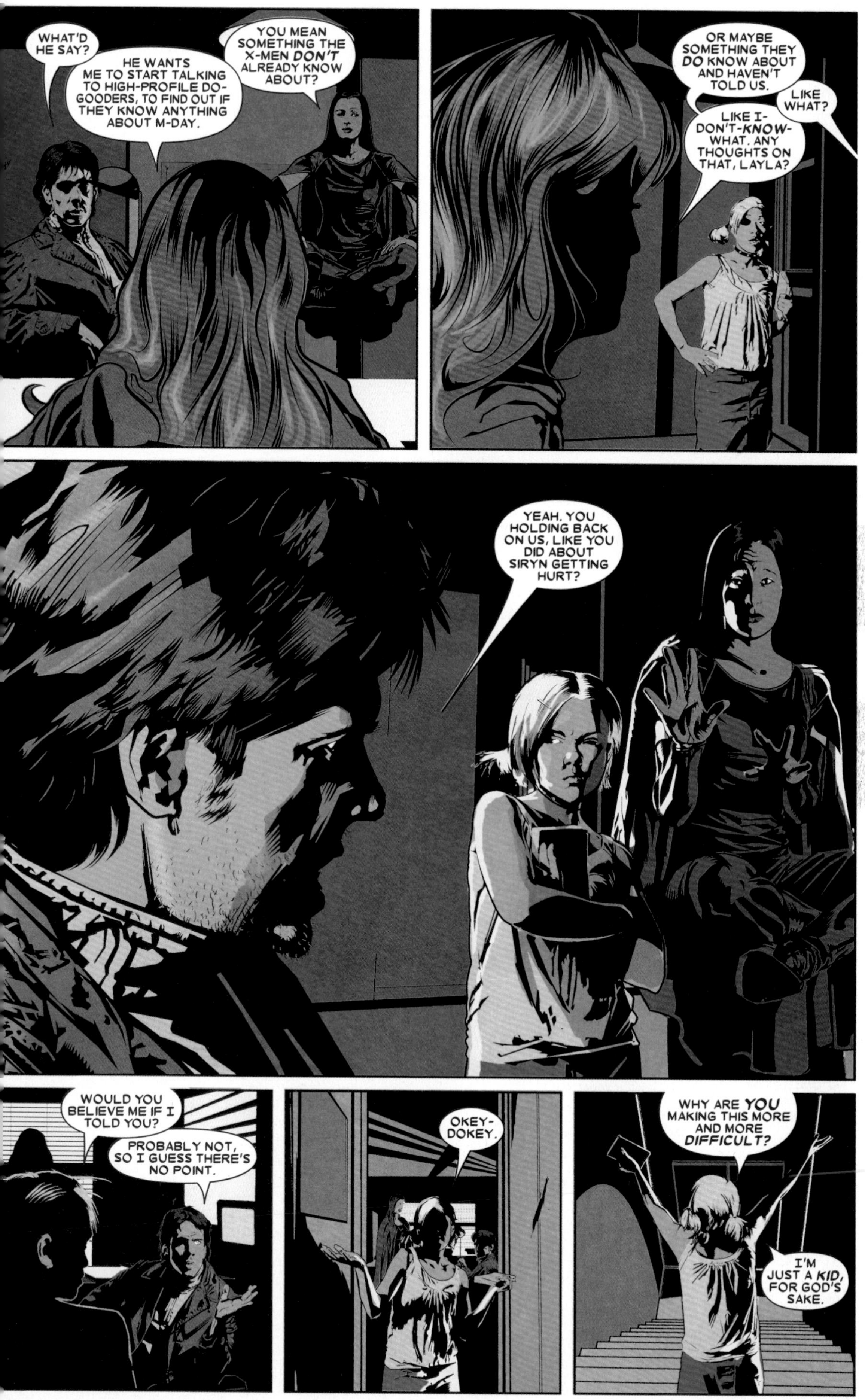
WHAT'D HE SAY?
HE WANTS ME TO START TALKING TO HIGH-PROFILE DO-GOODERS, TO FIND OUT IF THEY KNOW ANYTHING ABOUT M-DAY.
YOU MEAN SOMETHING THE X-MEN *DON'T* ALREADY KNOW ABOUT?
OR MAYBE SOMETHING THEY *DO* KNOW ABOUT AND HAVEN'T TOLD US.
LIKE WHAT?
LIKE I-DON'T-*KNOW*-WHAT. ANY THOUGHTS ON THAT, LAYLA?
YEAH. YOU HOLDING BACK ON US, LIKE YOU DID ABOUT SIRYN GETTING HURT?
WOULD YOU BELIEVE ME IF I TOLD YOU?
PROBABLY NOT, SO I GUESS THERE'S NO POINT.
OKEY-DOKEY.
WHY ARE *YOU* MAKING THIS MORE AND MORE *DIFFICULT*?
I'M JUST A *KID*, FOR GOD'S SAKE.

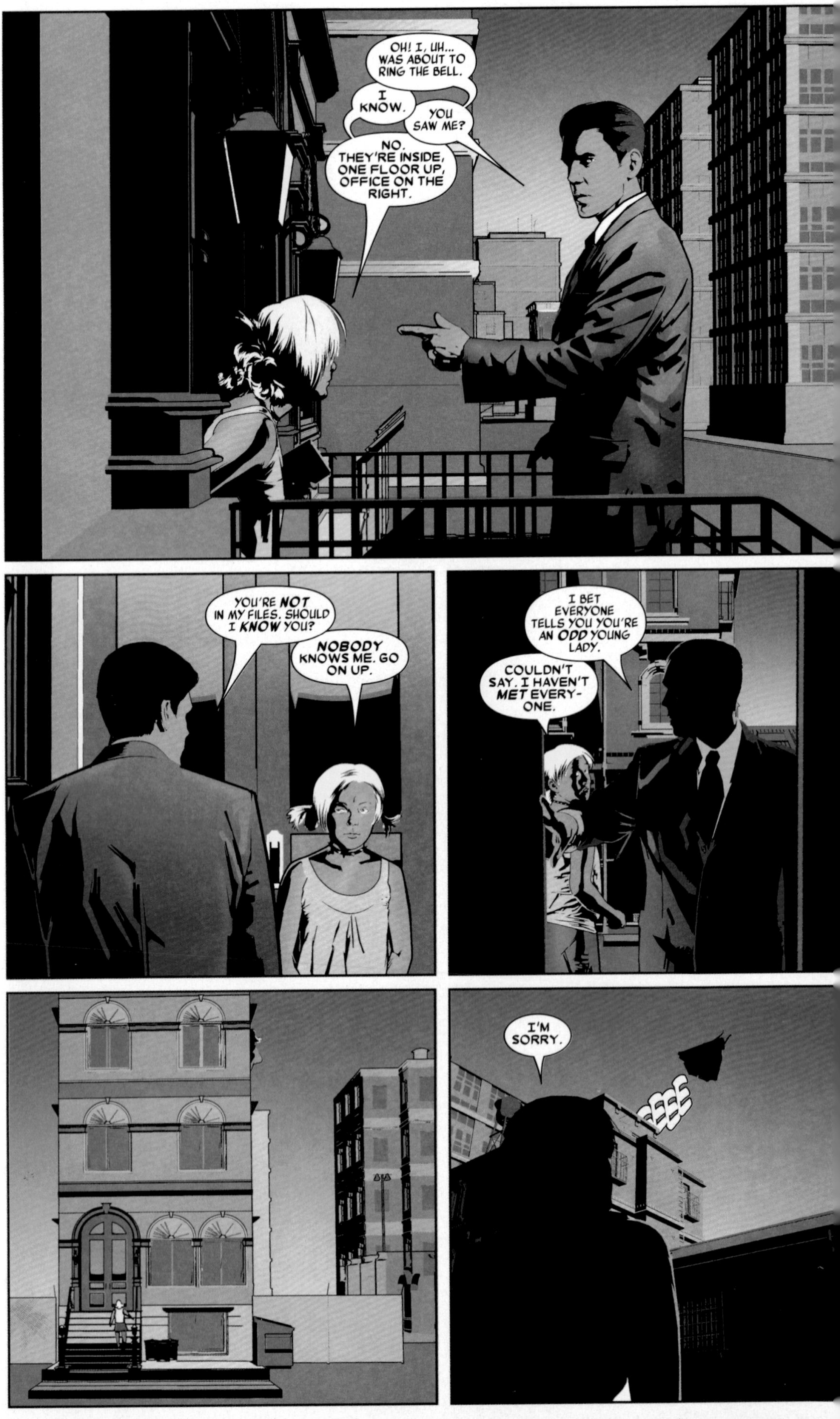
OH! I, UH... WAS ABOUT TO RING THE BELL.
I KNOW.
YOU SAW ME?
NO. THEY'RE INSIDE, ONE FLOOR UP, OFFICE ON THE RIGHT.
YOU'RE NOT IN MY FILES. SHOULD I KNOW YOU?
NOBODY KNOWS ME. GO ON UP.
I BET EVERYONE TELLS YOU YOU'RE AN ODD YOUNG LADY.
COULDN'T SAY. I HAVEN'T MET EVERY-ONE.
I'M SORRY.

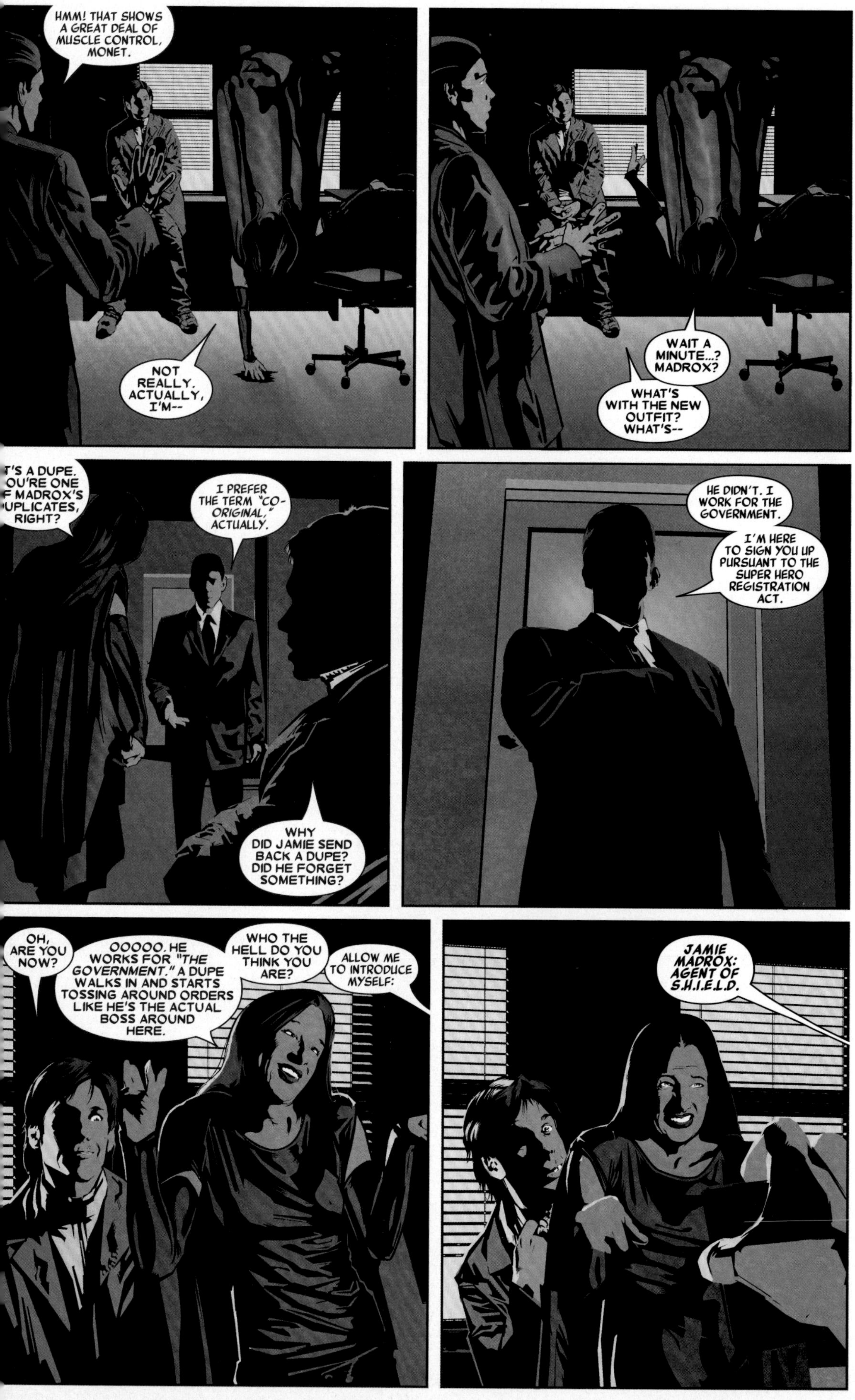

HMM! THAT SHOWS A GREAT DEAL OF MUSCLE CONTROL, MONET.
NOT REALLY. ACTUALLY, I'M--
WAIT A MINUTE...? MADROX?
WHAT'S WITH THE NEW OUTFIT? WHAT'S--
T'S A DUPE. OU'RE ONE F MADROX'S UPLICATES, RIGHT?
I PREFER THE TERM "CO-ORIGINAL," ACTUALLY.
WHY DID JAMIE SEND BACK A DUPE? DID HE FORGET SOMETHING?
HE DIDN'T. I WORK FOR THE GOVERNMENT.
I'M HERE TO SIGN YOU UP PURSUANT TO THE SUPER HERO REGISTRATION ACT.
OH, ARE YOU NOW?
OOOOO. HE WORKS FOR "THE GOVERNMENT." A DUPE WALKS IN AND STARTS TOSSING AROUND ORDERS LIKE HE'S THE ACTUAL BOSS AROUND HERE.
WHO THE HELL DO YOU THINK YOU ARE?
ALLOW ME TO INTRODUCE MYSELF:
JAMIE MADROX: AGENT OF S.H.I.E.L.D.

IT'S A MIRACLE! A FREAKIN' MIRACLE!

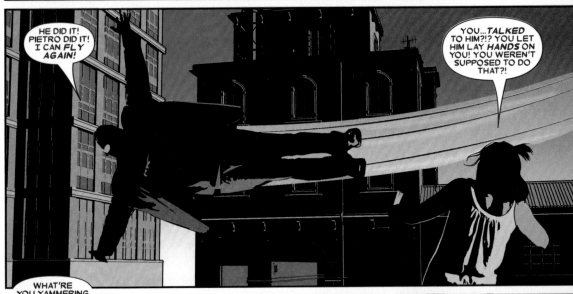

HE DID IT! PIETRO DID IT! I CAN FLY AGAIN!

YOU...*TALKED* TO HIM?!? YOU LET HIM LAY *HANDS* ON YOU! YOU WEREN'T SUPPOSED TO DO THAT?!

WHAT'RE YOU YAMMERING ABOUT, BRAT?!

YOU AND YOUR FRIEND WERE SUPPOSED TO *CHASE* HIM AND THEN HE WAS GOING TO SHUNT INTO THE NEAR FUTURE TO GET *AWAY*, AND HE WAS GONNA WIND UP IN THE PATH OF A TRUCK AND WHAM! YOU MESSED THINGS UP, YOU...YOU BIG DUMMY!

LOOK, I DUNNO WHAT YOUR PROBLEM IS, BUT I'M COMING DOWN THERE TO TEACH YOU SOME MAN--

WHA--?! I... I CAN'T LAND! NO! *NO!!!!*

NNNOOOOOOOOOO

I TRY TO DO THE RIGHT THING, AND IT TURNS OUT *WRONG.*

I KNOW THAT'S HOW IT IS FOR EVERYONE *ELSE*...BUT NOT FOR ME. IS THIS SOME KIND OF SICK JOKE?

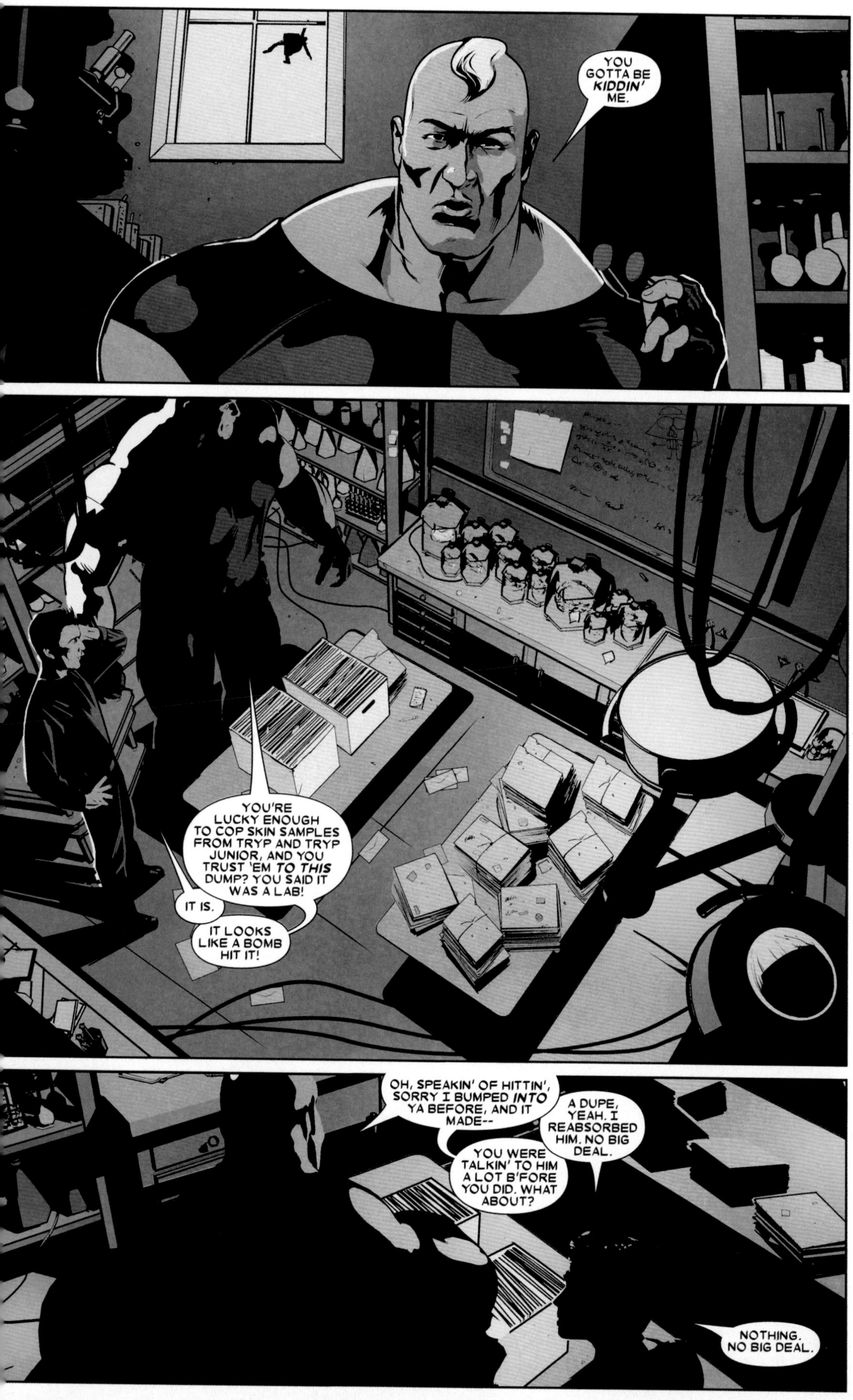

YOU GOTTA BE *KIDDIN'* ME.
YOU'RE LUCKY ENOUGH TO COP SKIN SAMPLES FROM TRYP AND TRYP JUNIOR, AND YOU TRUST 'EM *TO THIS* DUMP? YOU SAID IT WAS A LAB!
IT IS.
IT LOOKS LIKE A BOMB HIT IT!
OH, SPEAKIN' OF HITTIN', SORRY I BUMPED *INTO* YA BEFORE, AND IT MADE--
A DUPE, YEAH. I REABSORBED HIM. NO BIG DEAL.
YOU WERE TALKIN' TO HIM A LOT B'FORE YOU DID. WHAT ABOUT?
NOTHING. NO BIG DEAL.

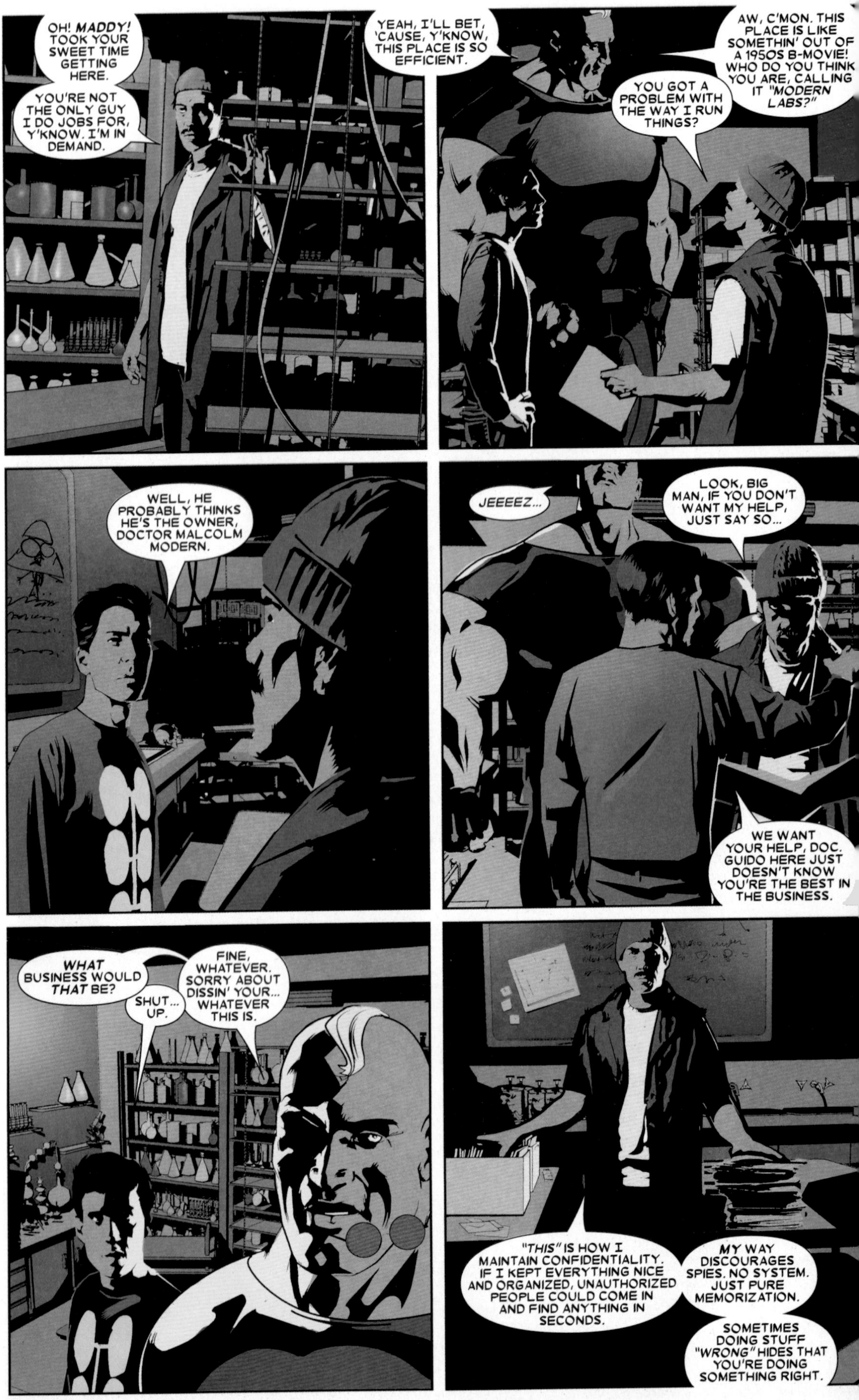
OH! MADDY! TOOK YOUR SWEET TIME GETTING HERE.
YOU'RE NOT THE ONLY GUY I DO JOBS FOR, Y'KNOW. I'M IN DEMAND.
YEAH, I'LL BET, 'CAUSE, Y'KNOW, THIS PLACE IS SO EFFICIENT.
AW, C'MON. THIS PLACE IS LIKE SOMETHIN' OUT OF A 1950S B-MOVIE! WHO DO YOU THINK YOU ARE, CALLING IT "MODERN LABS?"
YOU GOT A PROBLEM WITH THE WAY I RUN THINGS?
WELL, HE PROBABLY THINKS HE'S THE OWNER, DOCTOR MALCOLM MODERN.
JEEEEZ...
LOOK, BIG MAN, IF YOU DON'T WANT MY HELP, JUST SAY SO...
WE WANT YOUR HELP, DOC. GUIDO HERE JUST DOESN'T KNOW YOU'RE THE BEST IN THE BUSINESS.
WHAT BUSINESS WOULD THAT BE?
SHUT... UP.
FINE, WHATEVER. SORRY ABOUT DISSIN' YOUR... WHATEVER THIS IS.
"THIS" IS HOW I MAINTAIN CONFIDENTIALITY. IF I KEPT EVERYTHING NICE AND ORGANIZED, UNAUTHORIZED PEOPLE COULD COME IN AND FIND ANYTHING IN SECONDS.
MY WAY DISCOURAGES SPIES. NO SYSTEM. JUST PURE MEMORIZATION.
SOMETIMES DOING STUFF "WRONG" HIDES THAT YOU'RE DOING SOMETHING RIGHT.

HERE WE GO.

THE FOLDER'S MARKED "WEIRD."

THAT'S 'CAUSE WHAT I FOUND WAS WEIRD. THIS SAMPLE YOU BROUGHT IN...IT'S LIKE NOTHING I'VE EVER SEEN.

MEANING WHAT?

MEANING IF THERE'S ANYTHING LIKE IT, I HAVEN'T SEEN IT.

THERE'S SOME TOTALLY NEW DNA MARKERS IN HERE. COMPLETELY UNCHARTED.

YOU'RE SAYING HE'S... WHAT? ALIEN?

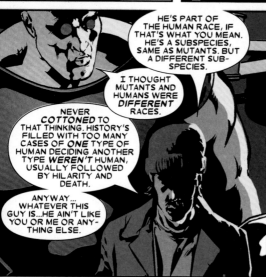

HE'S PART OF THE HUMAN RACE, IF THAT'S WHAT YOU MEAN. HE'S A SUBSPECIES, SAME AS MUTANTS. BUT A DIFFERENT SUBSPECIES.

I THOUGHT MUTANTS AND HUMANS WERE DIFFERENT RACES.

NEVER COTTONED TO THAT THINKING. HISTORY'S FILLED WITH TOO MANY CASES OF ONE TYPE OF HUMAN DECIDING ANOTHER TYPE WEREN'T HUMAN, USUALLY FOLLOWED BY HILARITY AND DEATH.

ANYWAY... WHATEVER THIS GUY IS...HE AIN'T LIKE YOU OR ME OR ANYTHING ELSE.

OKAY... THAT'S TRYP. WHAT ABOUT THE OTHER GUY?

WHAT OTHER GUY?

HIS SON. JUNIOR.

MADDY, I DUNNO WHAT THE HELL YOU'RE TALKIN' ABOUT.

THE TWO SAMPLES YOU GAVE ME...I JUST FIGURED YOU WERE PLAYING IT SAFE.

SAFE? I DON'T--?

THE TWO SAMPLES ARE EXACT DNA MATCHES. THEY'RE THE SAME GUY.

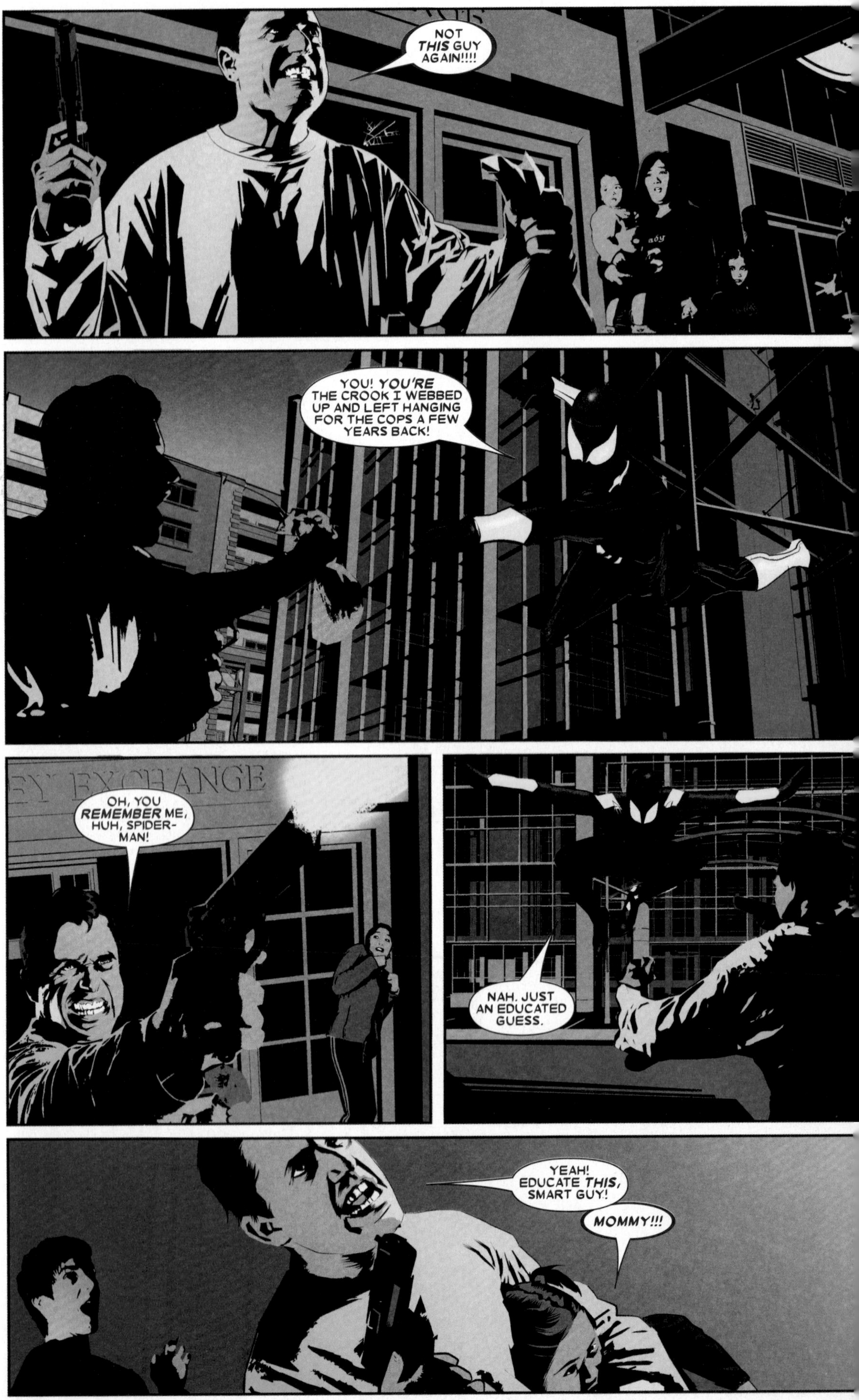
NOT THIS GUY AGAIN!!!!
YOU! YOU'RE THE CROOK I WEBBED UP AND LEFT HANGING FOR THE COPS A FEW YEARS BACK!
OH, YOU REMEMBER ME, HUH, SPIDER-MAN!
NAH. JUST AN EDUCATED GUESS.
YEAH! EDUCATE THIS, SMART GUY!
MOMMY!!!

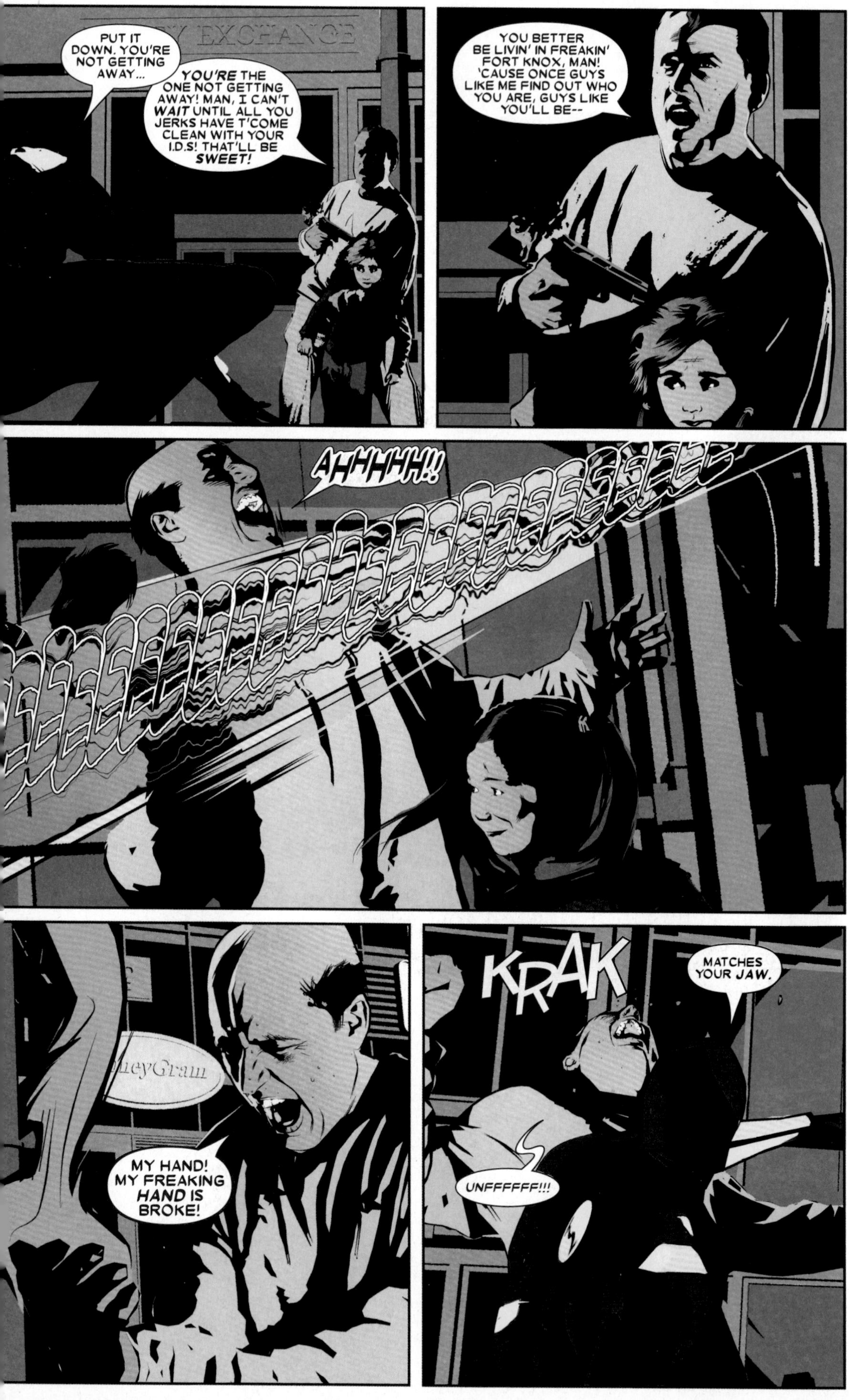

PUT IT DOWN. YOU'RE NOT GETTING AWAY...
YOU'RE THE ONE NOT GETTING AWAY! MAN, I CAN'T WAIT UNTIL ALL YOU JERKS HAVE T'COME CLEAN WITH YOUR I.D.S! THAT'LL BE SWEET!
YOU BETTER BE LIVIN' IN FREAKIN' FORT KNOX, MAN! 'CAUSE ONCE GUYS LIKE ME FIND OUT WHO YOU ARE, GUYS LIKE YOU'LL BE--
AHHHHH!!
MY HAND! MY FREAKING HAND IS BROKE!
KRAK
MATCHES YOUR JAW.
UNFFFFFF!!!

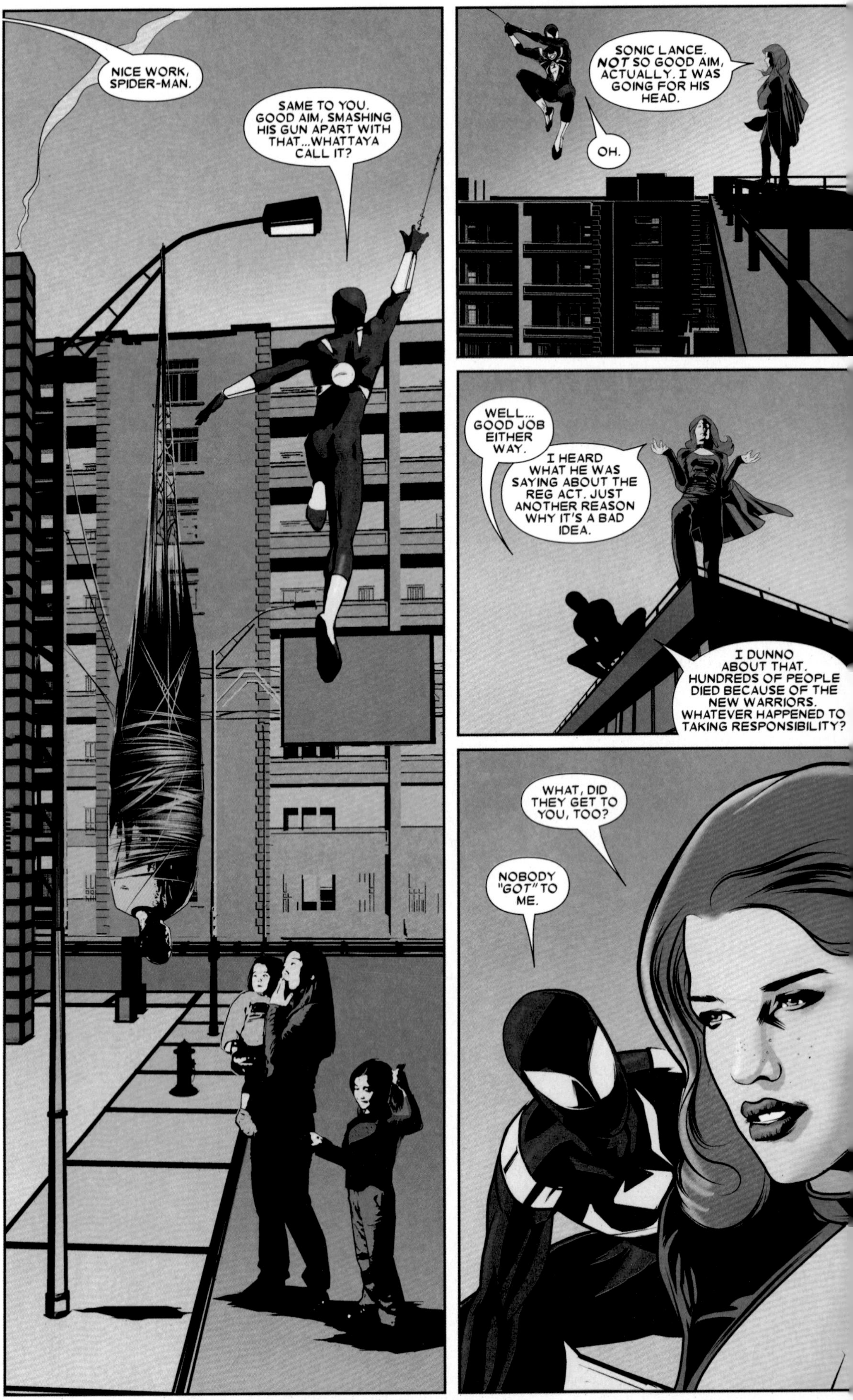
NICE WORK, SPIDER-MAN.
SAME TO YOU. GOOD AIM, SMASHING HIS GUN APART WITH THAT...WHATTAYA CALL IT?
SONIC LANCE. NOT SO GOOD AIM, ACTUALLY. I WAS GOING FOR HIS HEAD.
OH.
WELL... GOOD JOB EITHER WAY.
I HEARD WHAT HE WAS SAYING ABOUT THE REG ACT. JUST ANOTHER REASON WHY IT'S A BAD IDEA.
I DUNNO ABOUT THAT. HUNDREDS OF PEOPLE DIED BECAUSE OF THE NEW WARRIORS. WHATEVER HAPPENED TO TAKING RESPONSIBILITY?
WHAT, DID THEY GET TO YOU, TOO?
NOBODY "GOT" TO ME.

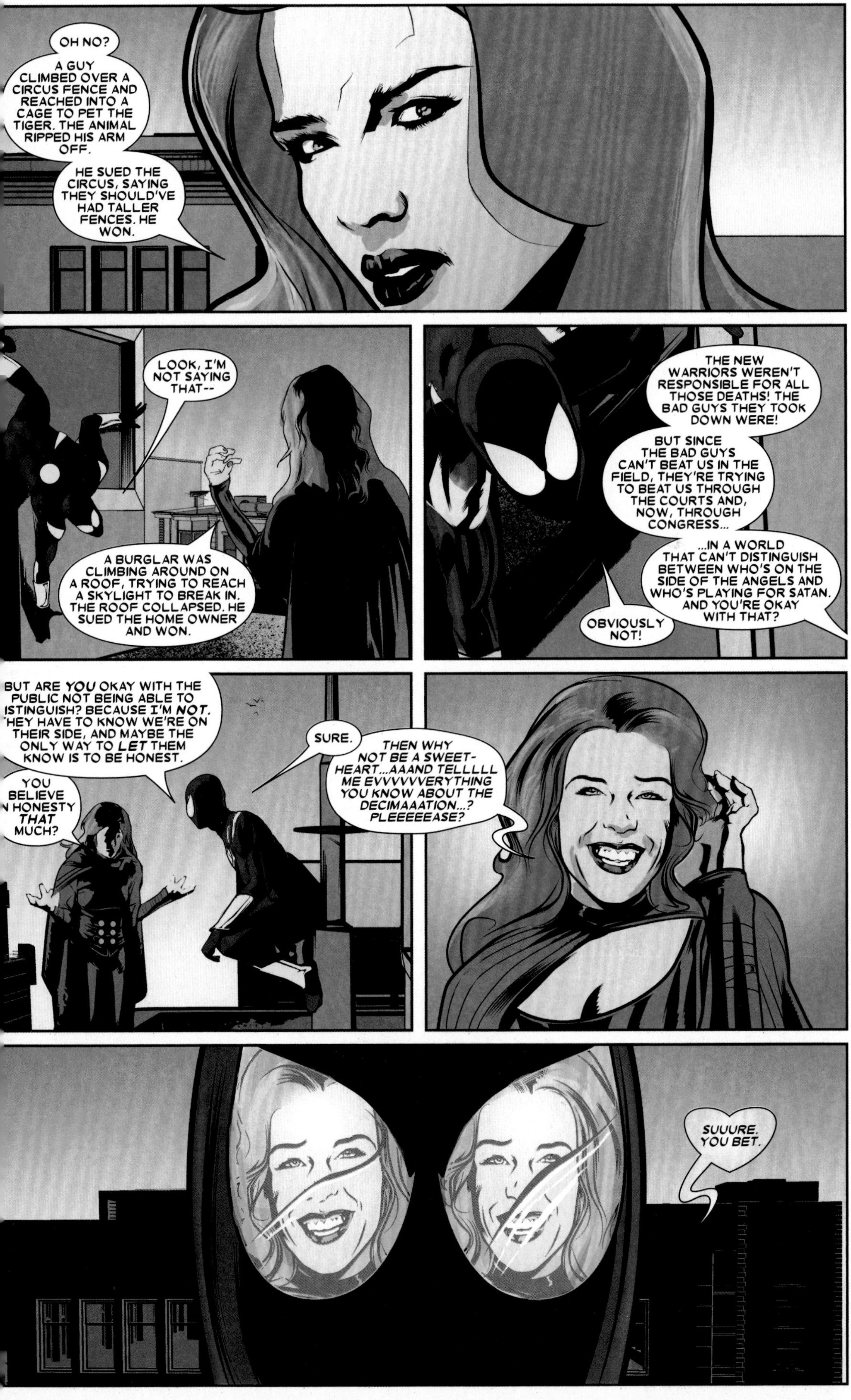
OH NO?
A GUY CLIMBED OVER A CIRCUS FENCE AND REACHED INTO A CAGE TO PET THE TIGER. THE ANIMAL RIPPED HIS ARM OFF.
HE SUED THE CIRCUS, SAYING THEY SHOULD'VE HAD TALLER FENCES. HE WON.
LOOK, I'M NOT SAYING THAT--
A BURGLAR WAS CLIMBING AROUND ON A ROOF, TRYING TO REACH A SKYLIGHT TO BREAK IN. THE ROOF COLLAPSED. HE SUED THE HOME OWNER AND WON.
THE NEW WARRIORS WEREN'T RESPONSIBLE FOR ALL THOSE DEATHS! THE BAD GUYS THEY TOOK DOWN WERE!
BUT SINCE THE BAD GUYS CAN'T BEAT US IN THE FIELD, THEY'RE TRYING TO BEAT US THROUGH THE COURTS AND, NOW, THROUGH CONGRESS...
...IN A WORLD THAT CAN'T DISTINGUISH BETWEEN WHO'S ON THE SIDE OF THE ANGELS AND WHO'S PLAYING FOR SATAN. AND YOU'RE OKAY WITH THAT?
OBVIOUSLY NOT!
BUT ARE YOU OKAY WITH THE PUBLIC NOT BEING ABLE TO ISTINGUISH? BECAUSE I'M NOT. 'HEY HAVE TO KNOW WE'RE ON THEIR SIDE, AND MAYBE THE ONLY WAY TO LET THEM KNOW IS TO BE HONEST.
YOU BELIEVE N HONESTY THAT MUCH?
SURE.
THEN WHY NOT BE A SWEET-HEART...AAAND TELLLLL ME EVVVVVVERYTHING YOU KNOW ABOUT THE DECIMAAATION...? PLEEEEEASE?
SUUURE. YOU BET.

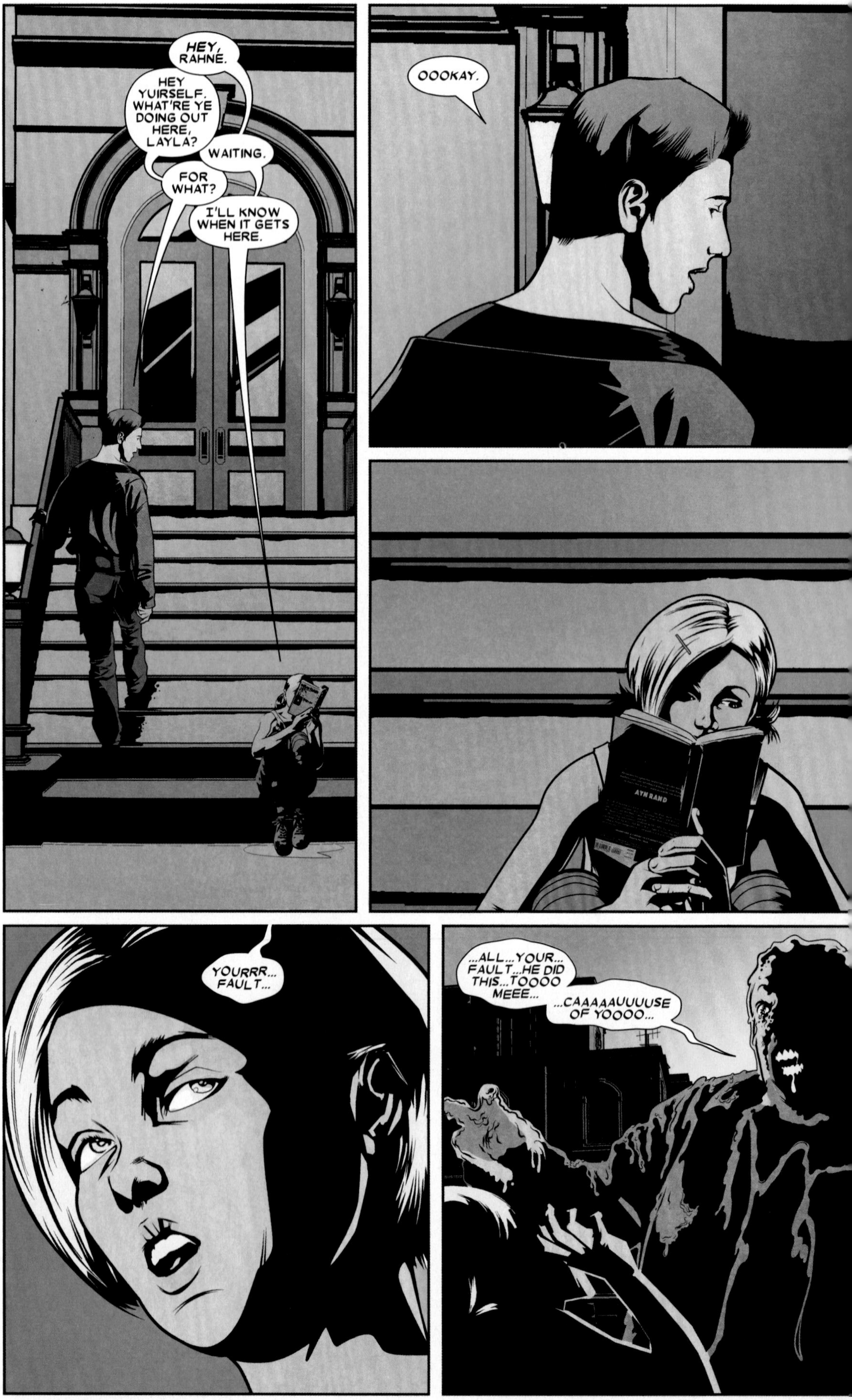

HEY, RAHNE.
HEY YUIRSELF. WHAT'RE YE DOING OUT HERE, LAYLA?
WAITING.
FOR WHAT?
I'LL KNOW WHEN IT GETS HERE.
OOOKAY.
AYN RAND
YOURRR... FAULT...
...ALL...YOUR... FAULT...HE DID THIS...TOOOO MEEE...
...CAAAAAUUUUSE OF YOOOO...

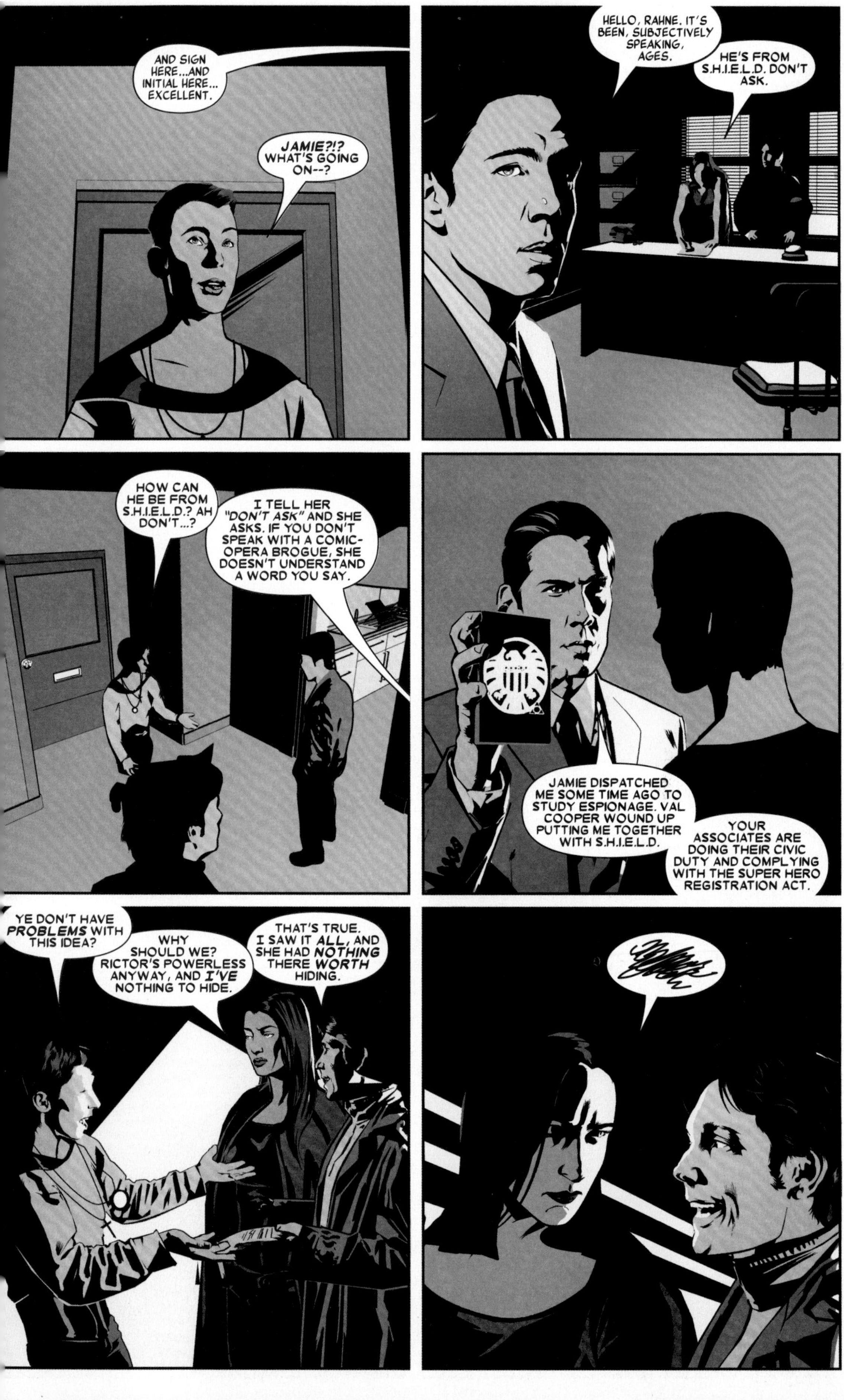
AND SIGN HERE...AND INITIAL HERE... EXCELLENT.
JAMIE?!? WHAT'S GOING ON--?
HELLO, RAHNE. IT'S BEEN, SUBJECTIVELY SPEAKING, AGES.
HE'S FROM S.H.I.E.L.D. DON'T ASK.
HOW CAN HE BE FROM S.H.I.E.L.D.? AH DON'T...?
I TELL HER "DON'T ASK" AND SHE ASKS. IF YOU DON'T SPEAK WITH A COMIC-OPERA BROGUE, SHE DOESN'T UNDERSTAND A WORD YOU SAY.
JAMIE DISPATCHED ME SOME TIME AGO TO STUDY ESPIONAGE. VAL COOPER WOUND UP PUTTING ME TOGETHER WITH S.H.I.E.L.D.
YOUR ASSOCIATES ARE DOING THEIR CIVIC DUTY AND COMPLYING WITH THE SUPER HERO REGISTRATION ACT.
YE DON'T HAVE PROBLEMS WITH THIS IDEA?
WHY SHOULD WE? RICTOR'S POWERLESS ANYWAY, AND I'VE NOTHING TO HIDE.
THAT'S TRUE. I SAW IT ALL, AND SHE HAD NOTHING THERE WORTH HIDING.

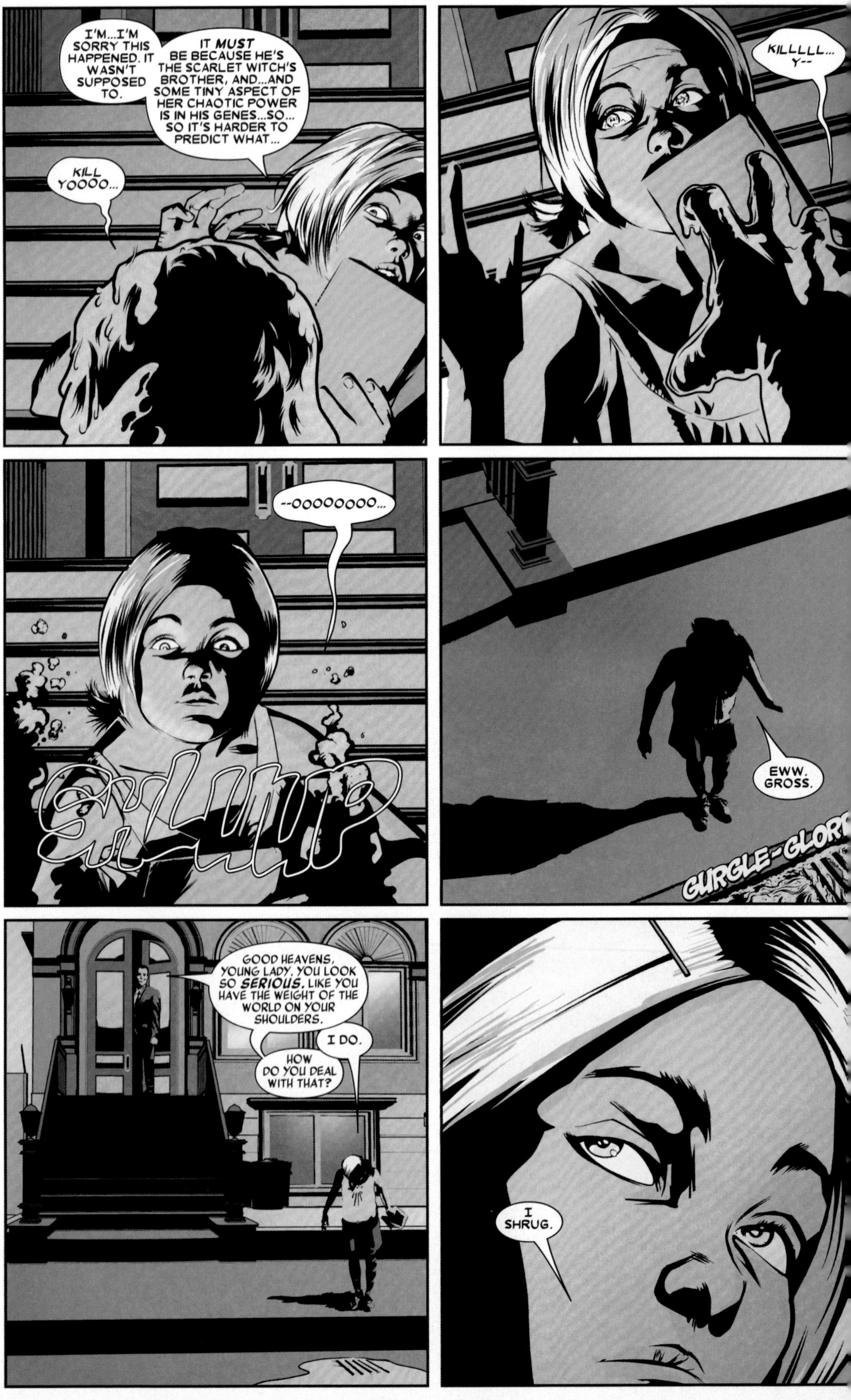
I'M...I'M SORRY THIS HAPPENED. IT WASN'T SUPPOSED TO.
IT MUST BE BECAUSE HE'S THE SCARLET WITCH'S BROTHER, AND...AND SOME TINY ASPECT OF HER CHAOTIC POWER IS IN HIS GENES...SO... SO IT'S HARDER TO PREDICT WHAT...
KILL YOOOO...
KILLLLLL... Y--
--OOOOOOOO...
EWW. GROSS.
GURGLE-GLOR
GOOD HEAVENS, YOUNG LADY. YOU LOOK SO SERIOUS, LIKE YOU HAVE THE WEIGHT OF THE WORLD ON YOUR SHOULDERS.
I DO.
HOW DO YOU DEAL WITH THAT?
I SHRUG.

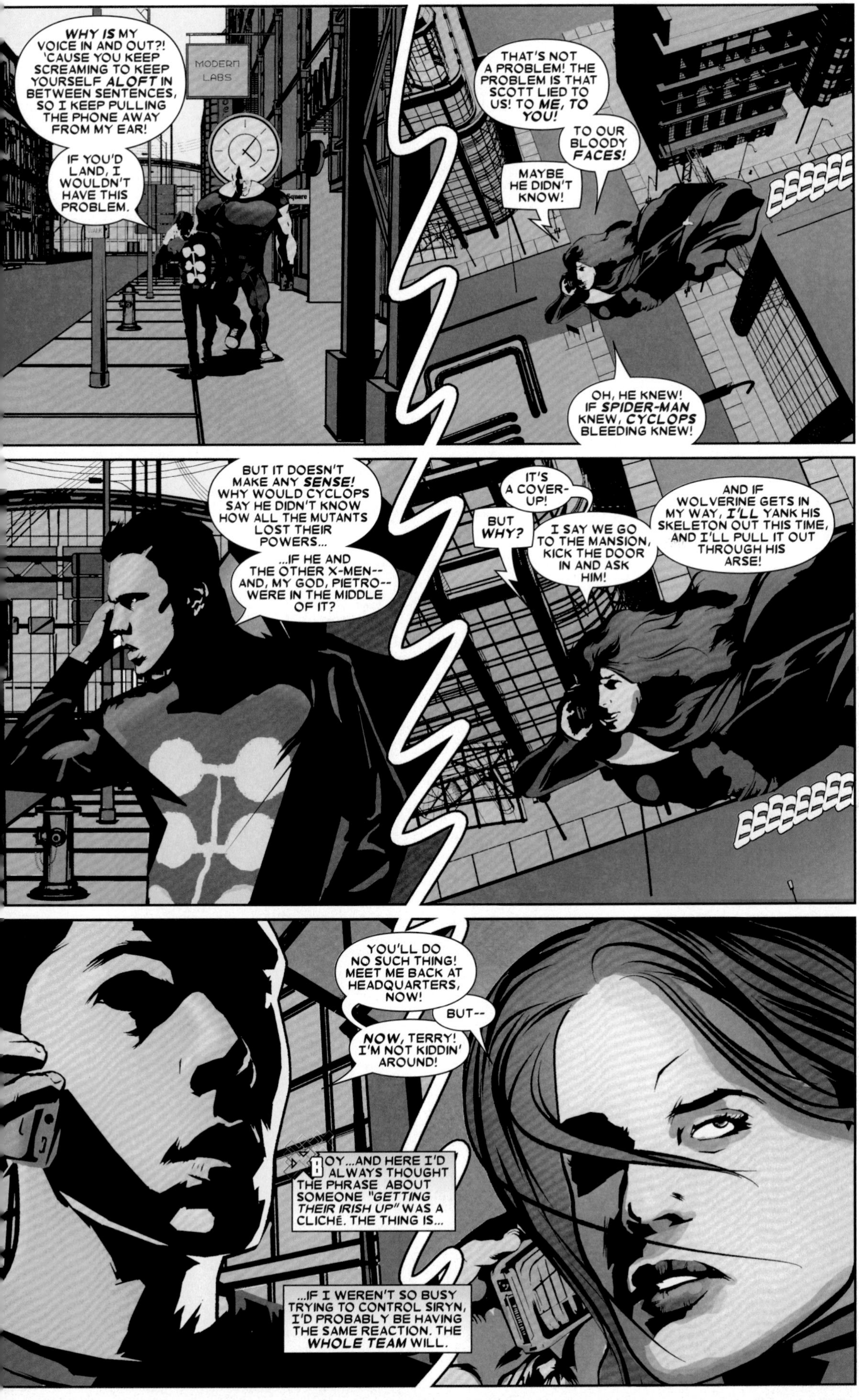
WHY IS MY VOICE IN AND OUT?! 'CAUSE YOU KEEP SCREAMING TO KEEP YOURSELF ALOFT IN BETWEEN SENTENCES, SO I KEEP PULLING THE PHONE AWAY FROM MY EAR!
IF YOU'D LAND, I WOULDN'T HAVE THIS PROBLEM.
MODERN LABS
THAT'S NOT A PROBLEM! THE PROBLEM IS THAT SCOTT LIED TO US! TO ME, TO YOU!
TO OUR BLOODY FACES!
MAYBE HE DIDN'T KNOW!
OH, HE KNEW! IF SPIDER-MAN KNEW, CYCLOPS BLEEDING KNEW!
EEEEEE
BUT IT DOESN'T MAKE ANY SENSE! WHY WOULD CYCLOPS SAY HE DIDN'T KNOW HOW ALL THE MUTANTS LOST THEIR POWERS...
...IF HE AND THE OTHER X-MEN-- AND, MY GOD, PIETRO-- WERE IN THE MIDDLE OF IT?
IT'S A COVER-UP!
BUT WHY?
I SAY WE GO TO THE MANSION, KICK THE DOOR IN AND ASK HIM!
AND IF WOLVERINE GETS IN MY WAY, I'LL YANK HIS SKELETON OUT THIS TIME, AND I'LL PULL IT OUT THROUGH HIS ARSE!
EEEEEEEE
YOU'LL DO NO SUCH THING! MEET ME BACK AT HEADQUARTERS, NOW!
BUT--
NOW, TERRY! I'M NOT KIDDIN' AROUND!
BOY...AND HERE I'D ALWAYS THOUGHT THE PHRASE ABOUT SOMEONE "GETTING THEIR IRISH UP" WAS A CLICHÉ. THE THING IS...
...IF I WEREN'T SO BUSY TRYING TO CONTROL SIRYN, I'D PROBABLY BE HAVING THE SAME REACTION. THE WHOLE TEAM WILL.

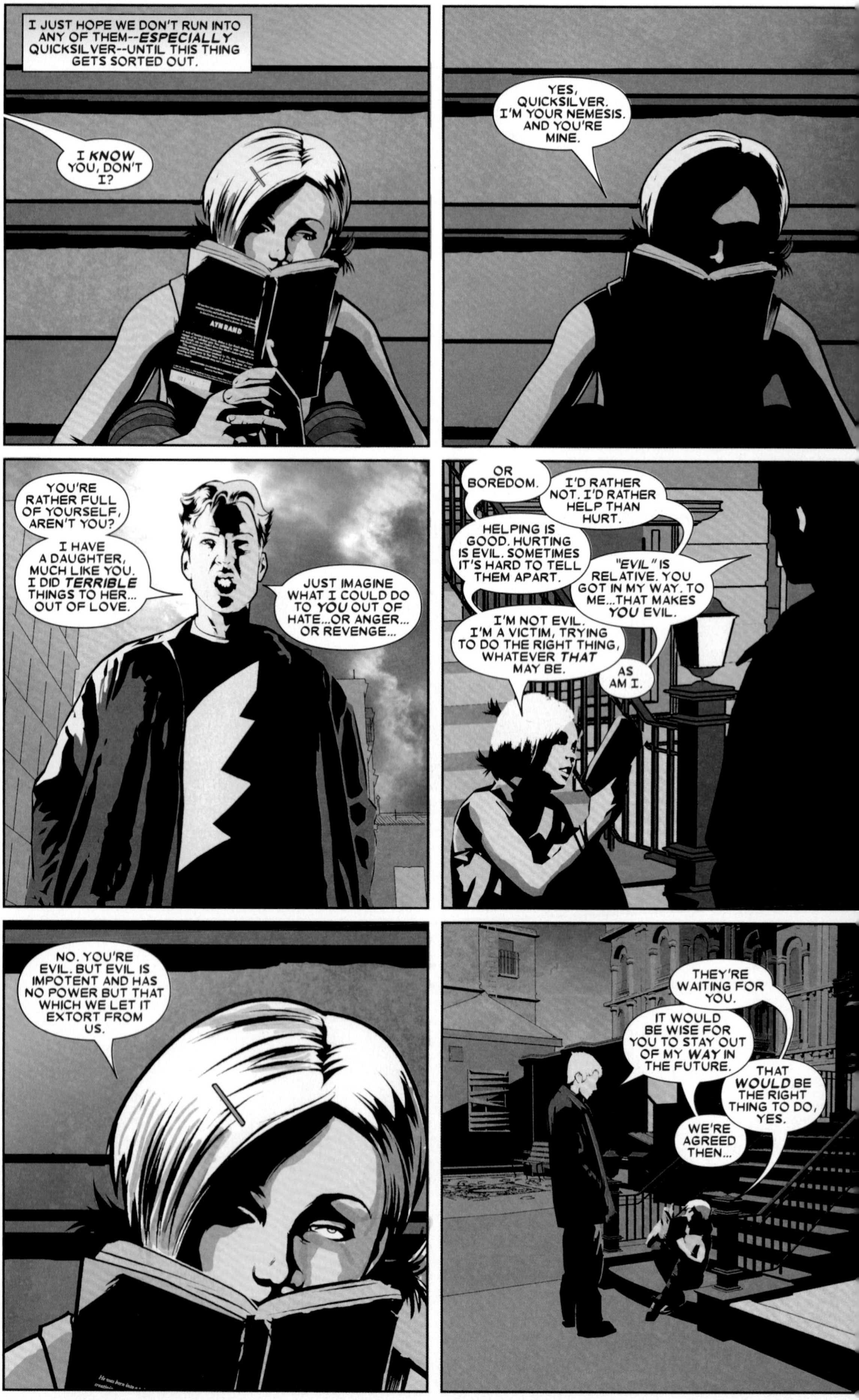
I JUST HOPE WE DON'T RUN INTO ANY OF THEM--ESPECIALLY QUICKSILVER--UNTIL THIS THING GETS SORTED OUT.
I KNOW YOU, DON'T I?
AYN RAND
YES, QUICKSILVER. I'M YOUR NEMESIS. AND YOU'RE MINE.
YOU'RE RATHER FULL OF YOURSELF, AREN'T YOU?
I HAVE A DAUGHTER, MUCH LIKE YOU. I DID TERRIBLE THINGS TO HER... OUT OF LOVE.
JUST IMAGINE WHAT I COULD DO TO YOU OUT OF HATE...OR ANGER... OR REVENGE...
OR BOREDOM.
I'D RATHER NOT. I'D RATHER HELP THAN HURT.
HELPING IS GOOD. HURTING IS EVIL. SOMETIMES IT'S HARD TO TELL THEM APART.
"EVIL" IS RELATIVE. YOU GOT IN MY WAY. TO ME...THAT MAKES YOU EVIL.
I'M NOT EVIL. I'M A VICTIM, TRYING TO DO THE RIGHT THING, WHATEVER THAT MAY BE.
AS AM I.
NO. YOU'RE EVIL. BUT EVIL IS IMPOTENT AND HAS NO POWER BUT THAT WHICH WE LET IT EXTORT FROM US.
THEY'RE WAITING FOR YOU.
IT WOULD BE WISE FOR YOU TO STAY OUT OF MY WAY IN THE FUTURE.
THAT WOULD BE THE RIGHT THING TO DO, YES.
WE'RE AGREED THEN...

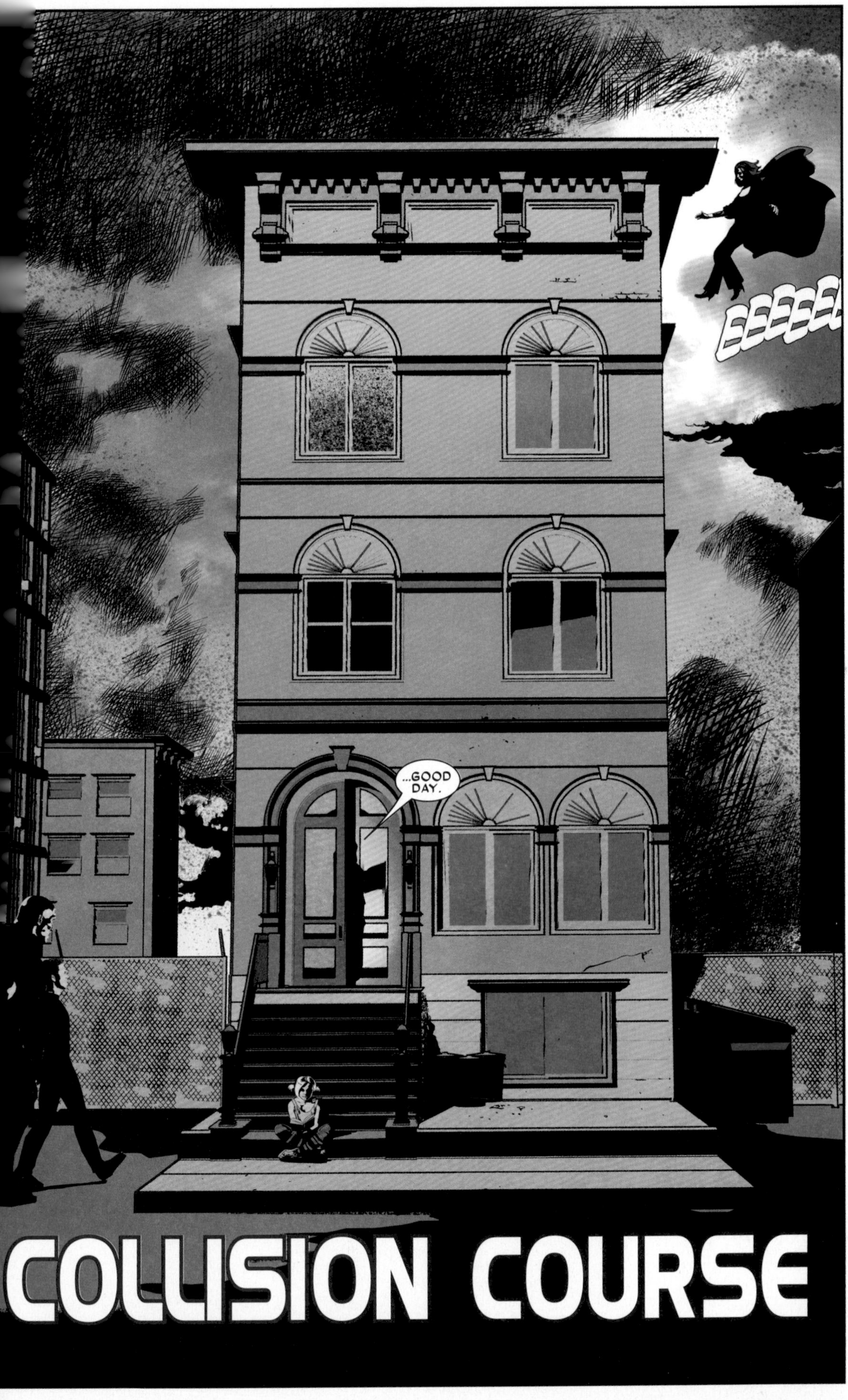
EEEEEE
...GOOD DAY.
COLLISION COURSE

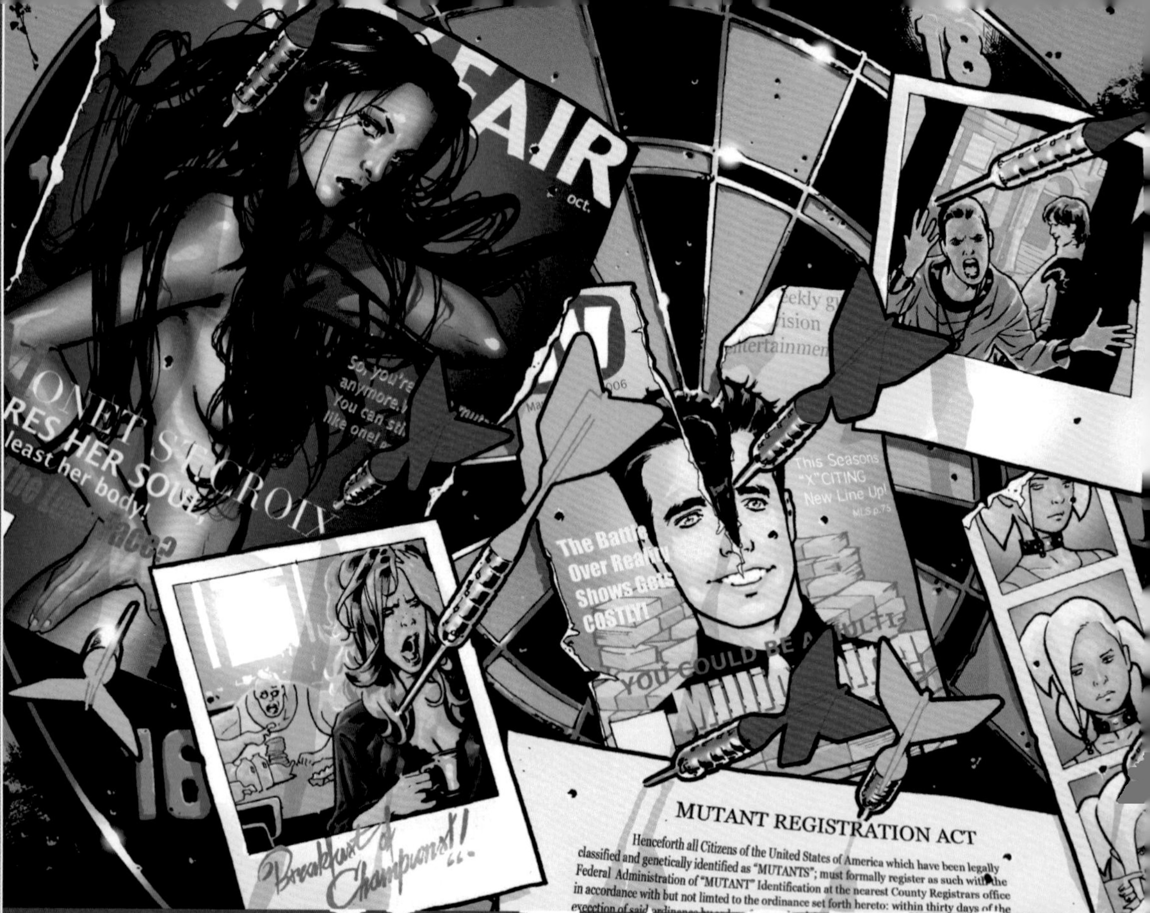

FAIR
oct.
So, you're anymore, you can still like one!
This Seasons "X"CITING New Line Up!
The Battle Over Reality Shows Gets COSTLY!
YOU COULD BE A MULTI-
Breakfast of Champions!!
MUTANT REGISTRATION ACT
Henceforth all Citizens of the United States of America which have been legally classified and genetically identified as "MUTANTS"; must formally register as such with the Federal Administration of "MUTANT" Identification at the nearest County Registrars office in accordance with but not limted to the ordinance set forth hereto: within thirty days of the

X-FACTOR

A MARVEL COMICS EVENT

CIVIL WAR

X-FACTOR #9

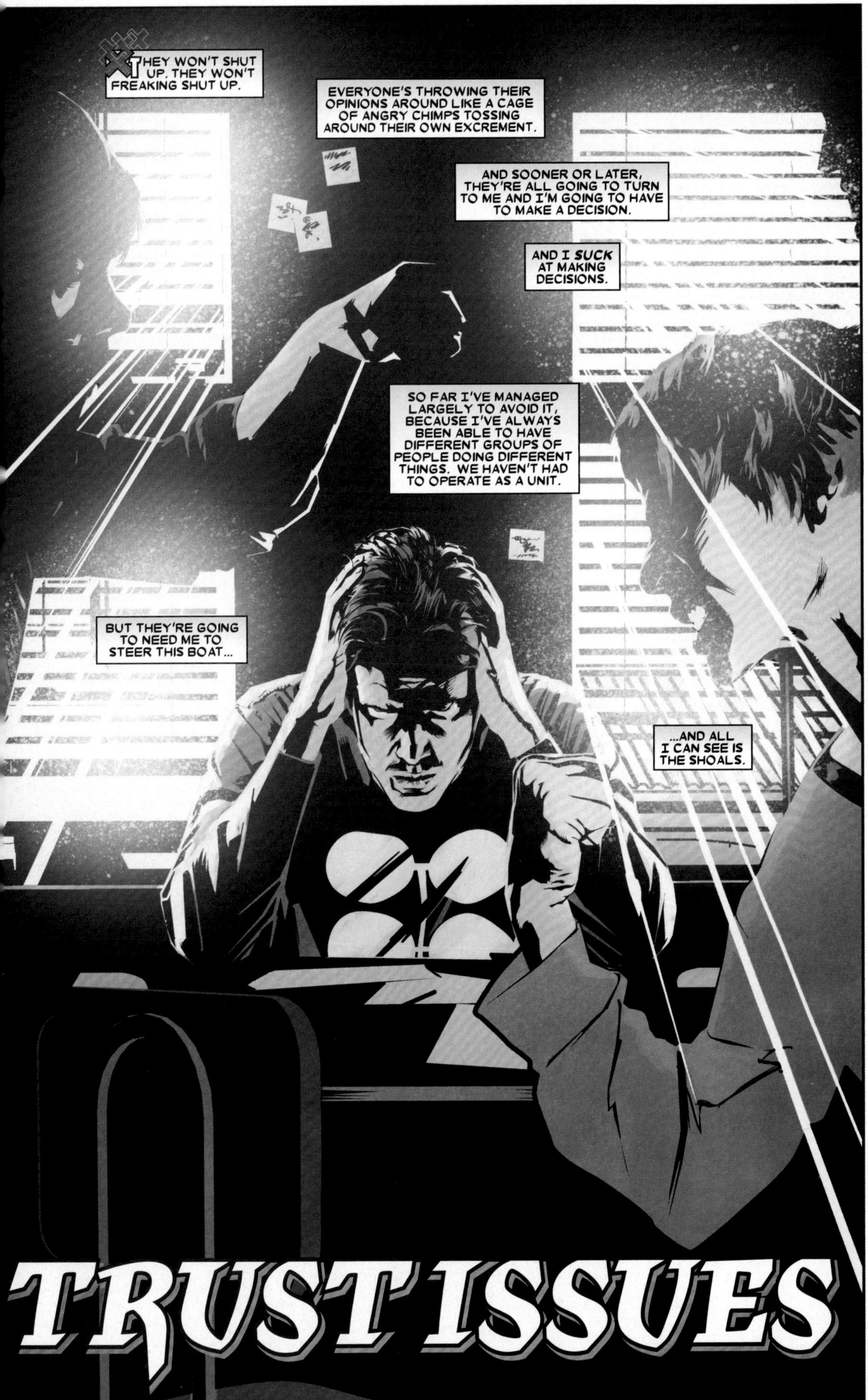
THEY WON'T SHUT UP. THEY WON'T FREAKING SHUT UP.
EVERYONE'S THROWING THEIR OPINIONS AROUND LIKE A CAGE OF ANGRY CHIMPS TOSSING AROUND THEIR OWN EXCREMENT.
AND SOONER OR LATER, THEY'RE ALL GOING TO TURN TO ME AND I'M GOING TO HAVE TO MAKE A DECISION.
AND I SUCK AT MAKING DECISIONS.
SO FAR I'VE MANAGED LARGELY TO AVOID IT, BECAUSE I'VE ALWAYS BEEN ABLE TO HAVE DIFFERENT GROUPS OF PEOPLE DOING DIFFERENT THINGS. WE HAVEN'T HAD TO OPERATE AS A UNIT.
BUT THEY'RE GOING TO NEED ME TO STEER THIS BOAT...
...AND ALL I CAN SEE IS THE SHOALS.
TRUST ISSUES

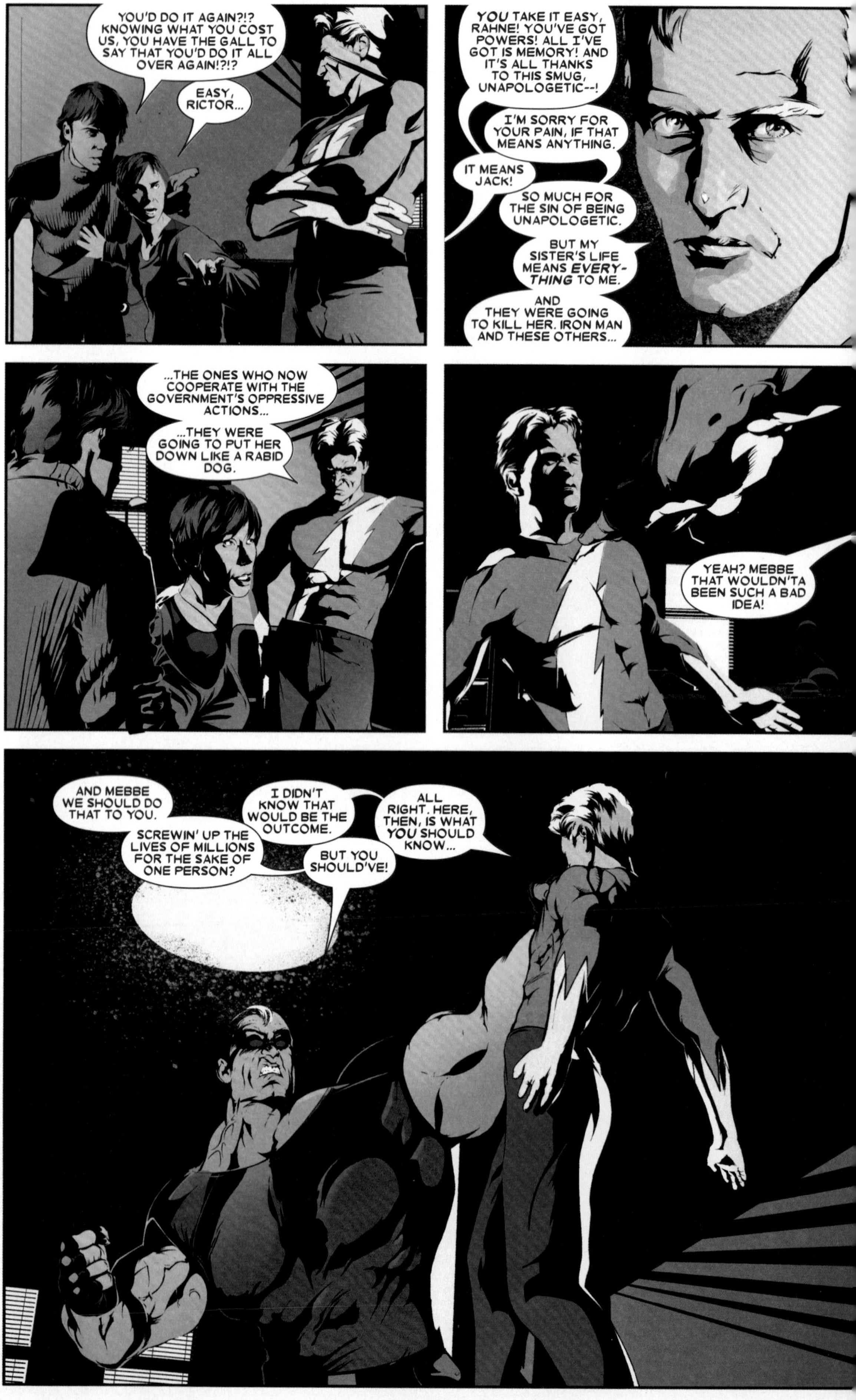
YOU'D DO IT AGAIN?!? KNOWING WHAT YOU COST US, YOU HAVE THE GALL TO SAY THAT YOU'D DO IT ALL OVER AGAIN!?!?
EASY, RICTOR...
YOU TAKE IT EASY, RAHNE! YOU'VE GOT POWERS! ALL I'VE GOT IS MEMORY! AND IT'S ALL THANKS TO THIS SMUG, UNAPOLOGETIC--!
I'M SORRY FOR YOUR PAIN, IF THAT MEANS ANYTHING.
IT MEANS JACK!
SO MUCH FOR THE SIN OF BEING UNAPOLOGETIC.
BUT MY SISTER'S LIFE MEANS EVERYTHING TO ME.
AND THEY WERE GOING TO KILL HER. IRON MAN AND THESE OTHERS...
...THE ONES WHO NOW COOPERATE WITH THE GOVERNMENT'S OPPRESSIVE ACTIONS...
...THEY WERE GOING TO PUT HER DOWN LIKE A RABID DOG.
YEAH? MEBBE THAT WOULDN'TA BEEN SUCH A BAD IDEA!
AND MEBBE WE SHOULD DO THAT TO YOU.
SCREWIN' UP THE LIVES OF MILLIONS FOR THE SAKE OF ONE PERSON?
I DIDN'T KNOW THAT WOULD BE THE OUTCOME.
BUT YOU SHOULD'VE!
ALL RIGHT. HERE, THEN, IS WHAT YOU SHOULD KNOW...

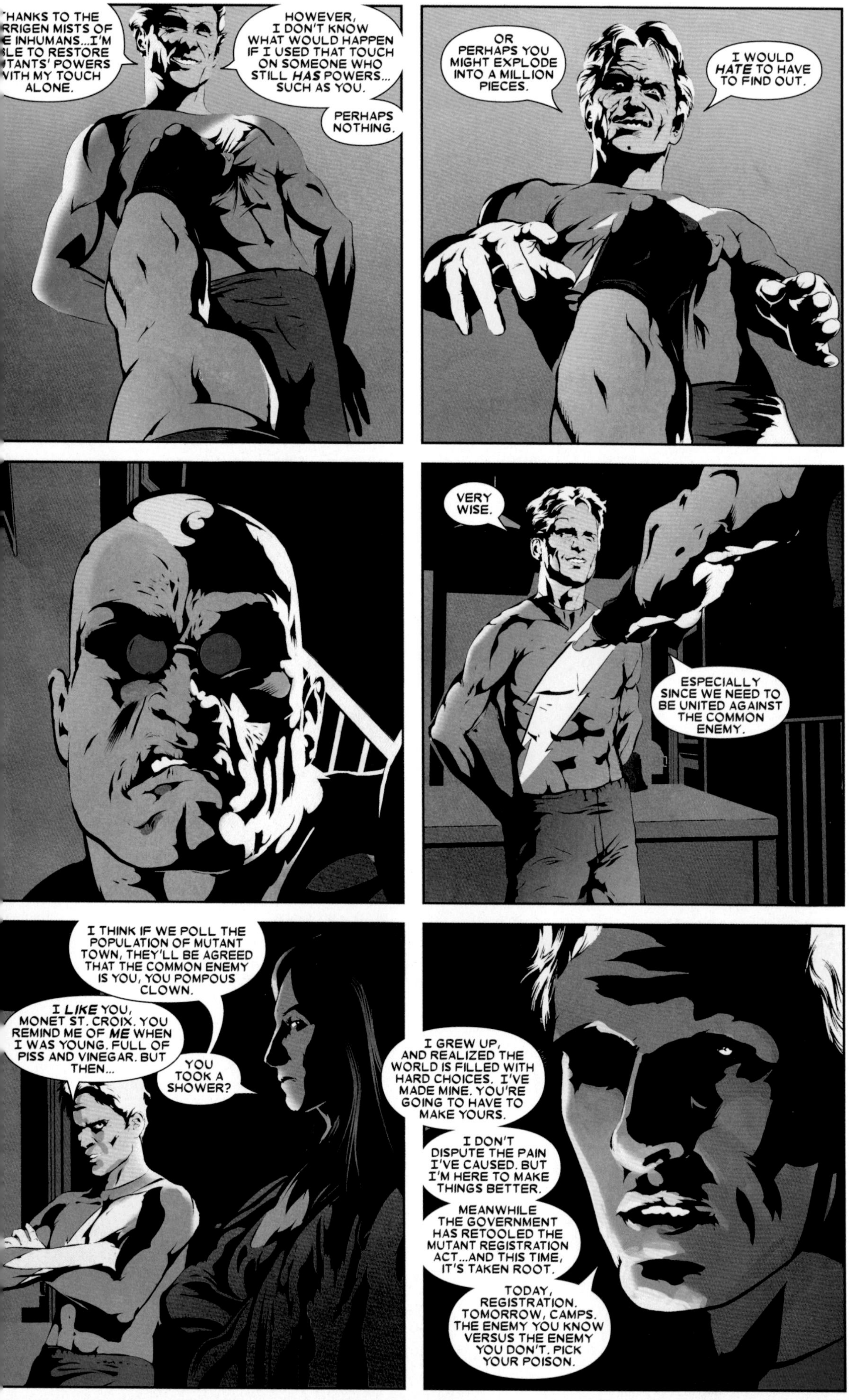
THANKS TO THE TERRIGEN MISTS OF THE INHUMANS...I'M ABLE TO RESTORE MUTANTS' POWERS WITH MY TOUCH ALONE.
HOWEVER, I DON'T KNOW WHAT WOULD HAPPEN IF I USED THAT TOUCH ON SOMEONE WHO STILL *HAS* POWERS... SUCH AS YOU.
PERHAPS NOTHING.
OR PERHAPS YOU MIGHT EXPLODE INTO A MILLION PIECES.
I WOULD *HATE* TO HAVE TO FIND OUT.
VERY WISE.
ESPECIALLY SINCE WE NEED TO BE UNITED AGAINST THE COMMON ENEMY.
I THINK IF WE POLL THE POPULATION OF MUTANT TOWN, THEY'LL BE AGREED THAT THE COMMON ENEMY IS YOU, YOU POMPOUS CLOWN.
I *LIKE* YOU, MONET ST. CROIX. YOU REMIND ME OF *ME* WHEN I WAS YOUNG. FULL OF PISS AND VINEGAR. BUT THEN...
YOU TOOK A SHOWER?
I GREW UP, AND REALIZED THE WORLD IS FILLED WITH HARD CHOICES. I'VE MADE MINE. YOU'RE GOING TO HAVE TO MAKE YOURS.
I DON'T DISPUTE THE PAIN I'VE CAUSED. BUT I'M HERE TO MAKE THINGS BETTER.
MEANWHILE THE GOVERNMENT HAS RETOOLED THE MUTANT REGISTRATION ACT...AND THIS TIME, IT'S TAKEN ROOT.
TODAY, REGISTRATION. TOMORROW, CAMPS. THE ENEMY YOU KNOW VERSUS THE ENEMY YOU DON'T. PICK YOUR POISON.

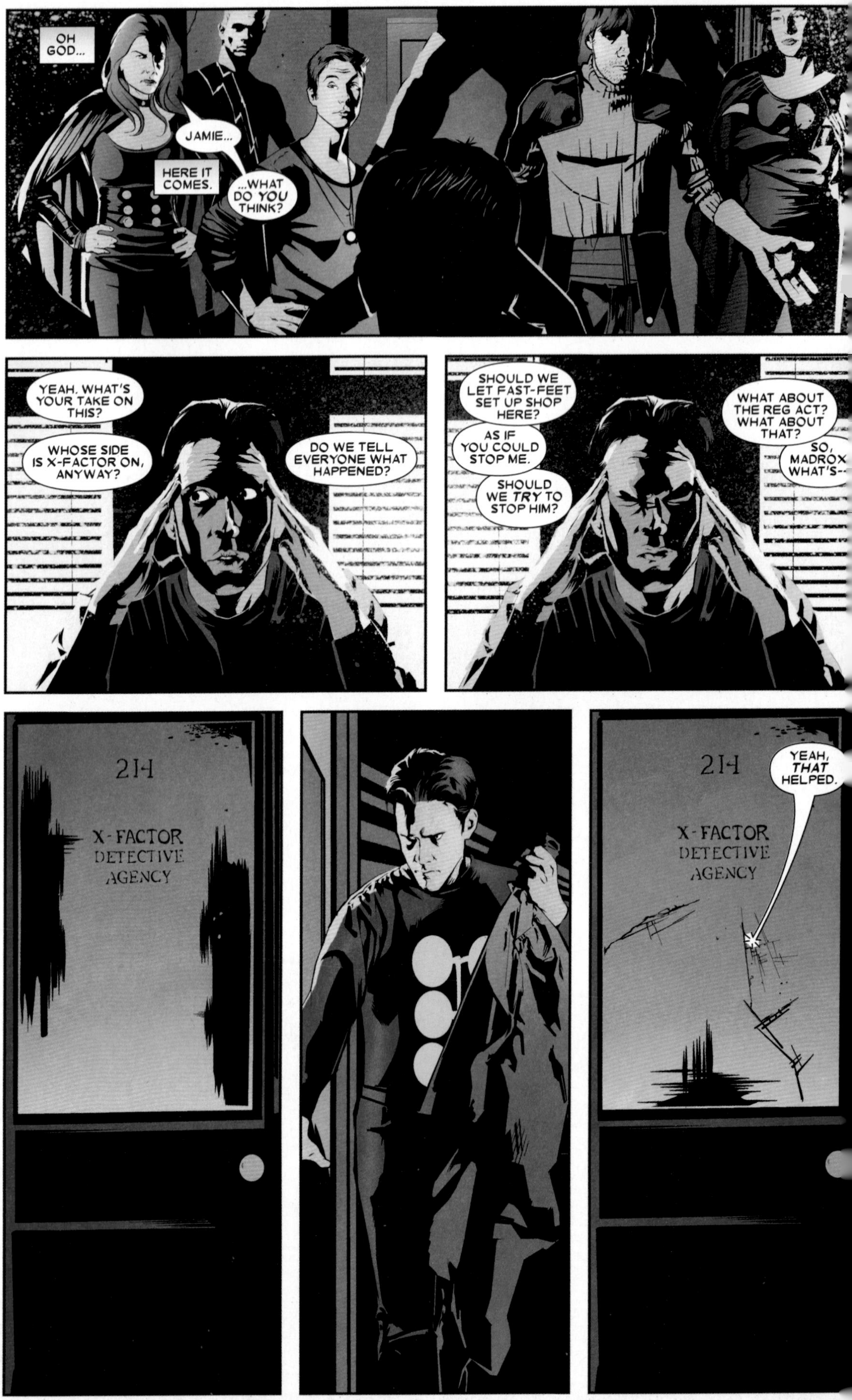

OH GOD...
JAMIE...
HERE IT COMES.
...WHAT DO YOU THINK?
YEAH. WHAT'S YOUR TAKE ON THIS?
WHOSE SIDE IS X-FACTOR ON, ANYWAY?
DO WE TELL EVERYONE WHAT HAPPENED?
SHOULD WE LET FAST-FEET SET UP SHOP HERE?
AS IF YOU COULD STOP ME.
SHOULD WE TRY TO STOP HIM?
WHAT ABOUT THE REG ACT? WHAT ABOUT THAT?
SO, MADROX WHAT'S--
214
X-FACTOR DETECTIVE AGENCY
214
X-FACTOR DETECTIVE AGENCY
YEAH, THAT HELPED.

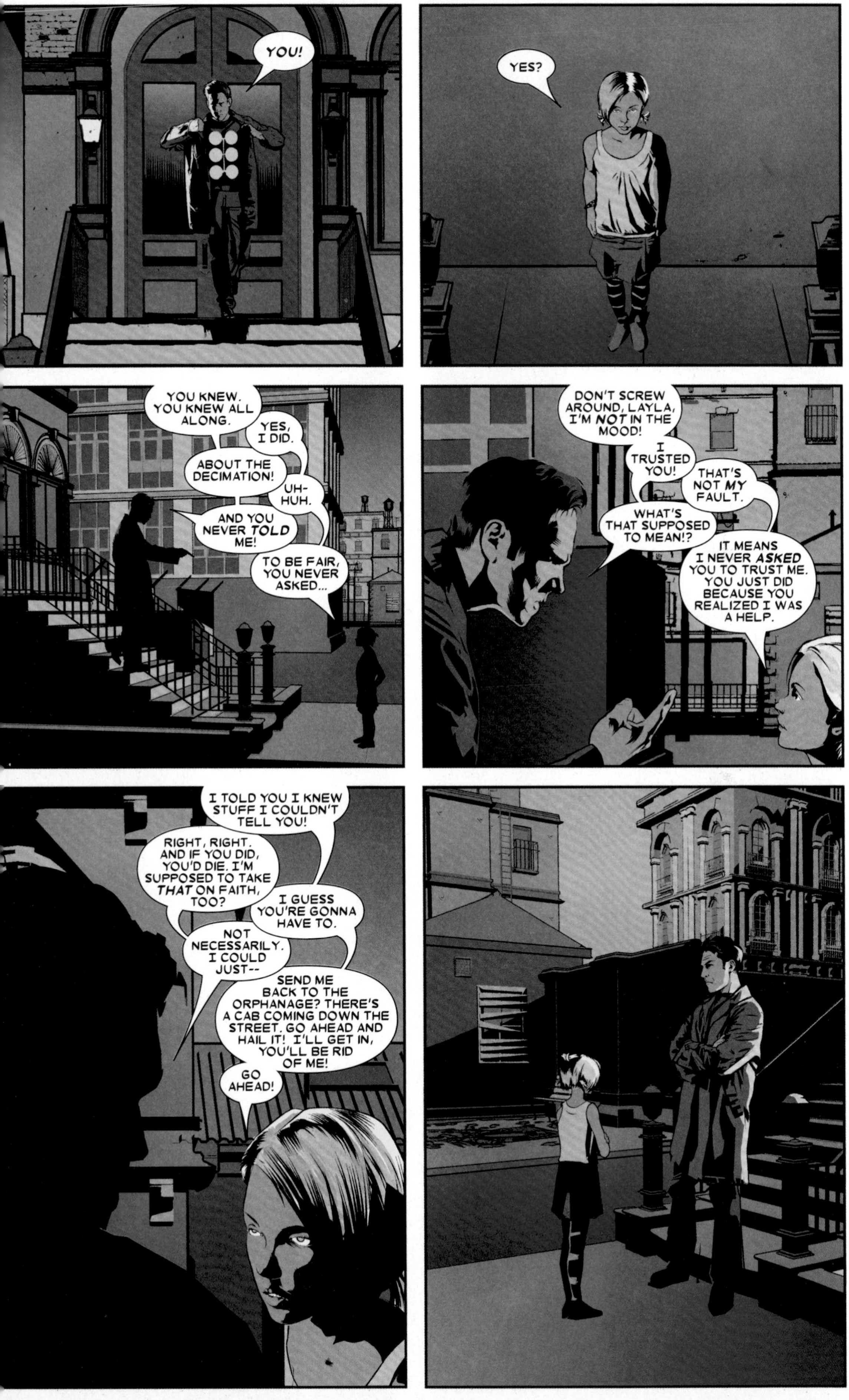
YOU!
YES?
YOU KNEW. YOU KNEW ALL ALONG.
YES, I DID.
ABOUT THE DECIMATION!
UH-HUH.
AND YOU NEVER TOLD ME!
TO BE FAIR, YOU NEVER ASKED...
DON'T SCREW AROUND, LAYLA, I'M NOT IN THE MOOD!
I TRUSTED YOU!
THAT'S NOT MY FAULT.
WHAT'S THAT SUPPOSED TO MEAN!?
IT MEANS I NEVER ASKED YOU TO TRUST ME. YOU JUST DID BECAUSE YOU REALIZED I WAS A HELP.
I TOLD YOU I KNEW STUFF I COULDN'T TELL YOU!
RIGHT, RIGHT. AND IF YOU DID, YOU'D DIE. I'M SUPPOSED TO TAKE THAT ON FAITH, TOO?
I GUESS YOU'RE GONNA HAVE TO.
NOT NECESSARILY. I COULD JUST--
SEND ME BACK TO THE ORPHANAGE? THERE'S A CAB COMING DOWN THE STREET. GO AHEAD AND HAIL IT! I'LL GET IN, YOU'LL BE RID OF ME!
GO AHEAD!

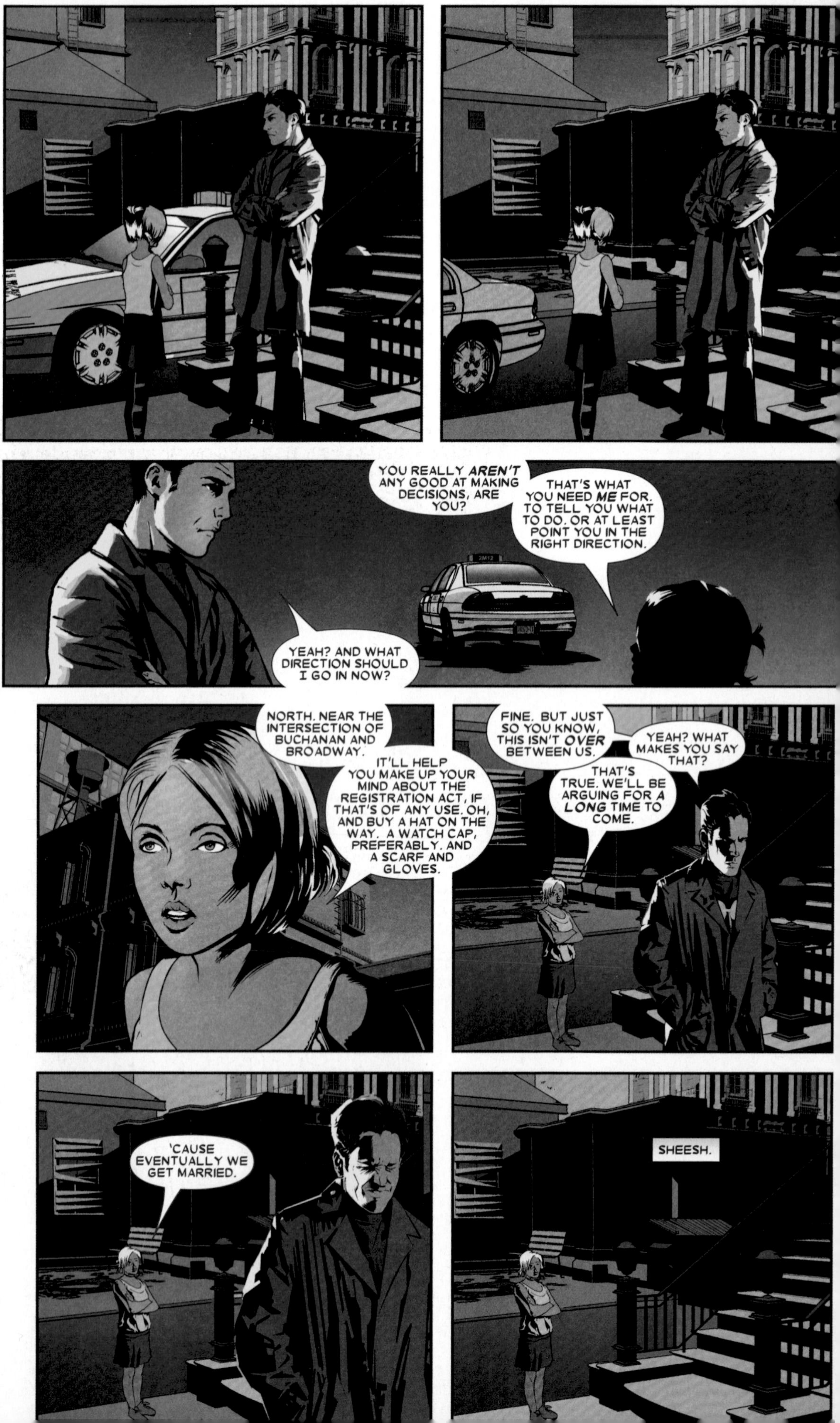
YOU REALLY AREN'T ANY GOOD AT MAKING DECISIONS, ARE YOU?
THAT'S WHAT YOU NEED ME FOR. TO TELL YOU WHAT TO DO. OR AT LEAST POINT YOU IN THE RIGHT DIRECTION.
YEAH? AND WHAT DIRECTION SHOULD I GO IN NOW?
NORTH. NEAR THE INTERSECTION OF BUCHANAN AND BROADWAY.
IT'LL HELP YOU MAKE UP YOUR MIND ABOUT THE REGISTRATION ACT, IF THAT'S OF ANY USE. OH, AND BUY A HAT ON THE WAY. A WATCH CAP, PREFERABLY. AND A SCARF AND GLOVES.
FINE. BUT JUST SO YOU KNOW, THIS ISN'T OVER BETWEEN US.
YEAH? WHAT MAKES YOU SAY THAT?
THAT'S TRUE. WE'LL BE ARGUING FOR A LONG TIME TO COME.
'CAUSE EVENTUALLY WE GET MARRIED.
SHEESH.

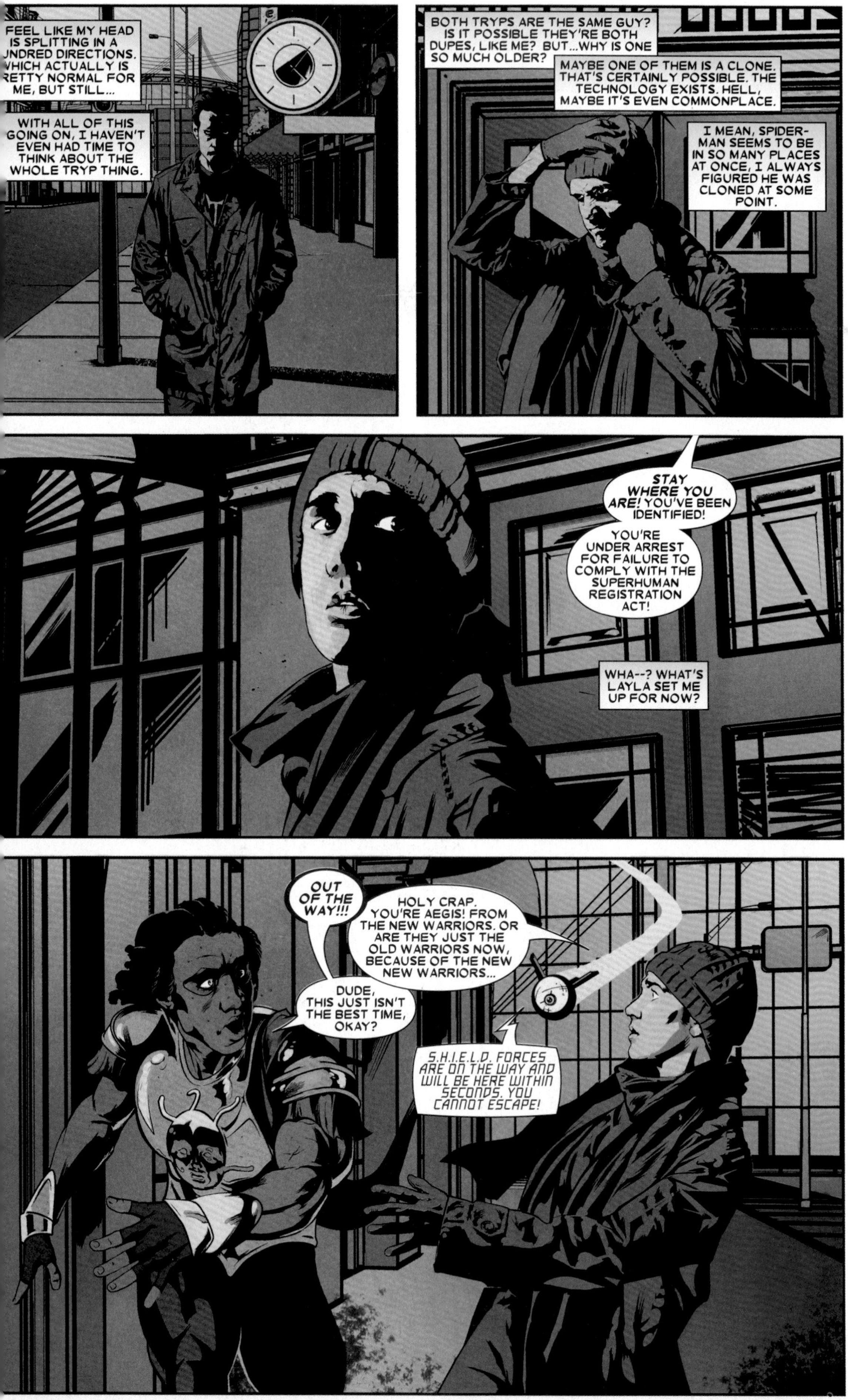

FEEL LIKE MY HEAD IS SPLITTING IN A UNDRED DIRECTIONS. WHICH ACTUALLY IS RETTY NORMAL FOR ME, BUT STILL...
WITH ALL OF THIS GOING ON, I HAVEN'T EVEN HAD TIME TO THINK ABOUT THE WHOLE TRYP THING.
BOTH TRYPS ARE THE SAME GUY? IS IT POSSIBLE THEY'RE BOTH DUPES, LIKE ME? BUT...WHY IS ONE SO MUCH OLDER?
MAYBE ONE OF THEM IS A CLONE. THAT'S CERTAINLY POSSIBLE. THE TECHNOLOGY EXISTS. HELL, MAYBE IT'S EVEN COMMONPLACE.
I MEAN, SPIDER-MAN SEEMS TO BE IN SO MANY PLACES AT ONCE, I ALWAYS FIGURED HE WAS CLONED AT SOME POINT.
STAY WHERE YOU ARE! YOU'VE BEEN IDENTIFIED!
YOU'RE UNDER ARREST FOR FAILURE TO COMPLY WITH THE SUPERHUMAN REGISTRATION ACT!
WHA--? WHAT'S LAYLA SET ME UP FOR NOW?
OUT OF THE WAY!!!
HOLY CRAP. YOU'RE AEGIS! FROM THE NEW WARRIORS. OR ARE THEY JUST THE OLD WARRIORS NOW, BECAUSE OF THE NEW NEW WARRIORS...
DUDE, THIS JUST ISN'T THE BEST TIME, OKAY?
S.H.I.E.L.D. FORCES ARE ON THE WAY AND WILL BE HERE WITHIN SECONDS. YOU CANNOT ESCAPE!

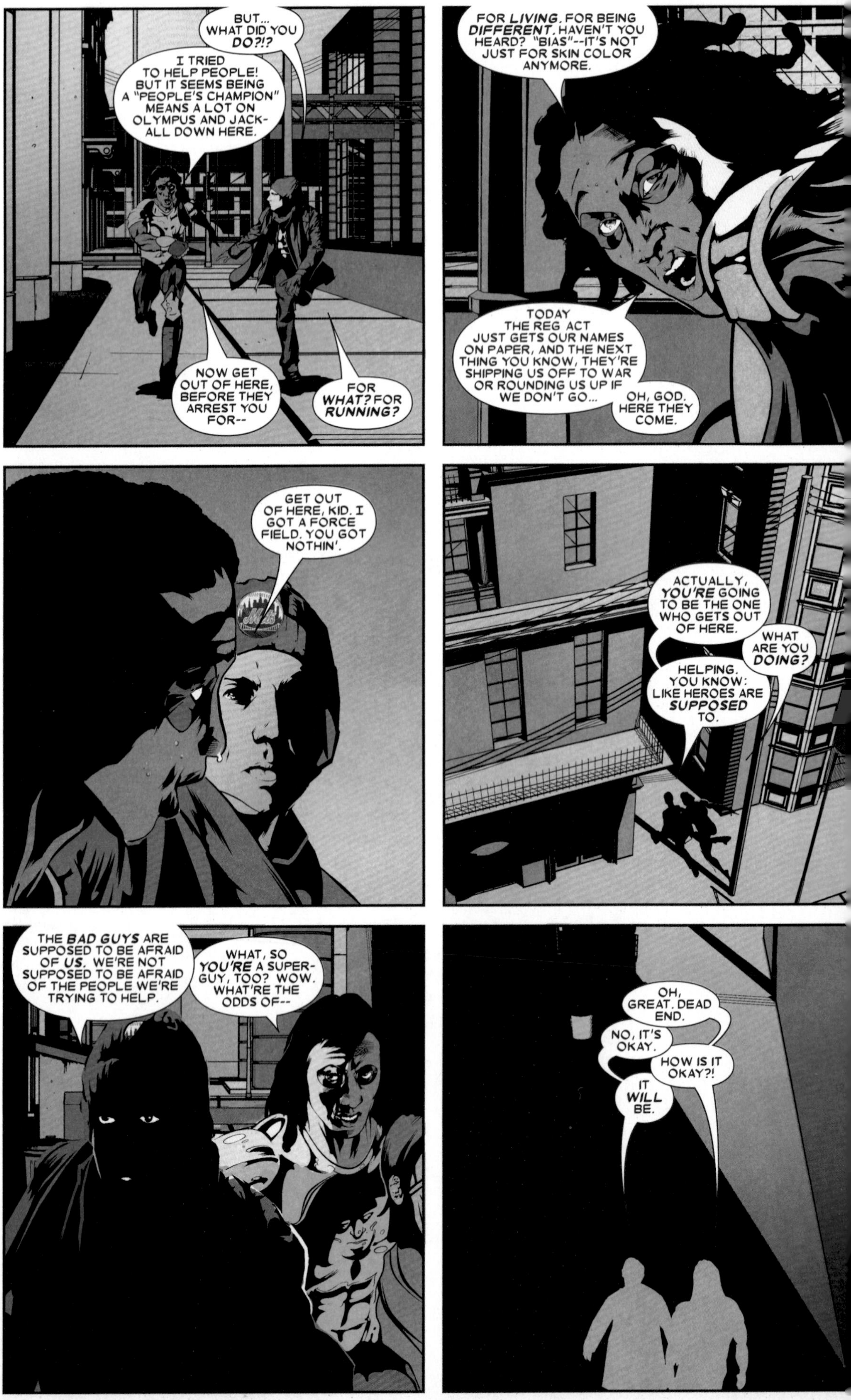
BUT... WHAT DID YOU DO?!?
I TRIED TO HELP PEOPLE! BUT IT SEEMS BEING A "PEOPLE'S CHAMPION" MEANS A LOT ON OLYMPUS AND JACK-ALL DOWN HERE.
NOW GET OUT OF HERE, BEFORE THEY ARREST YOU FOR--
FOR WHAT? FOR RUNNING?
FOR LIVING. FOR BEING DIFFERENT. HAVEN'T YOU HEARD? "BIAS"--IT'S NOT JUST FOR SKIN COLOR ANYMORE.
TODAY THE REG ACT JUST GETS OUR NAMES ON PAPER, AND THE NEXT THING YOU KNOW, THEY'RE SHIPPING US OFF TO WAR OR ROUNDING US UP IF WE DON'T GO...
OH, GOD. HERE THEY COME.
GET OUT OF HERE, KID. I GOT A FORCE FIELD. YOU GOT NOTHIN'.
ACTUALLY, YOU'RE GOING TO BE THE ONE WHO GETS OUT OF HERE.
WHAT ARE YOU DOING?
HELPING. YOU KNOW: LIKE HEROES ARE SUPPOSED TO.
THE BAD GUYS ARE SUPPOSED TO BE AFRAID OF US. WE'RE NOT SUPPOSED TO BE AFRAID OF THE PEOPLE WE'RE TRYING TO HELP.
WHAT, SO YOU'RE A SUPER-GUY, TOO? WOW. WHAT'RE THE ODDS OF--
OH, GREAT. DEAD END.
NO, IT'S OKAY.
HOW IS IT OKAY?!
IT WILL BE.

AEGIS! COME OUT SLOWLY AND MAKE NO SUDDEN MOVES.
WE HAVE WEAPONS THAT CAN PUNCH THROUGH EVEN YOUR FORCE FIELD, SON. BUT YOU WON'T BE INJURED IF YOU SURRENDER IMMEDIATELY!
COMPLY WITH THE LAW, OR WE WILL BE FORCED TO--
DO YOU HEAR SOMETHING? LIKE... THE GROUND RUMBLING?
SOUNDS LIKE...A STAMPEDE.
GIVE ME A VIDEO REPORT FROM THE 'BOT!
SCANNING NOW, SIR.
WHAT THE HECK IS GOING ON IN THERE? I THOUGHT ONLY TWO PEOPLE WENT IN THERE...OUR SUBJECT AND SOME BYSTANDER.
YES, SIR. BUT IT'S...MUCH MORE CROWDED NOW. I GOT A READING ON--
WHA--?

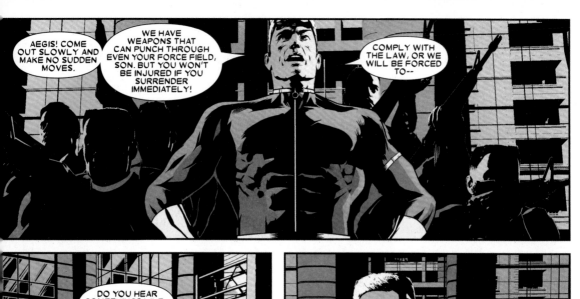

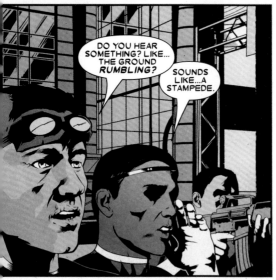

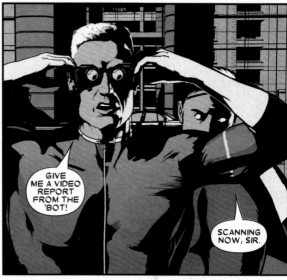

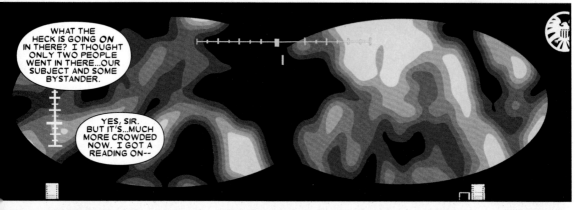

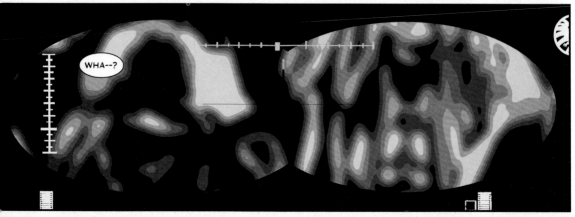

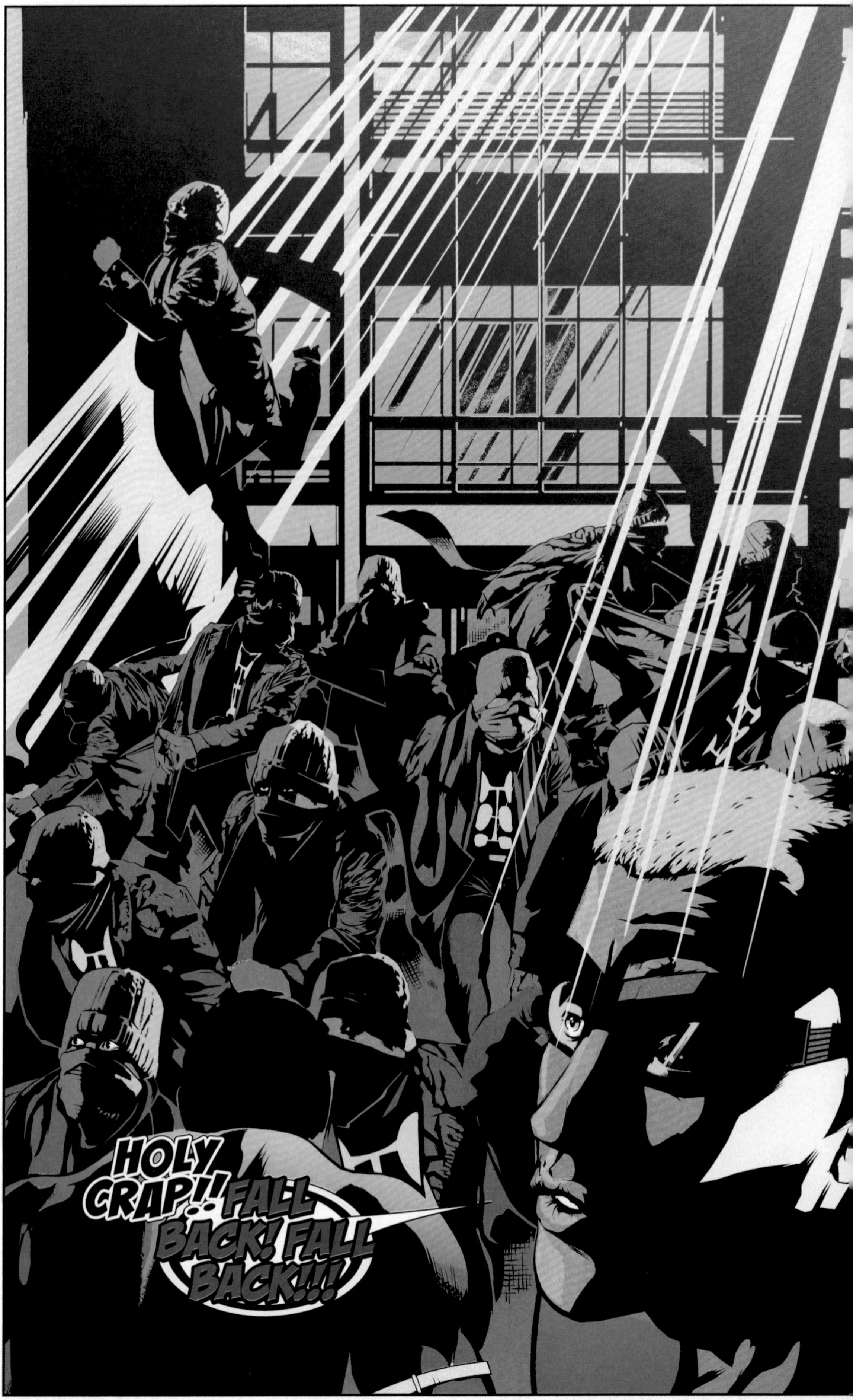
HOLY CRAP!! FALL BACK! FALL BACK!!!

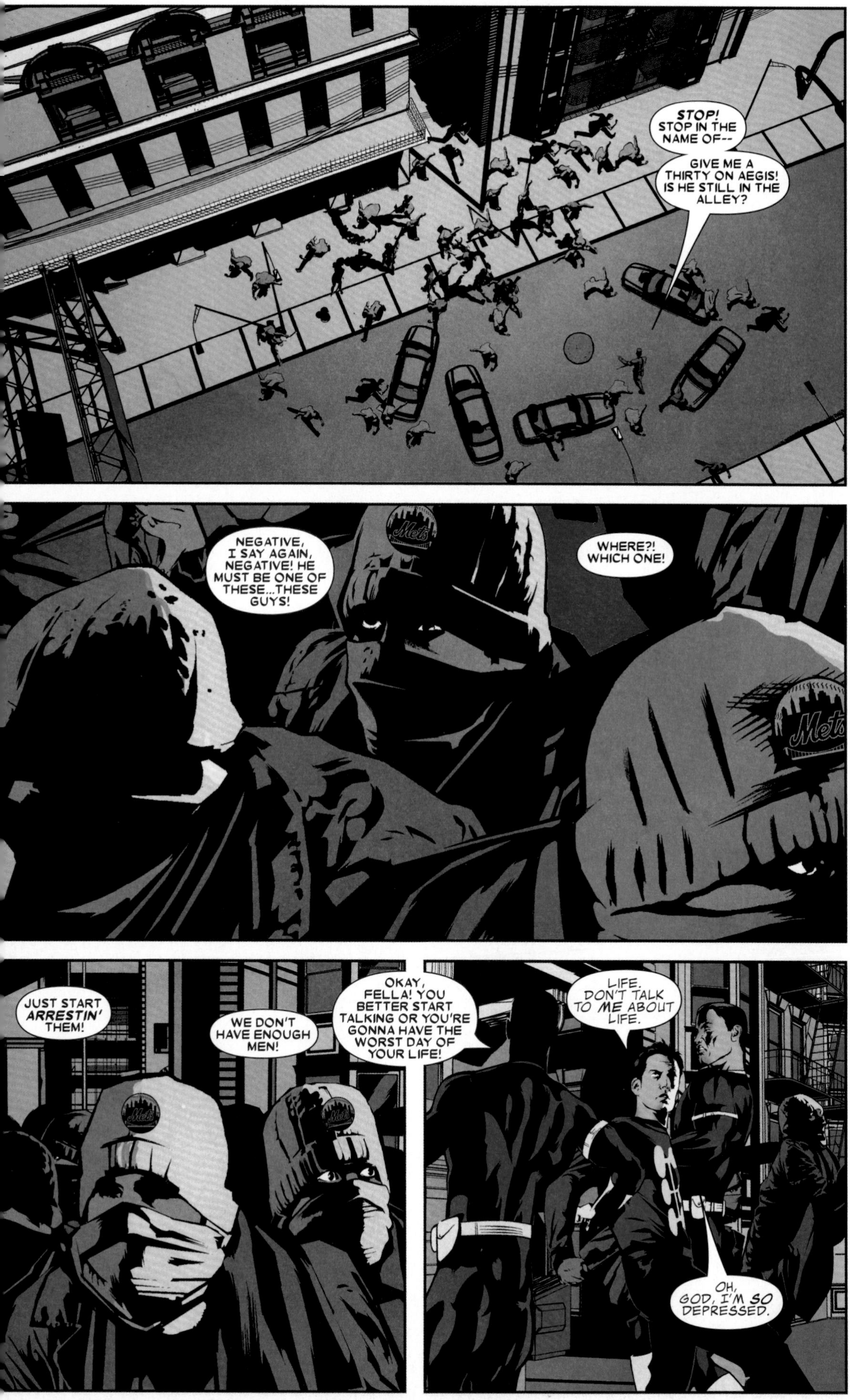
STOP! STOP IN THE NAME OF--
GIVE ME A THIRTY ON AEGIS! IS HE STILL IN THE ALLEY?
NEGATIVE, I SAY AGAIN, NEGATIVE! HE MUST BE ONE OF THESE...THESE GUYS!
WHERE?! WHICH ONE!
Mets
Mets
JUST START ARRESTIN' THEM!
WE DON'T HAVE ENOUGH MEN!
OKAY, FELLA! YOU BETTER START TALKING OR YOU'RE GONNA HAVE THE WORST DAY OF YOUR LIFE!
LIFE. DON'T TALK TO ME ABOUT LIFE.
OH, GOD, I'M SO DEPRESSED.

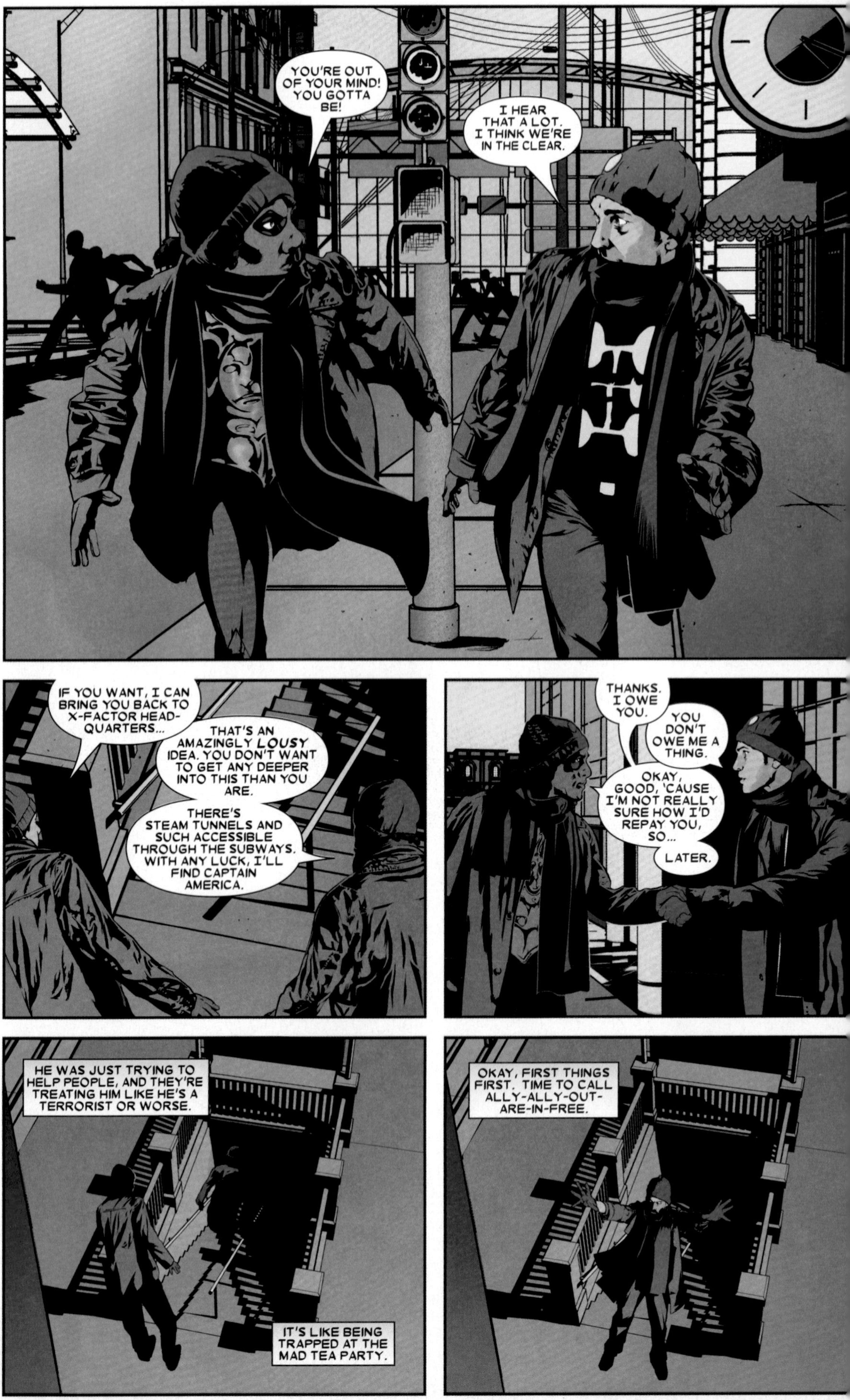
YOU'RE OUT OF YOUR MIND! YOU GOTTA BE!
I HEAR THAT A LOT. I THINK WE'RE IN THE CLEAR.
IF YOU WANT, I CAN BRING YOU BACK TO X-FACTOR HEAD-QUARTERS...
THAT'S AN AMAZINGLY LOUSY IDEA. YOU DON'T WANT TO GET ANY DEEPER INTO THIS THAN YOU ARE.
THERE'S STEAM TUNNELS AND SUCH ACCESSIBLE THROUGH THE SUBWAYS. WITH ANY LUCK, I'LL FIND CAPTAIN AMERICA.
THANKS. I OWE YOU.
YOU DON'T OWE ME A THING.
OKAY, GOOD, 'CAUSE I'M NOT REALLY SURE HOW I'D REPAY YOU, SO...
LATER.
HE WAS JUST TRYING TO HELP PEOPLE, AND THEY'RE TREATING HIM LIKE HE'S A TERRORIST OR WORSE.
IT'S LIKE BEING TRAPPED AT THE MAD TEA PARTY.
OKAY, FIRST THINGS FIRST. TIME TO CALL ALLY-ALLY-OUT-ARE-IN-FREE.

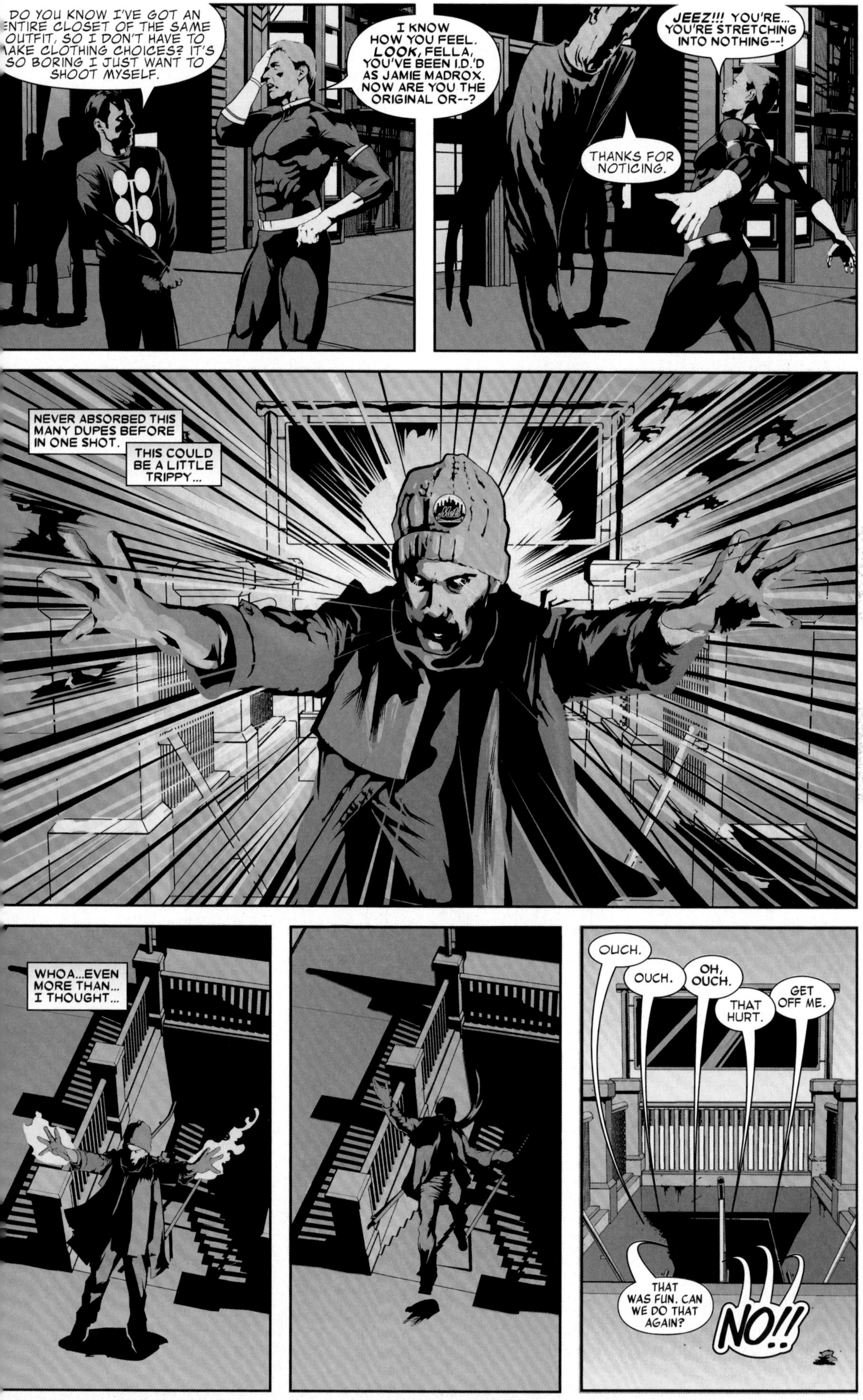
DO YOU KNOW I'VE GOT AN ENTIRE CLOSET OF THE SAME OUTFIT, SO I DON'T HAVE TO MAKE CLOTHING CHOICES? IT'S SO BORING I JUST WANT TO SHOOT MYSELF.
I KNOW HOW YOU FEEL. LOOK, FELLA, YOU'VE BEEN I.D.'D AS JAMIE MADROX. NOW ARE YOU THE ORIGINAL OR--?
JEEZ!!! YOU'RE... YOU'RE STRETCHING INTO NOTHING--!
THANKS FOR NOTICING.
NEVER ABSORBED THIS MANY DUPES BEFORE IN ONE SHOT.
THIS COULD BE A LITTLE TRIPPY...
WHOA...EVEN MORE THAN... I THOUGHT...
OUCH.
OUCH.
OH, OUCH.
THAT HURT.
GET OFF ME.
THAT WAS FUN. CAN WE DO THAT AGAIN?
NO!!

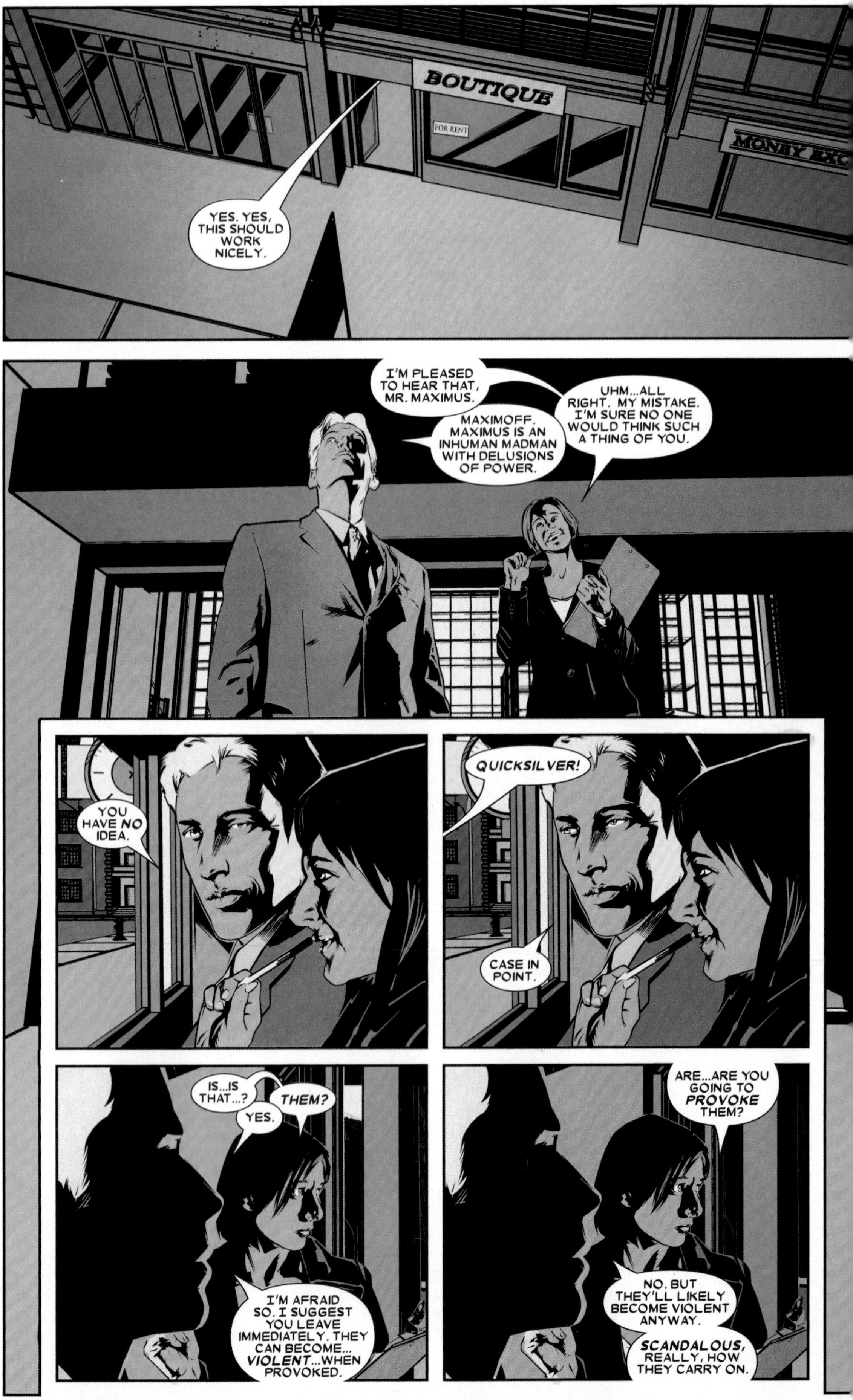
BOUTIQUE
FOR RENT
MONEY EXC
YES. YES, THIS SHOULD WORK NICELY.
I'M PLEASED TO HEAR THAT, MR. MAXIMUS.
MAXIMOFF. MAXIMUS IS AN INHUMAN MADMAN WITH DELUSIONS OF POWER.
UHM...ALL RIGHT. MY MISTAKE. I'M SURE NO ONE WOULD THINK SUCH A THING OF YOU.
YOU HAVE NO IDEA.
QUICKSILVER!
CASE IN POINT.
IS...IS THAT...?
YES.
THEM?
I'M AFRAID SO. I SUGGEST YOU LEAVE IMMEDIATELY. THEY CAN BECOME... VIOLENT...WHEN PROVOKED.
ARE...ARE YOU GOING TO PROVOKE THEM?
NO. BUT THEY'LL LIKELY BECOME VIOLENT ANYWAY.
SCANDALOUS, REALLY, HOW THEY CARRY ON.

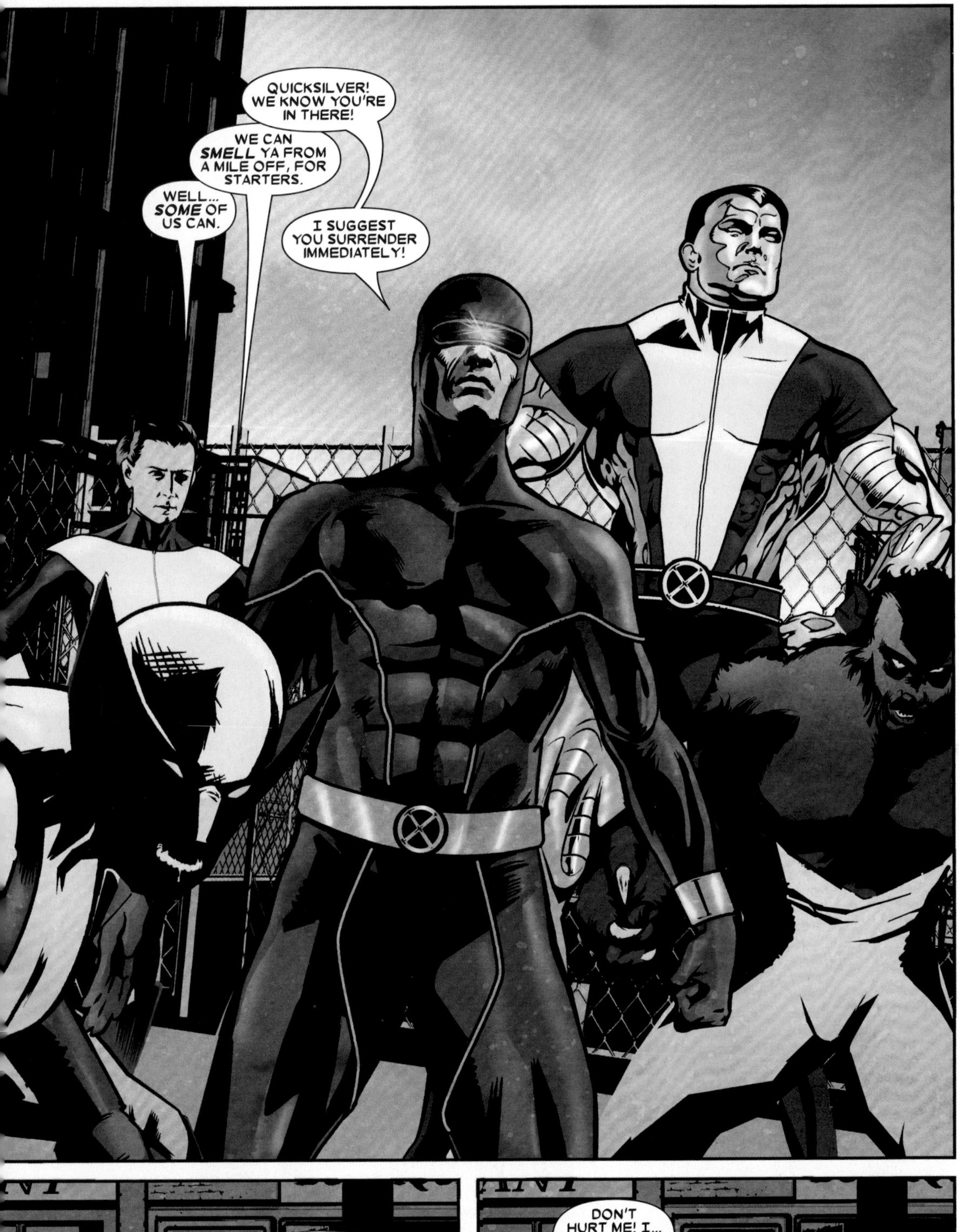
QUICKSILVER! WE KNOW YOU'RE IN THERE!
WE CAN *SMELL* YA FROM A MILE OFF, FOR STARTERS.
WELL... *SOME* OF US CAN.
I SUGGEST YOU SURRENDER IMMEDIATELY!

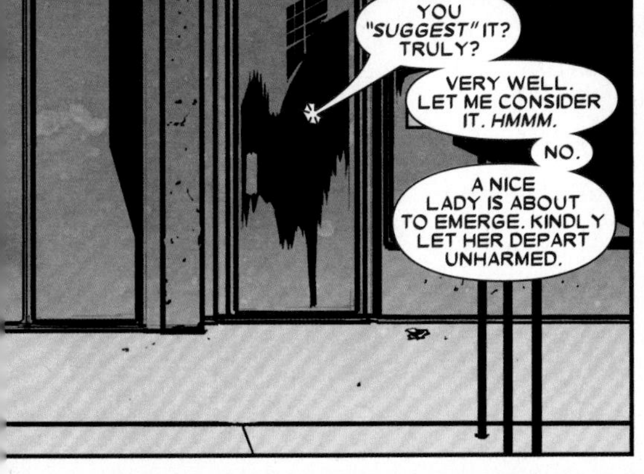
YOU "*SUGGEST*" IT? TRULY?
VERY WELL. LET ME CONSIDER IT. *HMMM.*
NO.
A NICE LADY IS ABOUT TO EMERGE. KINDLY LET HER DEPART UNHARMED.

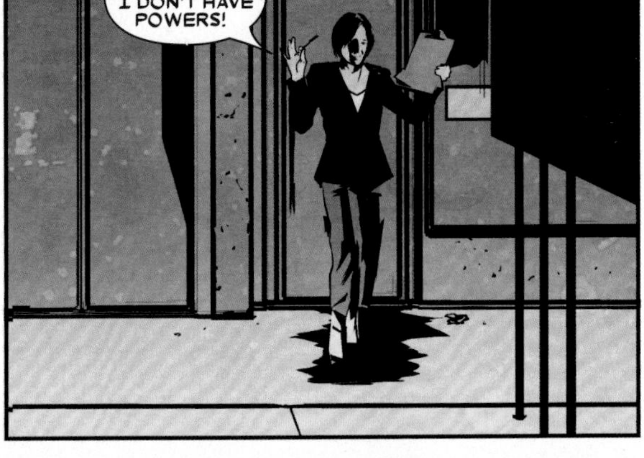
DON'T HURT ME! I... I DON'T HAVE POWERS!

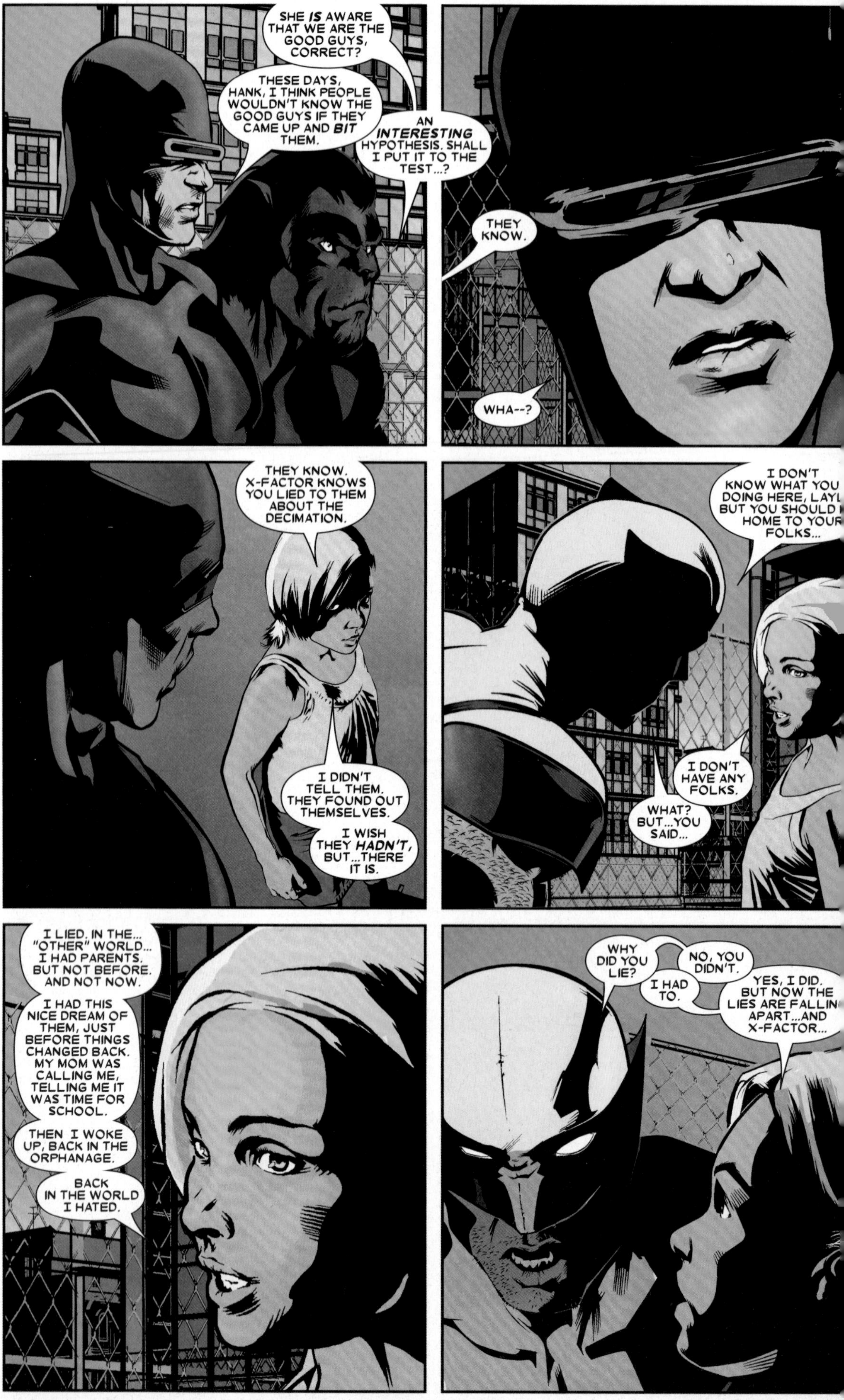
SHE *IS* AWARE THAT WE ARE THE GOOD GUYS, CORRECT?
THESE DAYS, HANK, I THINK PEOPLE WOULDN'T KNOW THE GOOD GUYS IF THEY CAME UP AND *BIT* THEM.
AN *INTERESTING* HYPOTHESIS. SHALL I PUT IT TO THE TEST...?
THEY KNOW.
WHA--?
THEY KNOW. X-FACTOR KNOWS YOU LIED TO THEM ABOUT THE DECIMATION.
I DIDN'T TELL THEM. THEY FOUND OUT THEMSELVES.
I WISH THEY *HADN'T,* BUT...THERE IT IS.
I DON'T KNOW WHAT YOU DOING HERE, LAYL BUT YOU SHOULD HOME TO YOUR FOLKS...
I DON'T HAVE ANY FOLKS.
WHAT? BUT...YOU SAID...
I LIED. IN THE... "OTHER" WORLD... I HAD PARENTS. BUT NOT BEFORE. AND NOT NOW.
I HAD THIS NICE DREAM OF THEM, JUST BEFORE THINGS CHANGED BACK. MY MOM WAS CALLING ME, TELLING ME IT WAS TIME FOR SCHOOL.
THEN I WOKE UP, BACK IN THE ORPHANAGE.
BACK IN THE WORLD I HATED.
WHY DID YOU LIE?
I HAD TO.
NO, YOU DIDN'T.
YES, I DID. BUT NOW THE LIES ARE FALLIN APART...AND X-FACTOR...

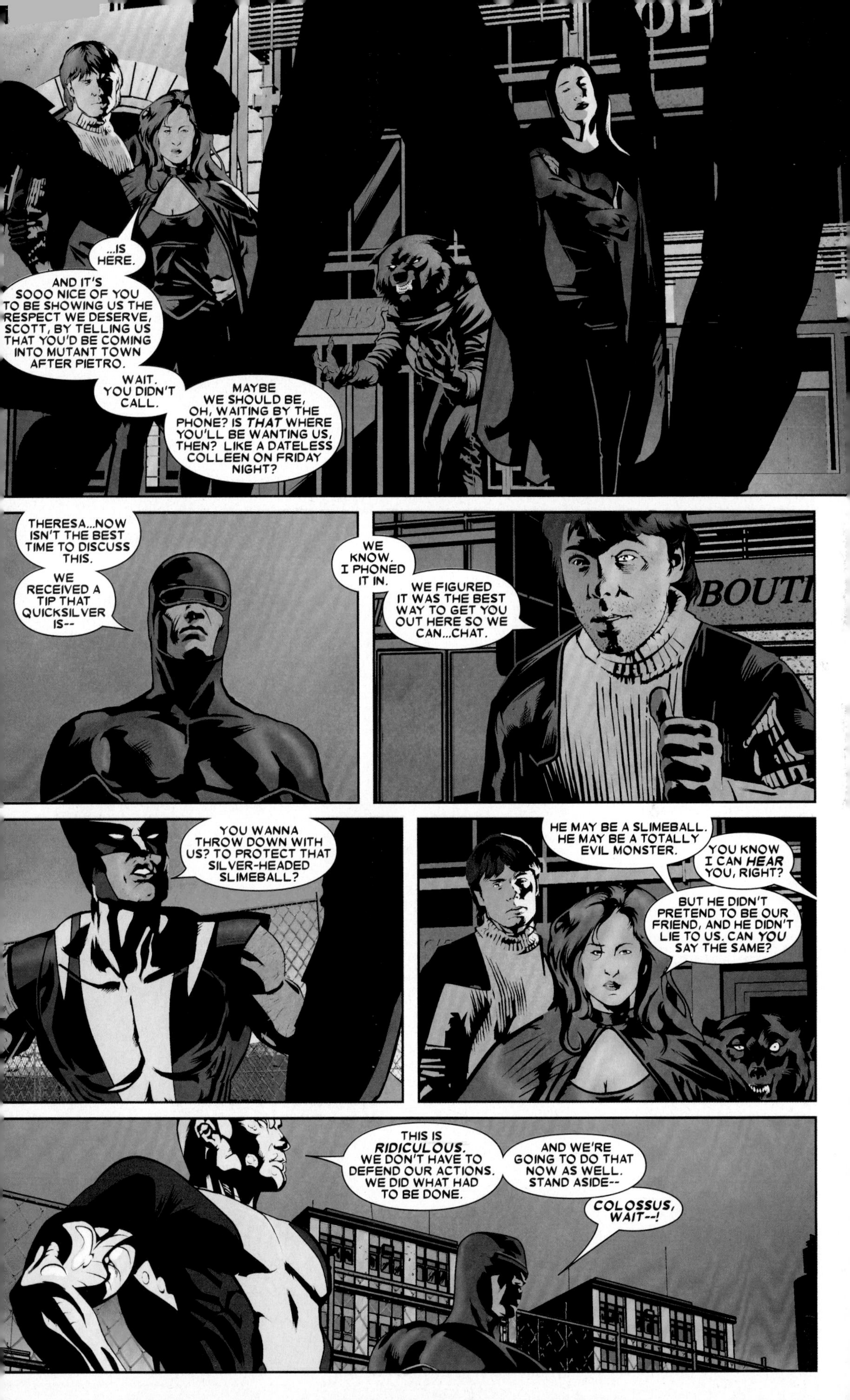

...IS HERE.
AND IT'S SOOO NICE OF YOU TO BE SHOWING US THE RESPECT WE DESERVE, SCOTT, BY TELLING US THAT YOU'D BE COMING INTO MUTANT TOWN AFTER PIETRO.
WAIT. YOU DIDN'T CALL.
MAYBE WE SHOULD BE, OH, WAITING BY THE PHONE? IS *THAT* WHERE YOU'LL BE WANTING US, THEN? LIKE A DATELESS COLLEEN ON FRIDAY NIGHT?
THERESA...NOW ISN'T THE BEST TIME TO DISCUSS THIS.
WE RECEIVED A TIP THAT QUICKSILVER IS--
WE KNOW. I PHONED IT IN.
WE FIGURED IT WAS THE BEST WAY TO GET YOU OUT HERE SO WE CAN...CHAT.
BOUTI
YOU WANNA THROW DOWN WITH US? TO PROTECT THAT SILVER-HEADED SLIMEBALL?
HE MAY BE A SLIMEBALL. HE MAY BE A TOTALLY EVIL MONSTER.
YOU KNOW I CAN *HEAR* YOU, RIGHT?
BUT HE DIDN'T PRETEND TO BE OUR FRIEND, AND HE DIDN'T LIE TO US. CAN *YOU* SAY THE SAME?
THIS IS *RIDICULOUS.* WE DON'T HAVE TO DEFEND OUR ACTIONS. WE DID WHAT HAD TO BE DONE.
AND WE'RE GOING TO DO THAT NOW AS WELL. STAND ASIDE--
COLOSSUS, WAIT--!

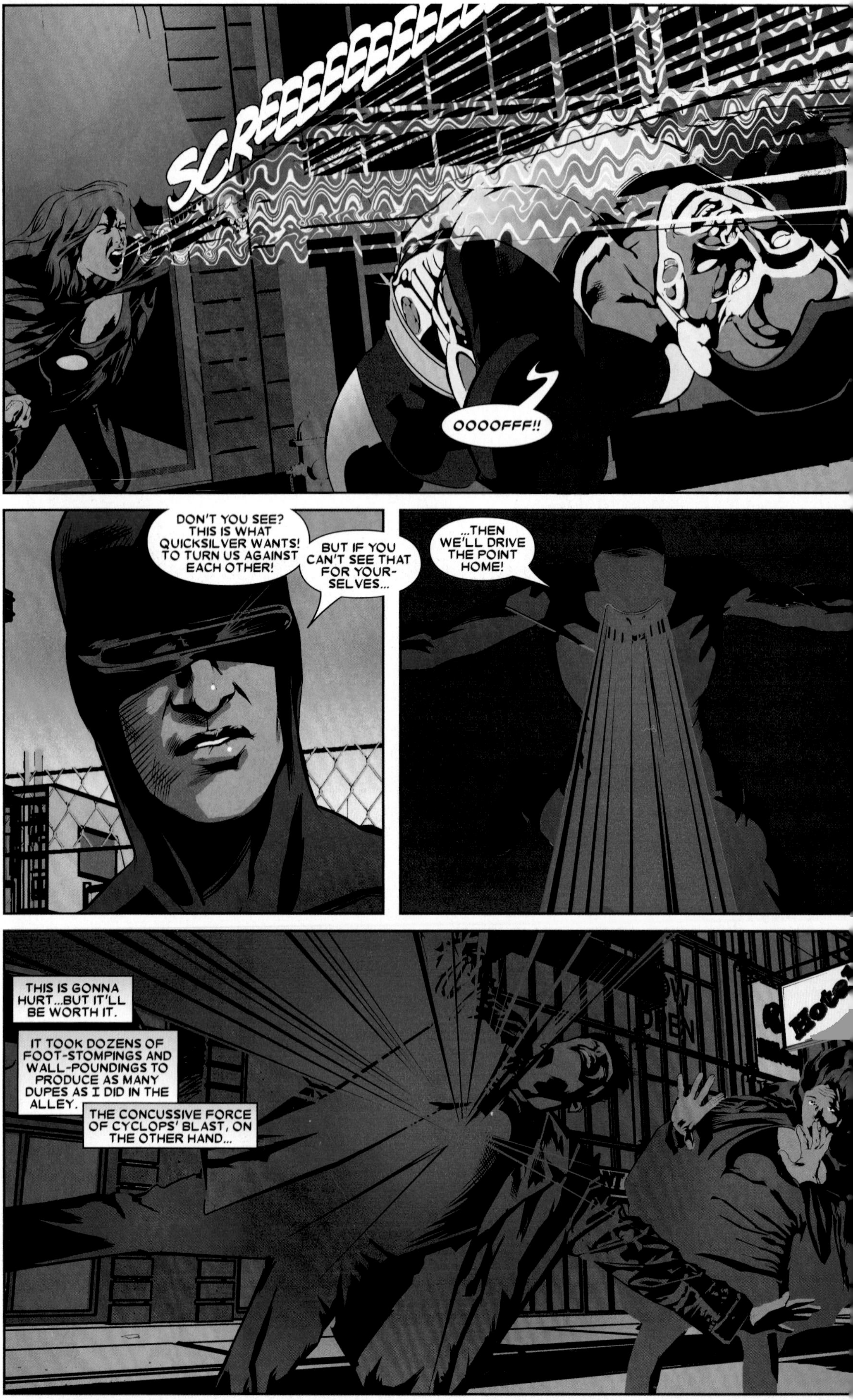

SCREEEEEEEEEE
OOOOFFF!!
DON'T YOU SEE? THIS IS WHAT QUICKSILVER WANTS! TO TURN US AGAINST EACH OTHER!
BUT IF YOU CAN'T SEE THAT FOR YOUR-SELVES...
...THEN WE'LL DRIVE THE POINT HOME!
THIS IS GONNA HURT...BUT IT'LL BE WORTH IT.
IT TOOK DOZENS OF FOOT-STOMPINGS AND WALL-POUNDINGS TO PRODUCE AS MANY DUPES AS I DID IN THE ALLEY.
THE CONCUSSIVE FORCE OF CYCLOPS' BLAST, ON THE OTHER HAND...

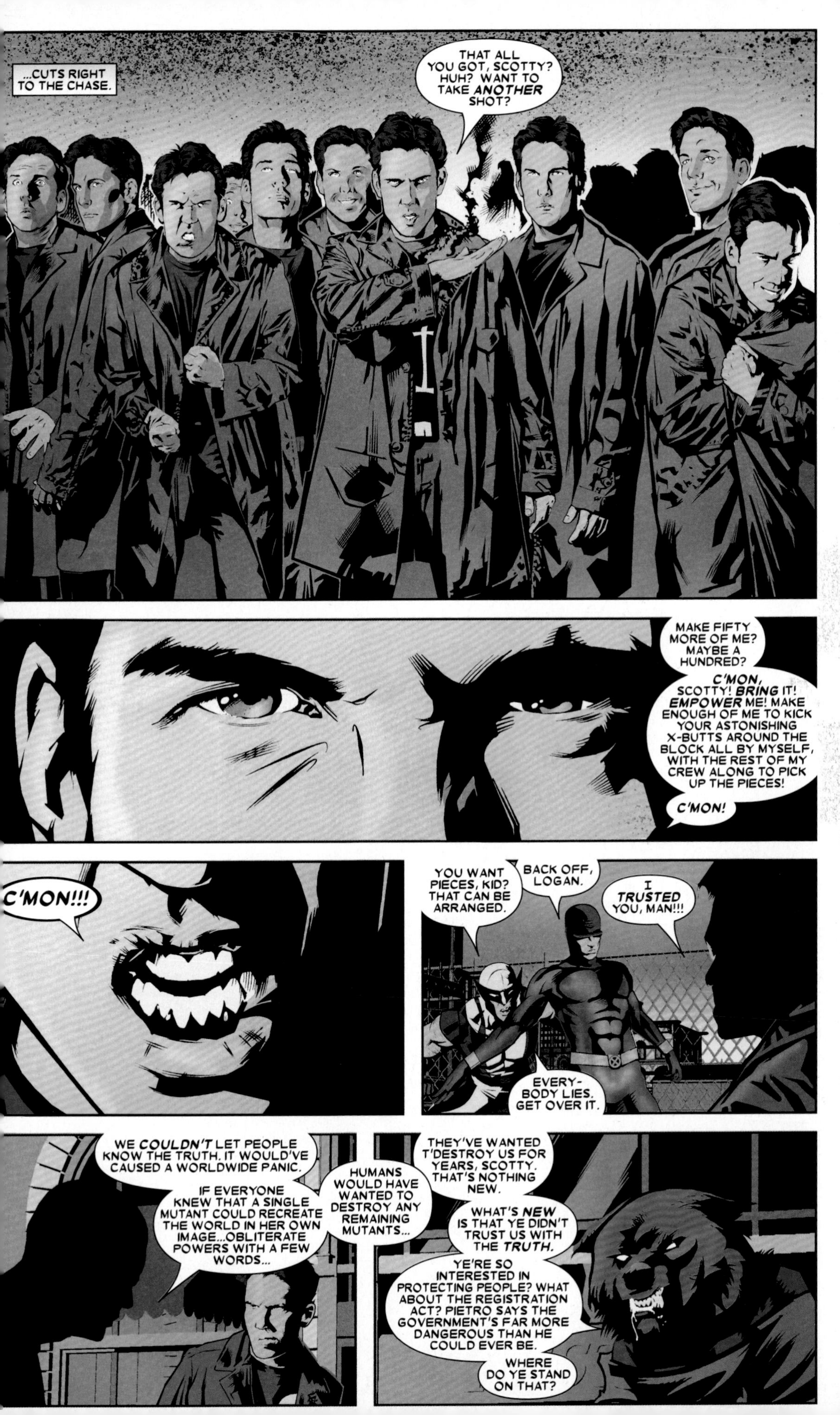
...CUTS RIGHT TO THE CHASE.
THAT ALL YOU GOT, SCOTTY? HUH? WANT TO TAKE ANOTHER SHOT?
MAKE FIFTY MORE OF ME? MAYBE A HUNDRED?
C'MON, SCOTTY! BRING IT! EMPOWER ME! MAKE ENOUGH OF ME TO KICK YOUR ASTONISHING X-BUTTS AROUND THE BLOCK ALL BY MYSELF, WITH THE REST OF MY CREW ALONG TO PICK UP THE PIECES!
C'MON!
C'MON!!!
YOU WANT PIECES, KID? THAT CAN BE ARRANGED.
BACK OFF, LOGAN.
I TRUSTED YOU, MAN!!!
EVERY-BODY LIES. GET OVER IT.
WE COULDN'T LET PEOPLE KNOW THE TRUTH. IT WOULD'VE CAUSED A WORLDWIDE PANIC.
IF EVERYONE KNEW THAT A SINGLE MUTANT COULD RECREATE THE WORLD IN HER OWN IMAGE...OBLITERATE POWERS WITH A FEW WORDS...
HUMANS WOULD HAVE WANTED TO DESTROY ANY REMAINING MUTANTS...
THEY'VE WANTED T'DESTROY US FOR YEARS, SCOTTY. THAT'S NOTHING NEW.
WHAT'S NEW IS THAT YE DIDN'T TRUST US WITH THE TRUTH.
YE'RE SO INTERESTED IN PROTECTING PEOPLE? WHAT ABOUT THE REGISTRATION ACT? PIETRO SAYS THE GOVERNMENT'S FAR MORE DANGEROUS THAN HE COULD EVER BE.
WHERE DO YE STAND ON THAT?

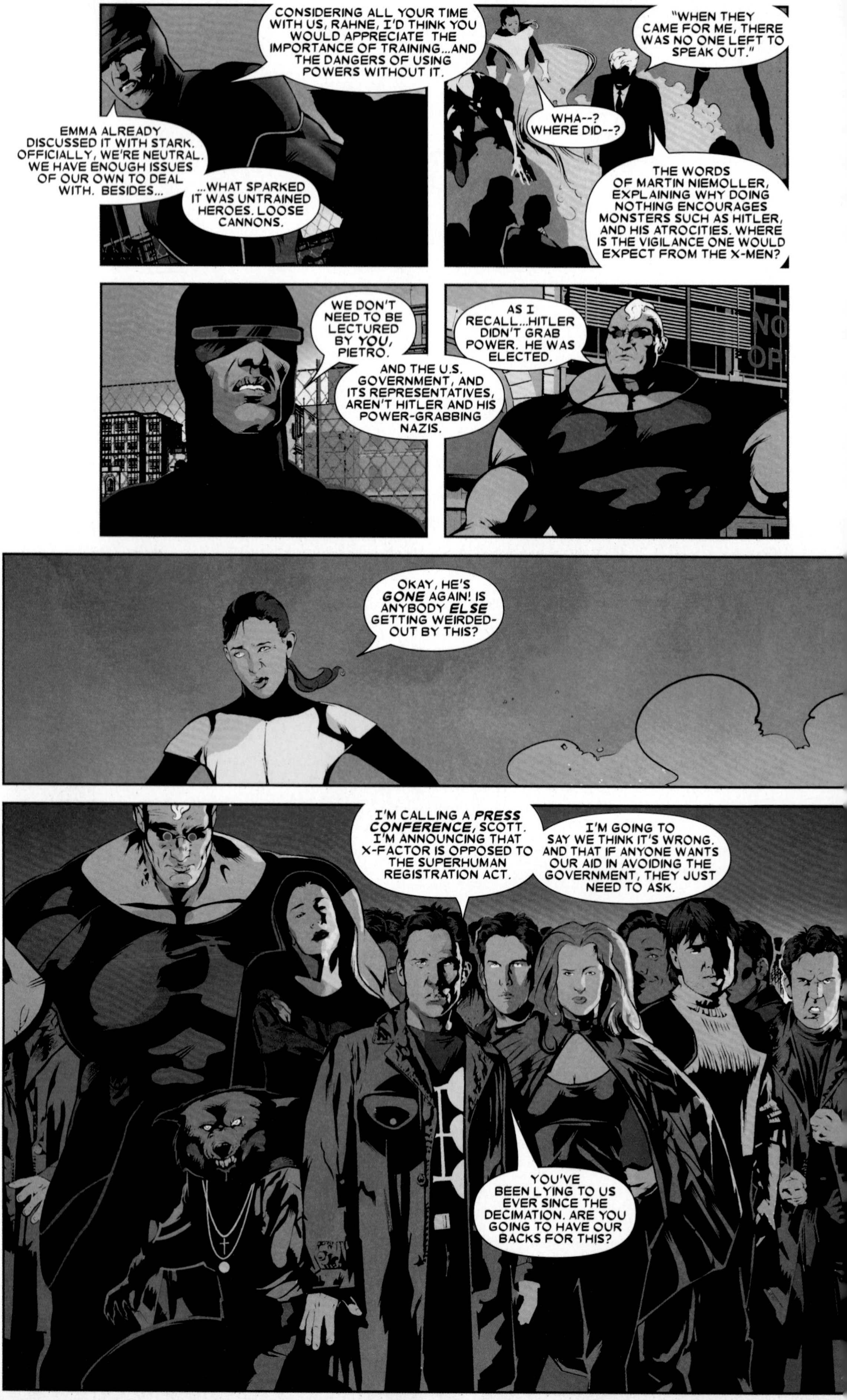

CONSIDERING ALL YOUR TIME WITH US, RAHNE, I'D THINK YOU WOULD APPRECIATE THE IMPORTANCE OF TRAINING...AND THE DANGERS OF USING POWERS WITHOUT IT.
EMMA ALREADY DISCUSSED IT WITH STARK. OFFICIALLY, WE'RE NEUTRAL. WE HAVE ENOUGH ISSUES OF OUR OWN TO DEAL WITH. BESIDES...
...WHAT SPARKED IT WAS UNTRAINED HEROES. LOOSE CANNONS.
"WHEN THEY CAME FOR ME, THERE WAS NO ONE LEFT TO SPEAK OUT."
WHA--? WHERE DID--?
THE WORDS OF MARTIN NIEMOLLER, EXPLAINING WHY DOING NOTHING ENCOURAGES MONSTERS SUCH AS HITLER, AND HIS ATROCITIES. WHERE IS THE VIGILANCE ONE WOULD EXPECT FROM THE X-MEN?
WE DON'T NEED TO BE LECTURED BY *YOU*, PIETRO.
AND THE U.S. GOVERNMENT, AND ITS REPRESENTATIVES, AREN'T HITLER AND HIS POWER-GRABBING NAZIS.
AS I RECALL...HITLER DIDN'T GRAB POWER. HE WAS ELECTED.
OKAY, HE'S *GONE* AGAIN! IS ANYBODY *ELSE* GETTING WEIRDED-OUT BY THIS?
I'M CALLING A *PRESS CONFERENCE*, SCOTT. I'M ANNOUNCING THAT X-FACTOR IS OPPOSED TO THE SUPERHUMAN REGISTRATION ACT.
I'M GOING TO SAY WE THINK IT'S WRONG. AND THAT IF ANYONE WANTS OUR AID IN AVOIDING THE GOVERNMENT, THEY JUST NEED TO ASK.
YOU'VE BEEN LYING TO US EVER SINCE THE DECIMATION. ARE YOU GOING TO HAVE OUR BACKS FOR THIS?

WE CAN'T. WE'VE ALREADY AGREED TO--

THEN GET THE HELL OUT OF MUTANT TOWN. OR IT'S GOING TO BE "GOOD GUY" MUTANT VERSUS "GOOD GUY" MUTANT, AND WE'LL HAVE OUR OWN LITTLE CIVIL WAR RIGHT HERE.

OKAY, THAT'S IT. I'M--

LET'S GO.

WHAT?

SCOTT, WE CAN--

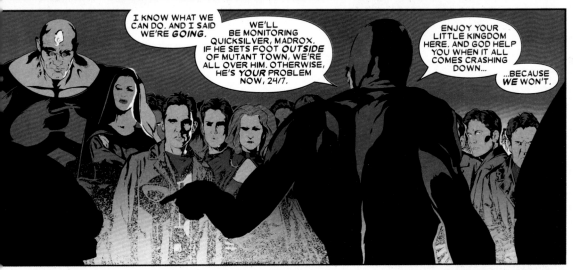

I KNOW WHAT WE CAN DO. AND I SAID WE'RE *GOING*.

WE'LL BE MONITORING QUICKSILVER, MADROX. IF HE SETS FOOT *OUTSIDE* OF MUTANT TOWN, WE'RE ALL OVER HIM. OTHERWISE, HE'S *YOUR* PROBLEM NOW, 24/7.

ENJOY YOUR LITTLE KINGDOM HERE. AND GOD HELP YOU WHEN IT ALL COMES CRASHING DOWN...

...BECAUSE *WE* WON'T.

MADROX... DID WE JUST WIN?

GOD AS MY WITNESS, RAHNE...I HAVEN'T THE *FAINTEST* IDEA.

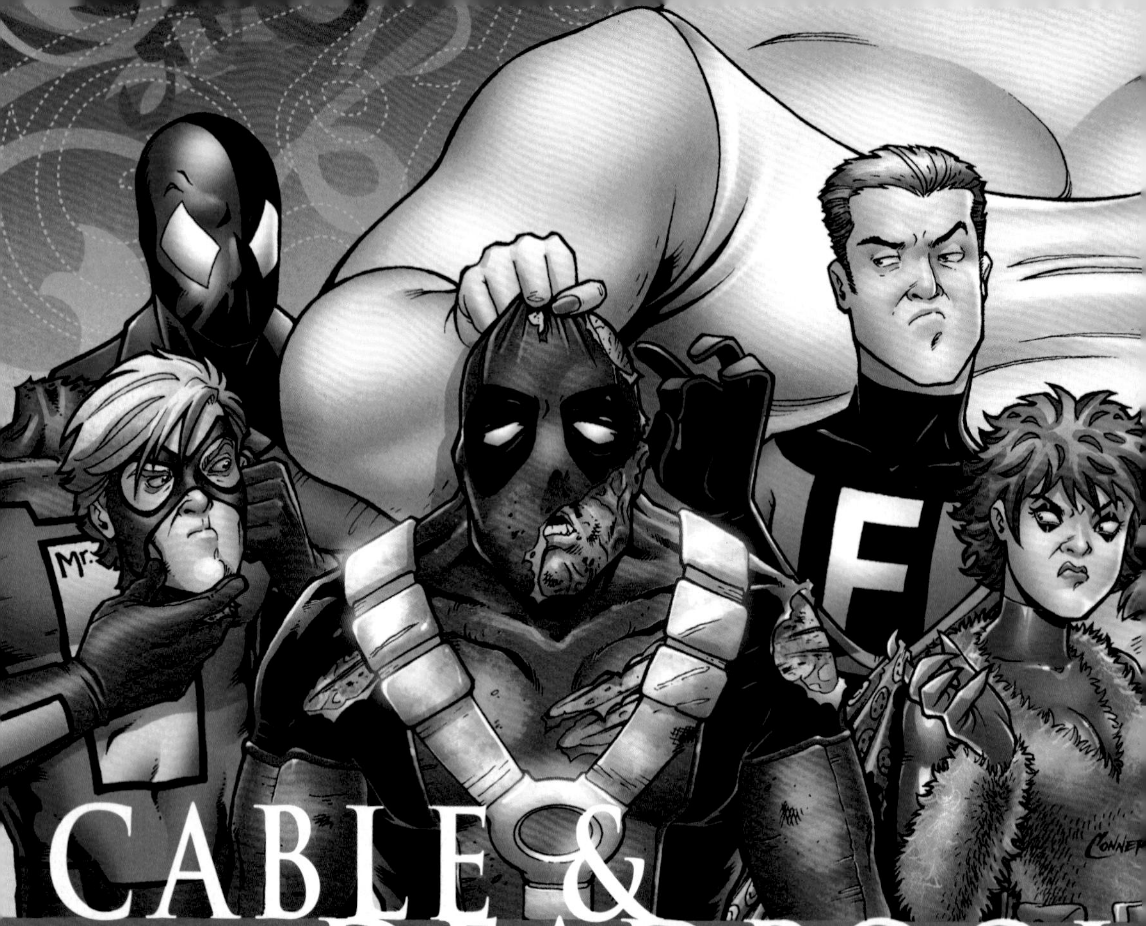

CABLE & DEADPOOL

A MARVEL® COMICS EVENT

CIVIL WAR

CABLE & DEADPOOL #30

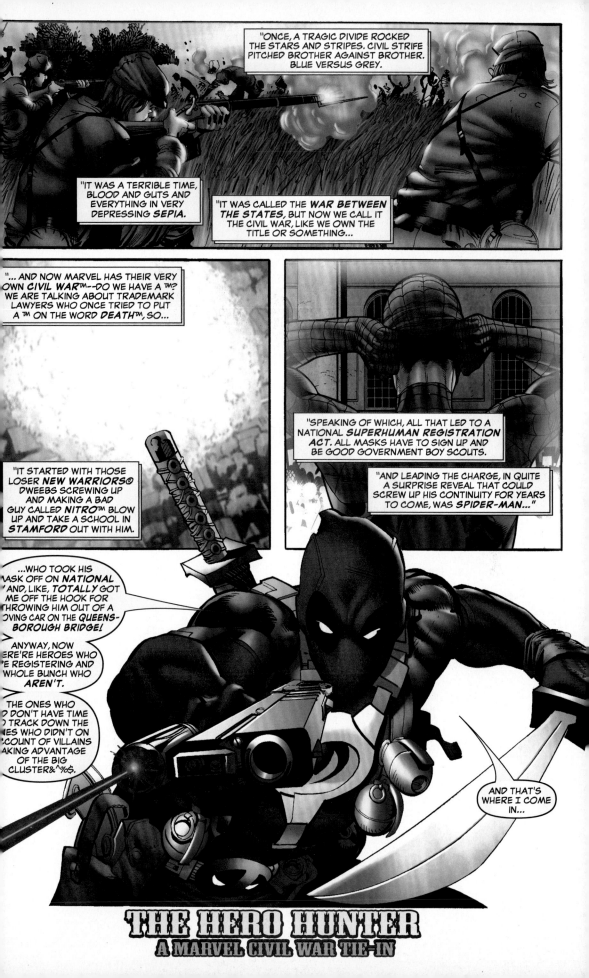

"ONCE, A TRAGIC DIVIDE ROCKED THE STARS AND STRIPES. CIVIL STRIFE PITCHED BROTHER AGAINST BROTHER. BLUE VERSUS GREY.

"IT WAS A TERRIBLE TIME, BLOOD AND GUTS AND EVERYTHING IN VERY DEPRESSING *SEPIA*.

"IT WAS CALLED THE *WAR BETWEEN THE STATES*, BUT NOW WE CALL IT THE CIVIL WAR, LIKE WE OWN THE TITLE OR SOMETHING...

"... AND NOW MARVEL HAS THEIR VERY OWN *CIVIL WAR*™--DO WE HAVE A ™? WE ARE TALKING ABOUT TRADEMARK LAWYERS WHO ONCE TRIED TO PUT A ™ ON THE WORD *DEATH*™, SO...

"IT STARTED WITH THOSE LOSER *NEW WARRIORS*® DWEEBS SCREWING UP AND MAKING A BAD GUY CALLED *NITRO*™ BLOW UP AND TAKE A SCHOOL IN *STAMFORD* OUT WITH HIM.

"SPEAKING OF WHICH, ALL THAT LED TO A NATIONAL *SUPERHUMAN REGISTRATION ACT*. ALL MASKS HAVE TO SIGN UP AND BE GOOD GOVERNMENT BOY SCOUTS.

"AND LEADING THE CHARGE, IN QUITE A SURPRISE REVEAL THAT COULD SCREW UP HIS CONTINUITY FOR YEARS TO COME, WAS *SPIDER-MAN*..."

...WHO TOOK HIS MASK OFF ON *NATIONAL* [T]V AND, LIKE, *TOTALLY* GOT ME OFF THE HOOK FOR THROWING HIM OUT OF A [M]OVING CAR ON THE *QUEENS-BOROUGH BRIDGE!*

ANYWAY, NOW [TH]ERE'RE HEROES WHO [AR]E REGISTERING AND [A] WHOLE BUNCH WHO *AREN'T*.

[AND] THE ONES WHO [THE]Y DON'T HAVE TIME [TO] TRACK DOWN THE [O]NES WHO DIDN'T ON [AC]COUNT OF VILLAINS [T]AKING ADVANTAGE OF THE BIG CLUSTER&^%$.

AND THAT'S WHERE I COME IN...

THE HERO HUNTER
A MARVEL CIVIL WAR TIE-IN

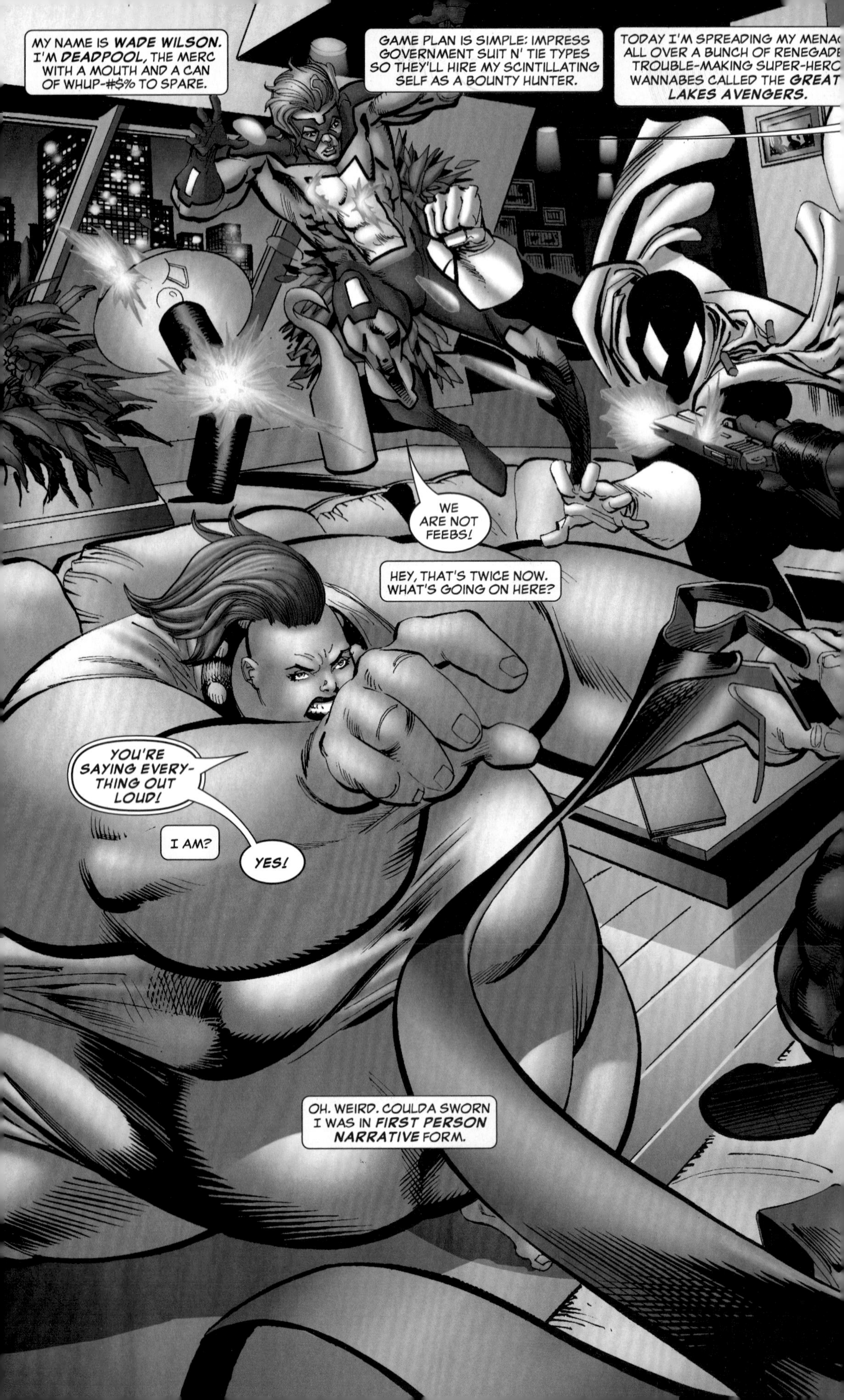
MY NAME IS WADE WILSON. I'M DEADPOOL, THE MERC WITH A MOUTH AND A CAN OF WHUP-#$% TO SPARE.
GAME PLAN IS SIMPLE: IMPRESS GOVERNMENT SUIT N' TIE TYPES SO THEY'LL HIRE MY SCINTILLATING SELF AS A BOUNTY HUNTER.
TODAY I'M SPREADING MY MENAC ALL OVER A BUNCH OF RENEGADE TROUBLE-MAKING SUPER-HERO WANNABES CALLED THE GREAT LAKES AVENGERS.
WE ARE NOT FEEBS!
HEY, THAT'S TWICE NOW. WHAT'S GOING ON HERE?
YOU'RE SAYING EVERY-THING OUT LOUD!
I AM?
YES!
OH. WEIRD. COULDA SWORN I WAS IN FIRST PERSON NARRATIVE FORM.

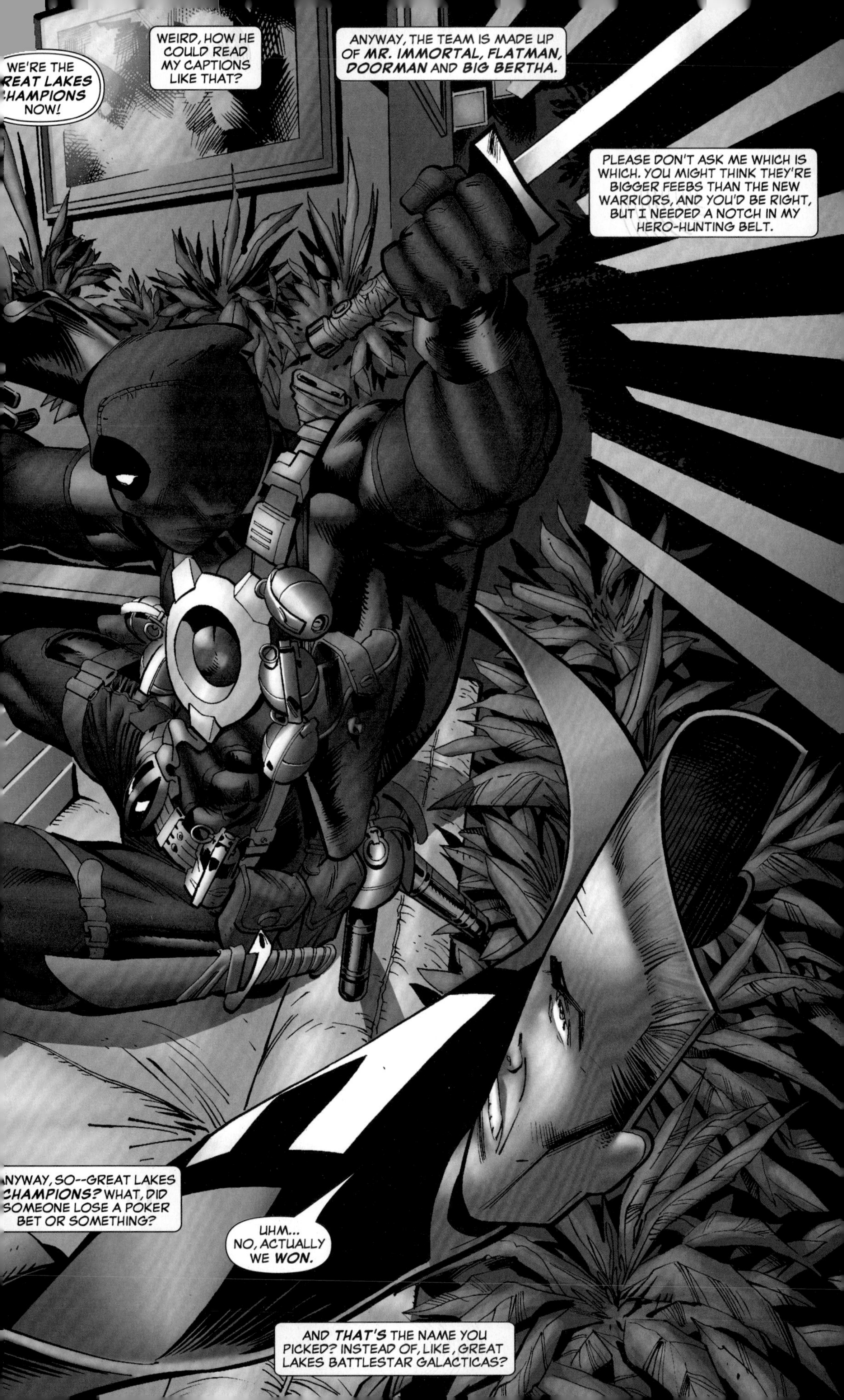
WE'RE THE
GREAT LAKES
CHAMPIONS
NOW!
WEIRD, HOW HE COULD READ MY CAPTIONS LIKE THAT?
ANYWAY, THE TEAM IS MADE UP OF MR. IMMORTAL, FLATMAN, DOORMAN AND BIG BERTHA.
PLEASE DON'T ASK ME WHICH IS WHICH. YOU MIGHT THINK THEY'RE BIGGER FEEBS THAN THE NEW WARRIORS, AND YOU'D BE RIGHT, BUT I NEEDED A NOTCH IN MY HERO-HUNTING BELT.
ANYWAY, SO--GREAT LAKES CHAMPIONS? WHAT, DID SOMEONE LOSE A POKER BET OR SOMETHING?
UHM... NO, ACTUALLY WE WON.
AND THAT'S THE NAME YOU PICKED? INSTEAD OF, LIKE, GREAT LAKES BATTLESTAR GALACTICAS?

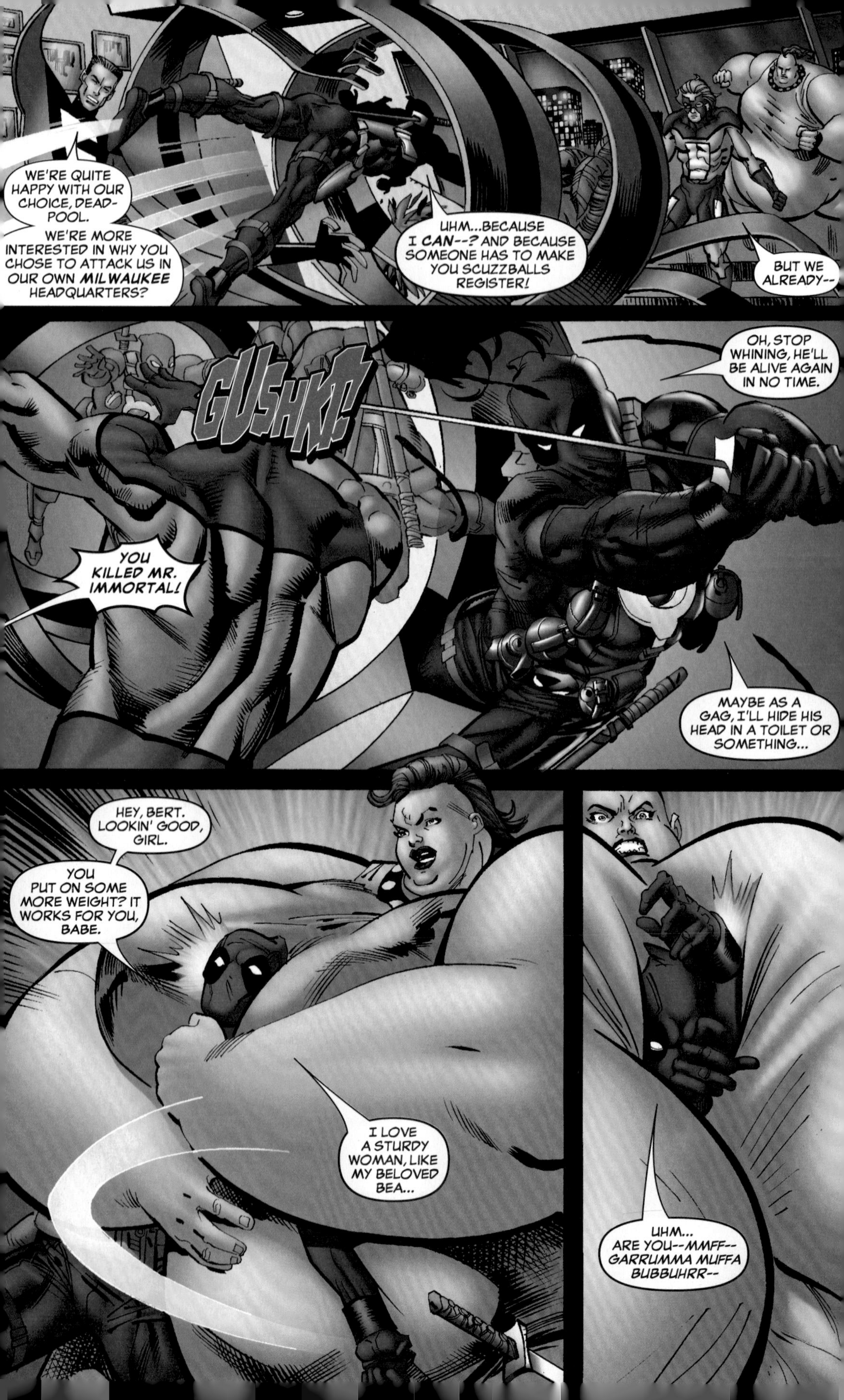
WE'RE QUITE HAPPY WITH OUR CHOICE, DEAD-POOL.
WE'RE MORE INTERESTED IN WHY YOU CHOSE TO ATTACK US IN OUR OWN MILWAUKEE HEADQUARTERS?
UHM...BECAUSE I CAN--? AND BECAUSE SOMEONE HAS TO MAKE YOU SCUZZBALLS REGISTER!
BUT WE ALREADY--
GUSHK!
OH, STOP WHINING, HE'LL BE ALIVE AGAIN IN NO TIME.
YOU KILLED MR. IMMORTAL!
MAYBE AS A GAG, I'LL HIDE HIS HEAD IN A TOILET OR SOMETHING...
HEY, BERT. LOOKIN' GOOD, GIRL.
YOU PUT ON SOME MORE WEIGHT? IT WORKS FOR YOU, BABE.
I LOVE A STURDY WOMAN, LIKE MY BELOVED BEA...
UHM... ARE YOU--MMFF-- GARRUMMA MUFFA BUBBUHRR--

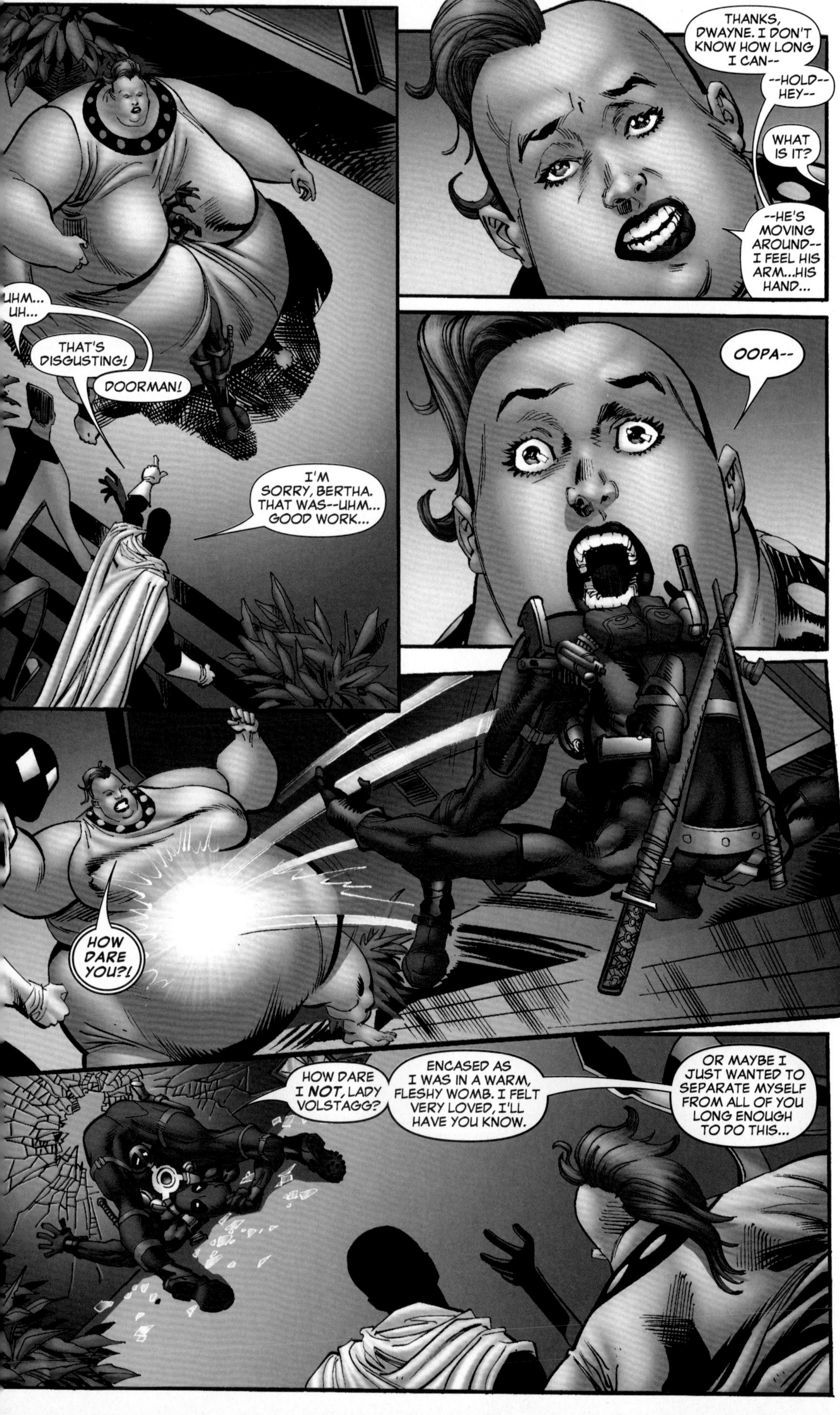
UHM... UH...
THAT'S DISGUSTING!
DOORMAN!
I'M SORRY, BERTHA. THAT WAS--UHM... GOOD WORK...
THANKS, DWAYNE. I DON'T KNOW HOW LONG I CAN--
--HOLD-- HEY--
WHAT IS IT?
--HE'S MOVING AROUND-- I FEEL HIS ARM...HIS HAND...
OOPA--
HOW DARE YOU?!
HOW DARE I NOT, LADY VOLSTAGG?
ENCASED AS I WAS IN A WARM, FLESHY WOMB. I FELT VERY LOVED, I'LL HAVE YOU KNOW.
OR MAYBE I JUST WANTED TO SEPARATE MYSELF FROM ALL OF YOU LONG ENOUGH TO DO THIS...

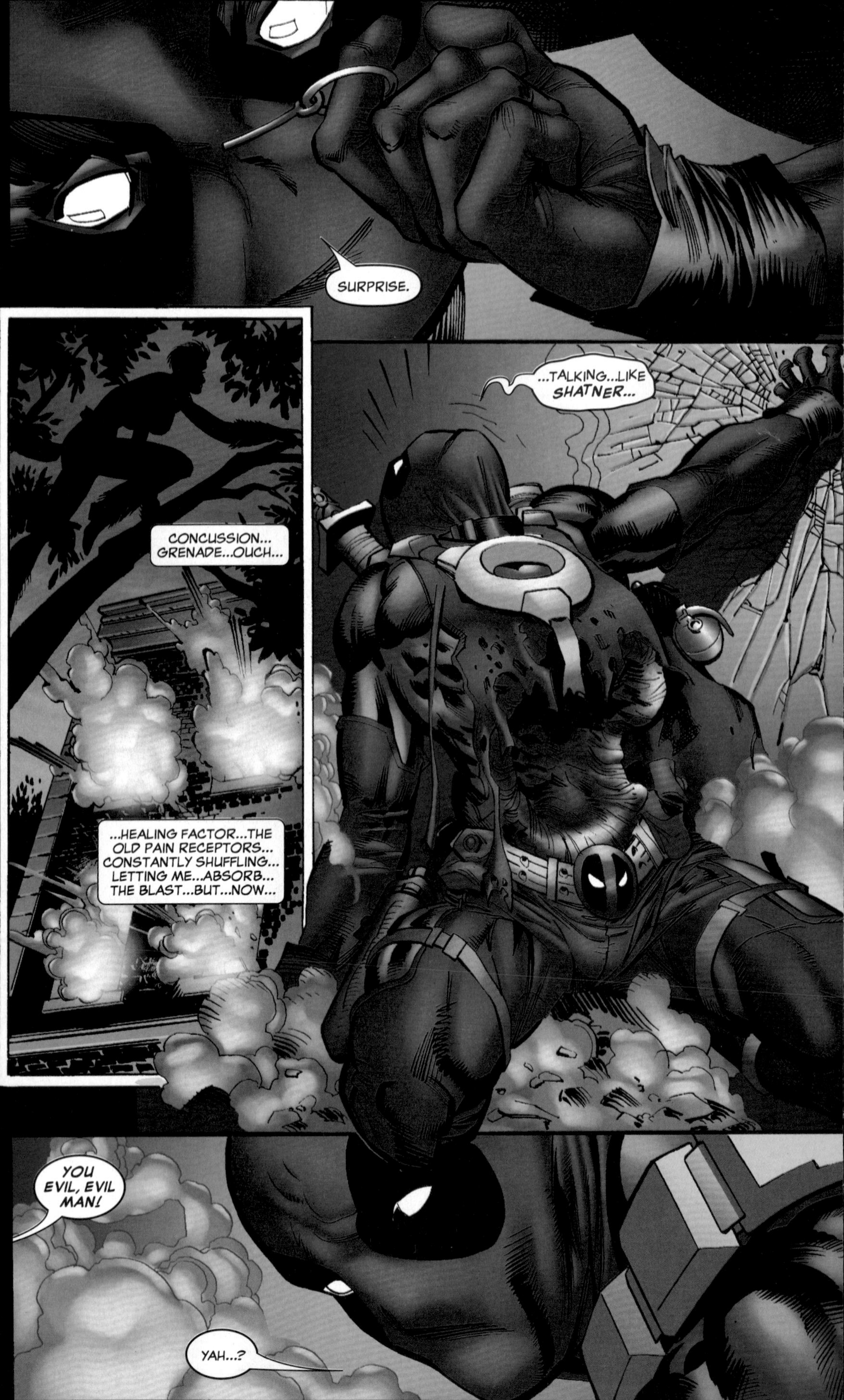
SURPRISE.
...TALKING...LIKE SHATNER...
CONCUSSION... GRENADE...OUCH...
...HEALING FACTOR...THE OLD PAIN RECEPTORS... CONSTANTLY SHUFFLING... LETTING ME...ABSORB... THE BLAST...BUT...NOW...
YOU EVIL, EVIL MAN!
YAH...?

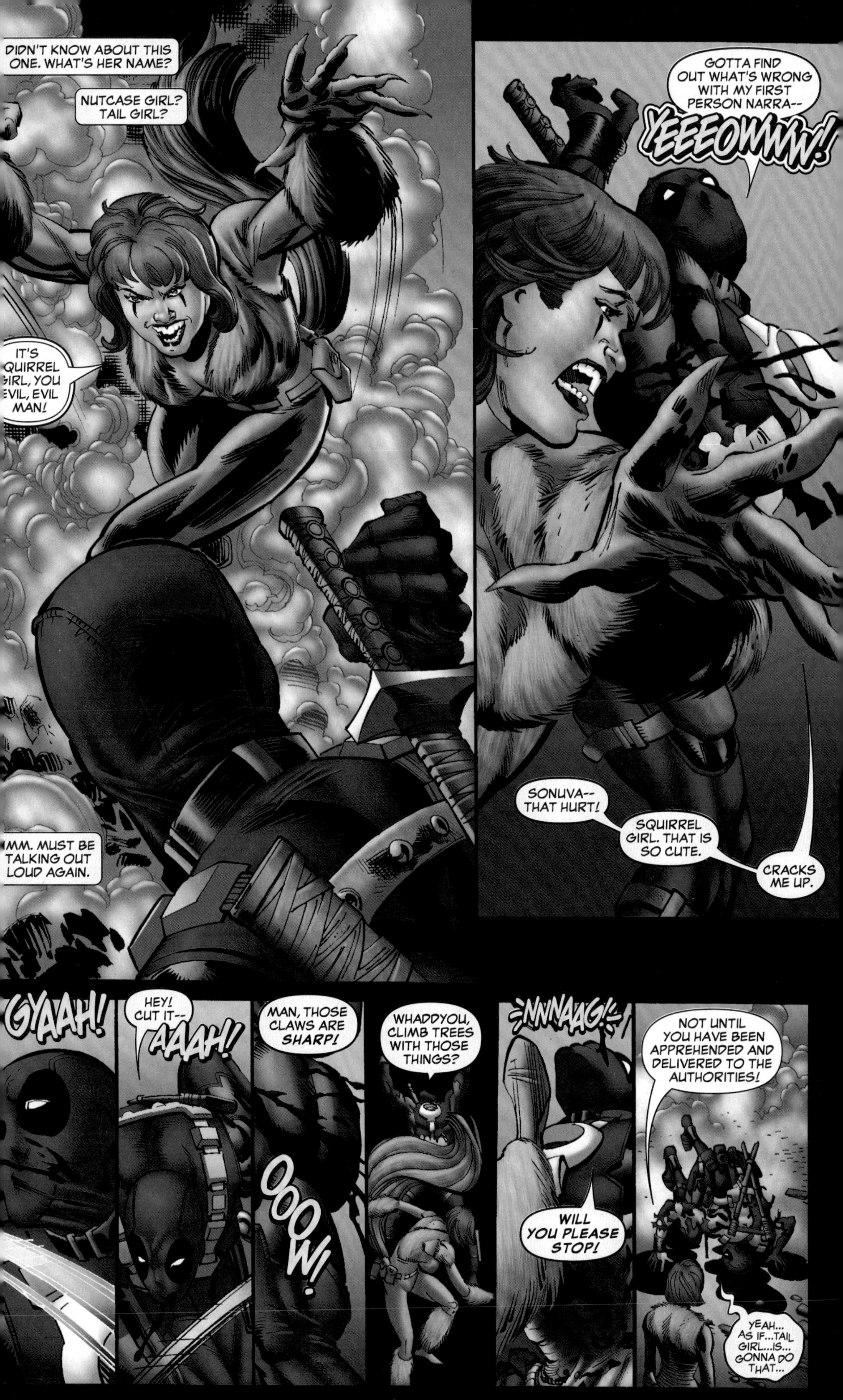
DIDN'T KNOW ABOUT THIS ONE. WHAT'S HER NAME?
NUTCASE GIRL? TAIL GIRL?
IT'S SQUIRREL GIRL, YOU EVIL, EVIL MAN!
MM. MUST BE TALKING OUT LOUD AGAIN.
GOTTA FIND OUT WHAT'S WRONG WITH MY FIRST PERSON NARRA--
YEEEOWWW!
SONUVA-- THAT HURT!
SQUIRREL GIRL. THAT IS SO CUTE.
CRACKS ME UP.
GYAAH!
HEY! CUT IT--
AAAH!
MAN, THOSE CLAWS ARE SHARP!
OOOW!
WHADDYOU, CLIMB TREES WITH THOSE THINGS?
NNNAAG!
WILL YOU PLEASE STOP!
NOT UNTIL YOU HAVE BEEN APPREHENDED AND DELIVERED TO THE AUTHORITIES!
YEAH... AS IF...TAIL GIRL...IS... GONNA DO THAT...

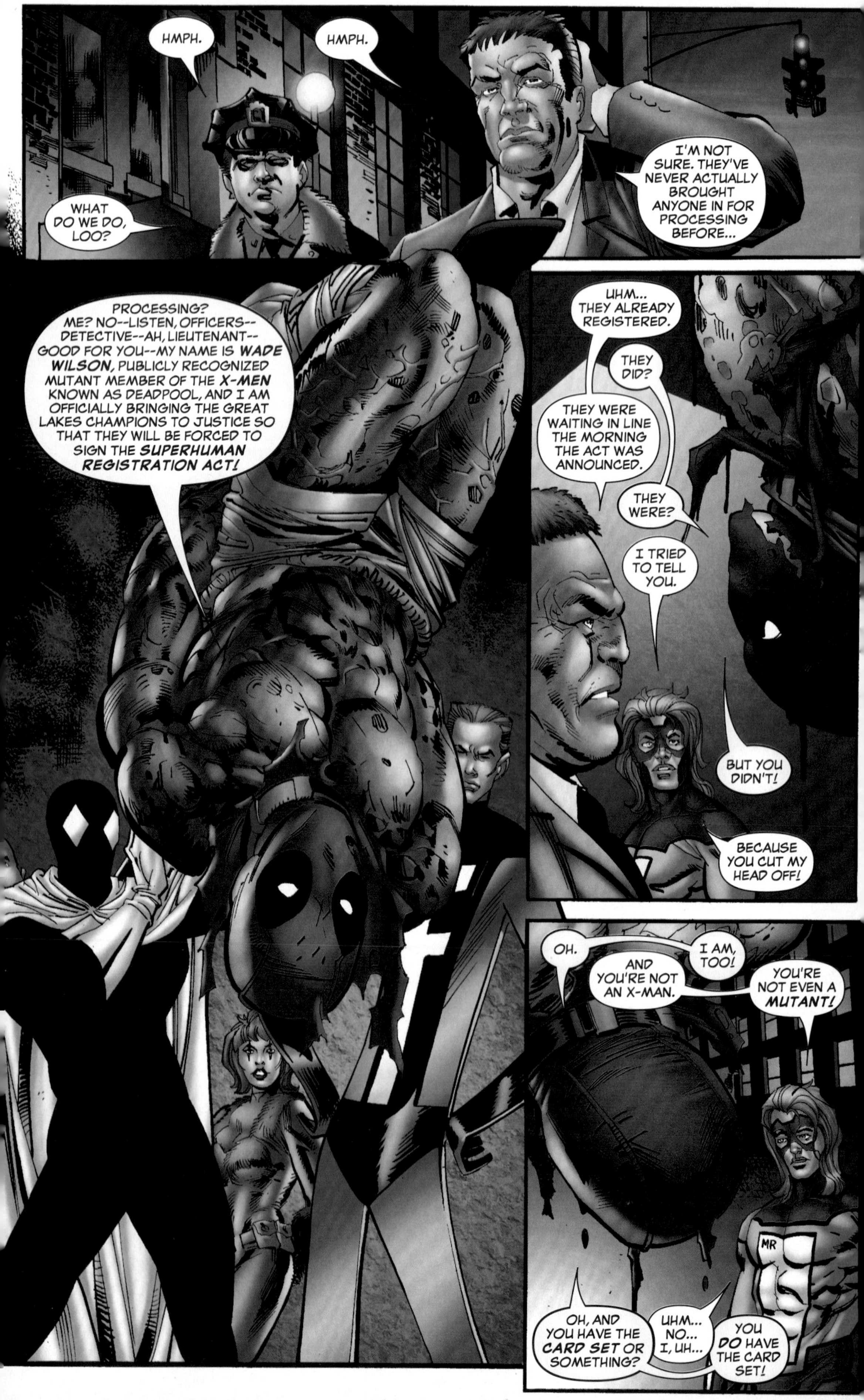
HMPH.
HMPH.
WHAT DO WE DO, LOO?
I'M NOT SURE. THEY'VE NEVER ACTUALLY BROUGHT ANYONE IN FOR PROCESSING BEFORE...
PROCESSING? ME? NO--LISTEN, OFFICERS--DETECTIVE--AH, LIEUTENANT--GOOD FOR YOU--MY NAME IS WADE WILSON, PUBLICLY RECOGNIZED MUTANT MEMBER OF THE X-MEN KNOWN AS DEADPOOL, AND I AM OFFICIALLY BRINGING THE GREAT LAKES CHAMPIONS TO JUSTICE SO THAT THEY WILL BE FORCED TO SIGN THE SUPERHUMAN REGISTRATION ACT!
UHM... THEY ALREADY REGISTERED.
THEY DID?
THEY WERE WAITING IN LINE THE MORNING THE ACT WAS ANNOUNCED.
THEY WERE?
I TRIED TO TELL YOU.
BUT YOU DIDN'T!
BECAUSE YOU CUT MY HEAD OFF!
OH.
I AM, TOO!
AND YOU'RE NOT AN X-MAN.
YOU'RE NOT EVEN A MUTANT!
MR
OH, AND YOU HAVE THE CARD SET OR SOMETHING?
UHM... NO... I, UH...
YOU DO HAVE THE CARD SET!

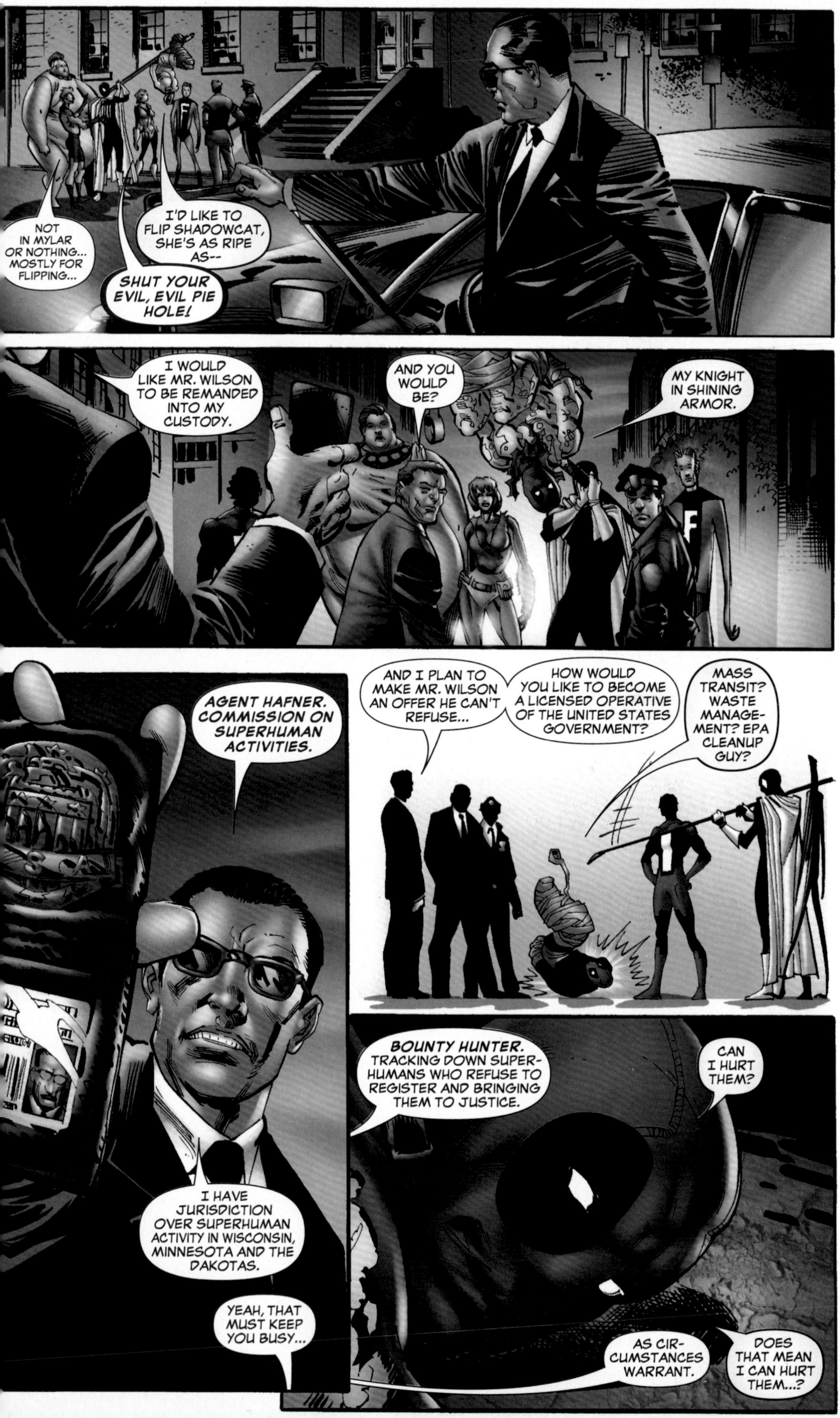
NOT IN MYLAR OR NOTHING... MOSTLY FOR FLIPPING...
I'D LIKE TO FLIP SHADOWCAT, SHE'S AS RIPE AS--
SHUT YOUR EVIL, EVIL PIE HOLE!
I WOULD LIKE MR. WILSON TO BE REMANDED INTO MY CUSTODY.
AND YOU WOULD BE?
MY KNIGHT IN SHINING ARMOR.
AGENT HAFNER. COMMISSION ON SUPERHUMAN ACTIVITIES.
I HAVE JURISDICTION OVER SUPERHUMAN ACTIVITY IN WISCONSIN, MINNESOTA AND THE DAKOTAS.
YEAH, THAT MUST KEEP YOU BUSY...
AND I PLAN TO MAKE MR. WILSON AN OFFER HE CAN'T REFUSE...
HOW WOULD YOU LIKE TO BECOME A LICENSED OPERATIVE OF THE UNITED STATES GOVERNMENT?
MASS TRANSIT? WASTE MANAGEMENT? EPA CLEANUP GUY?
BOUNTY HUNTER. TRACKING DOWN SUPERHUMANS WHO REFUSE TO REGISTER AND BRINGING THEM TO JUSTICE.
CAN I HURT THEM?
AS CIRCUMSTANCES WARRANT.
DOES THAT MEAN I CAN HURT THEM...?

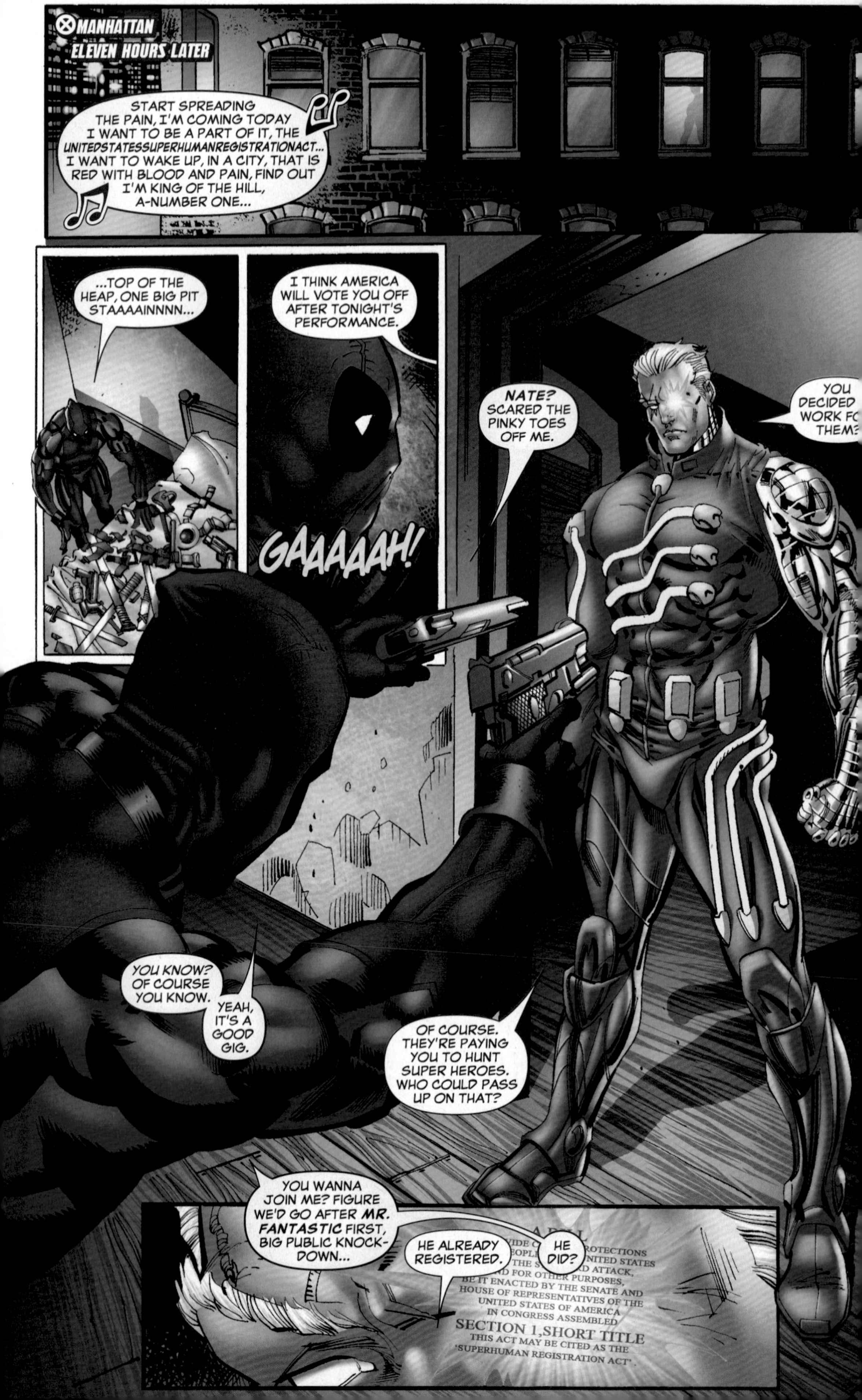
MANHATTAN
ELEVEN HOURS LATER
START SPREADING THE PAIN, I'M COMING TODAY I WANT TO BE A PART OF IT, THE UNITEDSTATESSUPERHUMANREGISTRATIONACT... I WANT TO WAKE UP, IN A CITY, THAT IS RED WITH BLOOD AND PAIN, FIND OUT I'M KING OF THE HILL, A-NUMBER ONE...
...TOP OF THE HEAP, ONE BIG PIT STAAAAINNNN...
I THINK AMERICA WILL VOTE YOU OFF AFTER TONIGHT'S PERFORMANCE.
GAAAAAH!
NATE? SCARED THE PINKY TOES OFF ME.
YOU DECIDED WORK FO THEM?
YOU KNOW? OF COURSE YOU KNOW.
YEAH, IT'S A GOOD GIG.
OF COURSE. THEY'RE PAYING YOU TO HUNT SUPER HEROES. WHO COULD PASS UP ON THAT?
YOU WANNA JOIN ME? FIGURE WE'D GO AFTER MR. FANTASTIC FIRST, BIG PUBLIC KNOCK-DOWN...
HE ALREADY REGISTERED.
HE DID?
BE IT ENACTED BY THE SENATE AND HOUSE OF REPRESENTATIVES OF THE UNITED STATES OF AMERICA IN CONGRESS ASSEMBLED
SECTION 1, SHORT TITLE
THIS ACT MAY BE CITED AS THE 'SUPERHUMAN REGISTRATION ACT'.

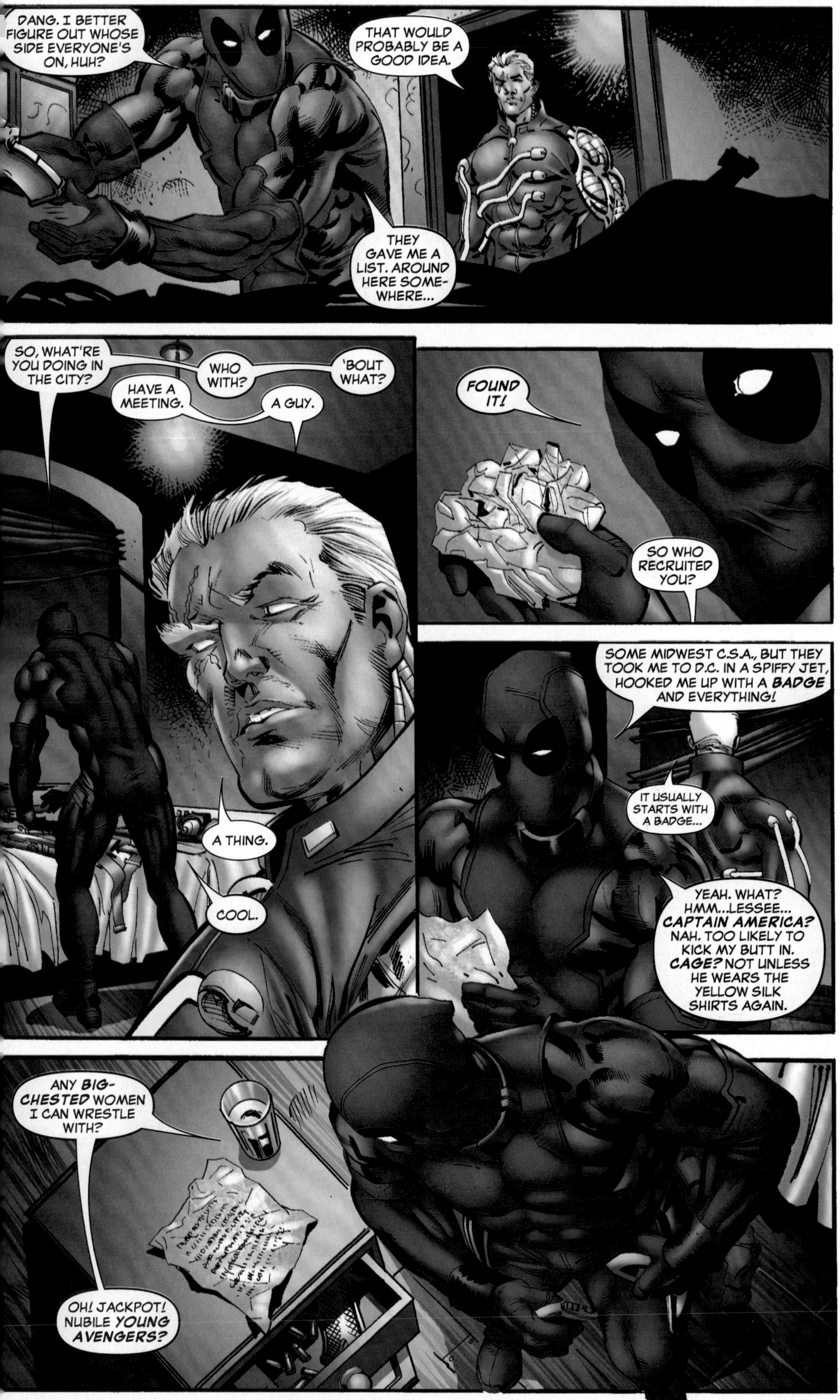

DANG. I BETTER FIGURE OUT WHOSE SIDE EVERYONE'S ON, HUH?
THAT WOULD PROBABLY BE A GOOD IDEA.
THEY GAVE ME A LIST. AROUND HERE SOME-WHERE...
SO, WHAT'RE YOU DOING IN THE CITY?
HAVE A MEETING.
WHO WITH?
A GUY.
'BOUT WHAT?
A THING.
COOL.
FOUND IT!
SO WHO RECRUITED YOU?
SOME MIDWEST C.S.A., BUT THEY TOOK ME TO D.C. IN A SPIFFY JET, HOOKED ME UP WITH A BADGE AND EVERYTHING!
IT USUALLY STARTS WITH A BADGE...
YEAH. WHAT? HMM...LESSEE... CAPTAIN AMERICA? NAH. TOO LIKELY TO KICK MY BUTT IN. CAGE? NOT UNLESS HE WEARS THE YELLOW SILK SHIRTS AGAIN.
ANY BIG-CHESTED WOMEN I CAN WRESTLE WITH?
OH! JACKPOT! NUBILE YOUNG AVENGERS?

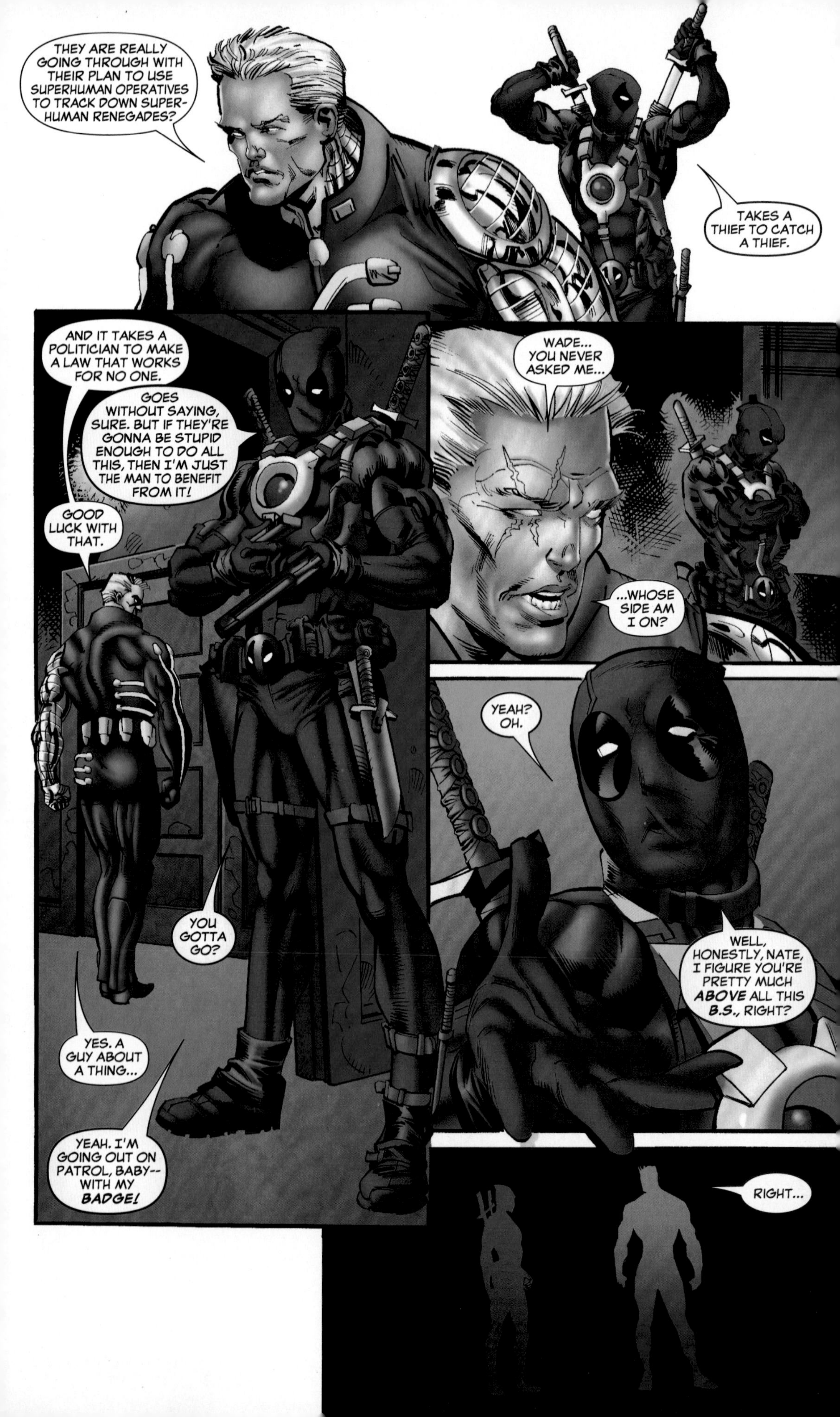
THEY ARE REALLY GOING THROUGH WITH THEIR PLAN TO USE SUPERHUMAN OPERATIVES TO TRACK DOWN SUPER-HUMAN RENEGADES?
TAKES A THIEF TO CATCH A THIEF.
AND IT TAKES A POLITICIAN TO MAKE A LAW THAT WORKS FOR NO ONE.
GOES WITHOUT SAYING, SURE. BUT IF THEY'RE GONNA BE STUPID ENOUGH TO DO ALL THIS, THEN I'M JUST THE MAN TO BENEFIT FROM IT!
GOOD LUCK WITH THAT.
YOU GOTTA GO?
YES. A GUY ABOUT A THING...
YEAH. I'M GOING OUT ON PATROL, BABY-- WITH MY BADGE!
WADE... YOU NEVER ASKED ME...
...WHOSE SIDE AM I ON?
YEAH? OH.
WELL, HONESTLY, NATE, I FIGURE YOU'RE PRETTY MUCH ABOVE ALL THIS B.S., RIGHT?
RIGHT...

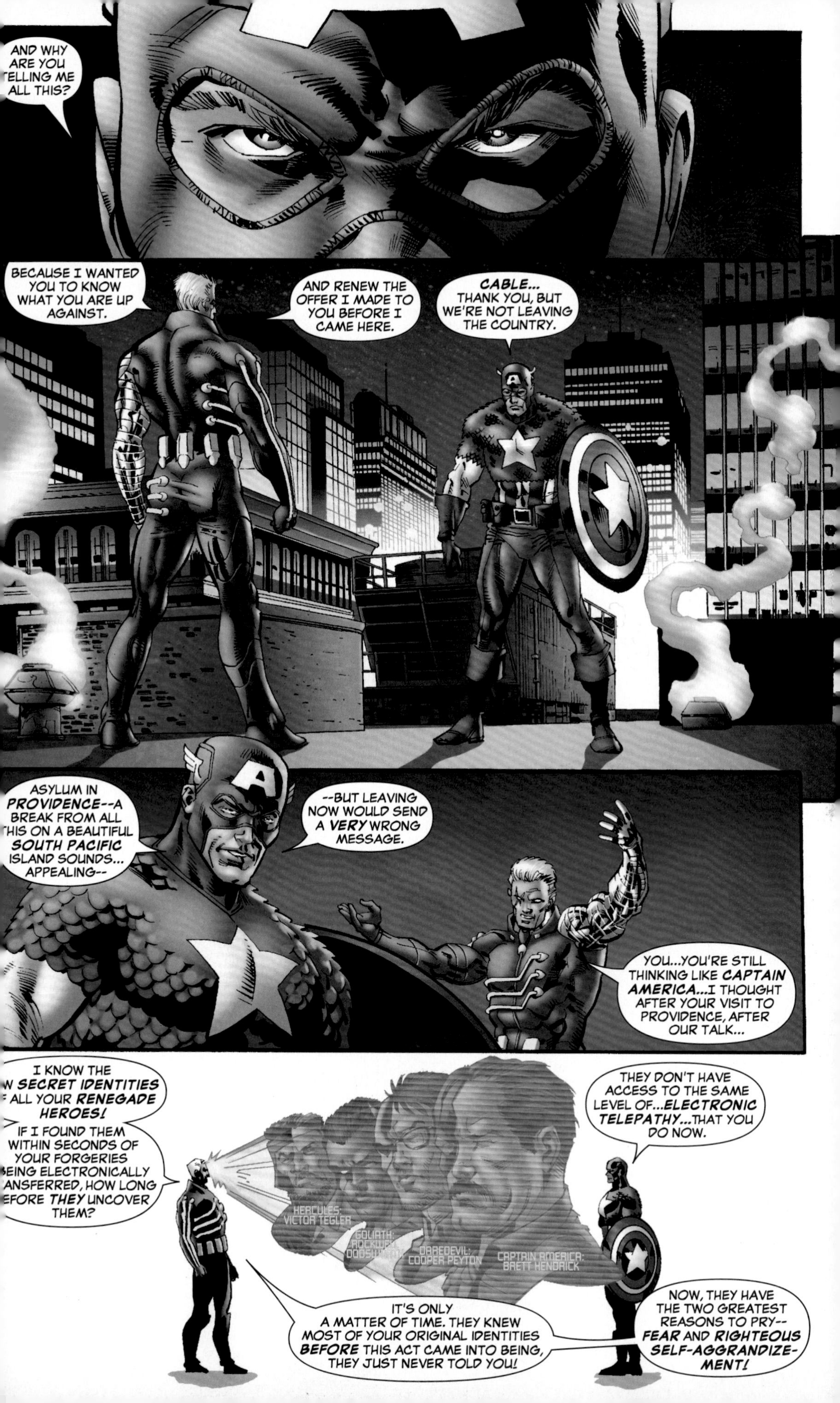

AND WHY ARE YOU TELLING ME ALL THIS?
BECAUSE I WANTED YOU TO KNOW WHAT YOU ARE UP AGAINST.
AND RENEW THE OFFER I MADE TO YOU BEFORE I CAME HERE.
CABLE... THANK YOU, BUT WE'RE NOT LEAVING THE COUNTRY.
ASYLUM IN PROVIDENCE--A BREAK FROM ALL THIS ON A BEAUTIFUL SOUTH PACIFIC ISLAND SOUNDS... APPEALING--
--BUT LEAVING NOW WOULD SEND A VERY WRONG MESSAGE.
YOU...YOU'RE STILL THINKING LIKE CAPTAIN AMERICA...I THOUGHT AFTER YOUR VISIT TO PROVIDENCE, AFTER OUR TALK...
I KNOW THE NEW SECRET IDENTITIES OF ALL YOUR RENEGADE HEROES!
IF I FOUND THEM WITHIN SECONDS OF YOUR FORGERIES BEING ELECTRONICALLY TRANSFERRED, HOW LONG BEFORE THEY UNCOVER THEM?
THEY DON'T HAVE ACCESS TO THE SAME LEVEL OF...ELECTRONIC TELEPATHY...THAT YOU DO NOW.
HERCULES: VICTOR TEGLER
DAREDEVIL: COOPER PEYTON
CAPTAIN AMERICA: BRETT HENDRICK
IT'S ONLY A MATTER OF TIME. THEY KNEW MOST OF YOUR ORIGINAL IDENTITIES BEFORE THIS ACT CAME INTO BEING, THEY JUST NEVER TOLD YOU!
NOW, THEY HAVE THE TWO GREATEST REASONS TO PRY-- FEAR AND RIGHTEOUS SELF-AGGRANDIZEMENT!

YOU'RE SAYING WE'RE GOING TO LOSE?

I'M SAYING YOU'VE *ALREADY* LOST!

YOU KNOW THIS BECAUSE YOU'RE FROM THE *FUTURE* AND KNOW EVERYTHING, RIGHT?

NO...I'M SAYING THIS BECAUSE I'VE SEEN WHAT THEY HAVE PLANNED.

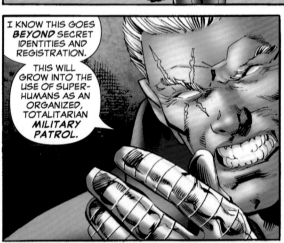

I KNOW THIS GOES *BEYOND* SECRET IDENTITIES AND REGISTRATION.

THIS WILL GROW INTO THE USE OF SUPER-HUMANS AS AN ORGANIZED, TOTALITARIAN *MILITARY* PATROL.

I KNOW *IRON MAN. TONY STARK* WOULD *NEVER* AGREE TO SOMETHING LIKE THAT.

AND WE'RE BACK TO SQUARE ONE. YOU'RE THINKING IN TERMS OF *MONTHS* AND *YEARS*, I'M TALKING ABOUT *DECADES* AND *CENTURIES*.

NATHAN...I'VE THOUGHT ABOUT OUR TALK A LOT...YOU CAN'T FIGHT TIME, YOU CAN'T CHANGE THE BIG PICTURE IN A *DAILY* STRUGGLE...

NO, BUT THROUGHOUT THE COURSE OF HISTORY, THE ACTIONS AND DECISIONS OF INDIVIDUALS--OR THEIR *NON-ACTIONS*--HAVE AFFECTED THE *"BIG PICTURE."*

MY OFFER OF ASYLUM IS IN CONSIDERATION OF THE BIG PICTURE-- THE *WORLD* PICTURE.

I AM PRESIDENT PRO TEM OF *RUMEKISTAN* NOW. EUROPEAN AND FORMER SOVIET BLOC COUNTRIES HAVE ALWAYS CONSIDERED SUPER-HUMANS A DANGEROUSLY *"AMERICAN THING."*

AND YOU CAN HELP MAKE IT A *"DANGEROUSLY GLOBAL THING"*--?

CYNICAL HUMOR DOESN'T WORK FOR YOU. GIVE UP THIS FIGHT TO WIN A MUCH, MUCH *BIGGER* ONE. THE FIGHT FOR THE *FUTURE!*

I CAN'T DO THAT.

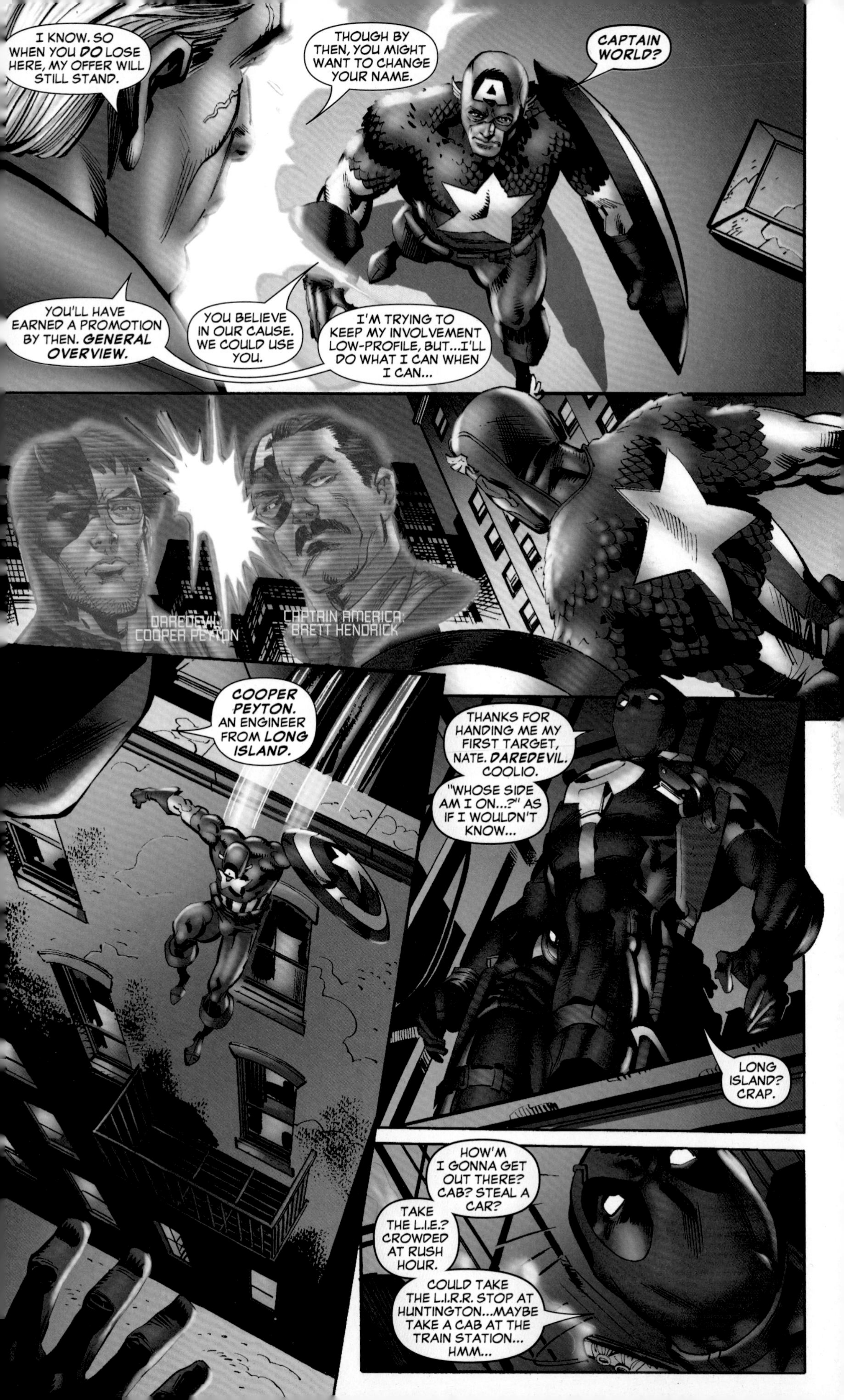
I KNOW. SO WHEN YOU DO LOSE HERE, MY OFFER WILL STILL STAND.
THOUGH BY THEN, YOU MIGHT WANT TO CHANGE YOUR NAME.
CAPTAIN WORLD?
YOU'LL HAVE EARNED A PROMOTION BY THEN. GENERAL OVERVIEW.
YOU BELIEVE IN OUR CAUSE. WE COULD USE YOU.
I'M TRYING TO KEEP MY INVOLVEMENT LOW-PROFILE, BUT...I'LL DO WHAT I CAN WHEN I CAN...
DAREDEVIL: COOPER PEYTON
CAPTAIN AMERICA: BRETT HENDRICK
COOPER PEYTON. AN ENGINEER FROM LONG ISLAND.
THANKS FOR HANDING ME MY FIRST TARGET, NATE. DAREDEVIL. COOLIO.
"WHOSE SIDE AM I ON...?" AS IF I WOULDN'T KNOW...
LONG ISLAND? CRAP.
HOW'M I GONNA GET OUT THERE? CAB? STEAL A CAR?
TAKE THE L.I.E.? CROWDED AT RUSH HOUR.
COULD TAKE THE L.I.R.R. STOP AT HUNTINGTON...MAYBE TAKE A CAB AT THE TRAIN STATION... HMM...

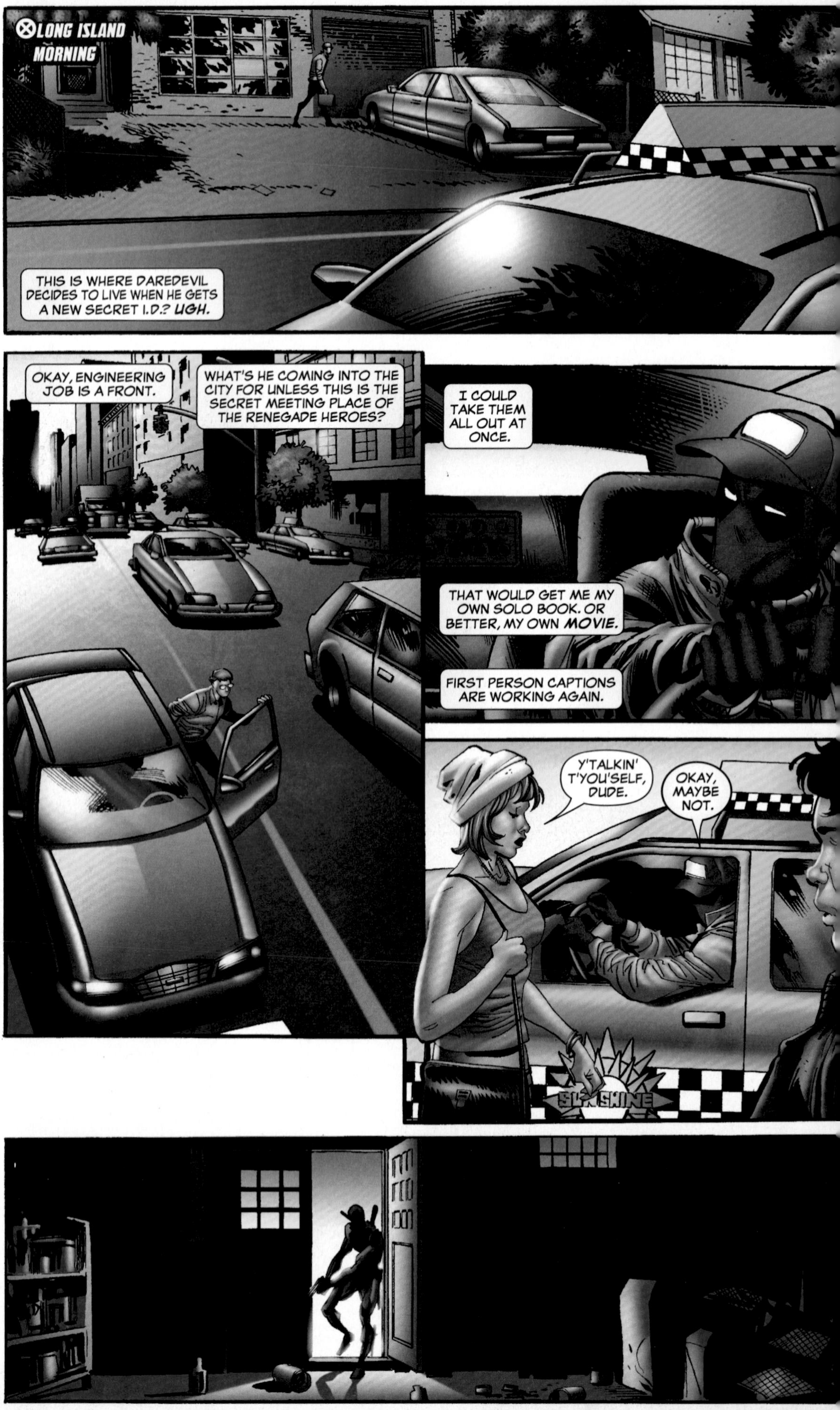
LONG ISLAND
MORNING
THIS IS WHERE DAREDEVIL DECIDES TO LIVE WHEN HE GETS A NEW SECRET I.D.? UGH.
OKAY, ENGINEERING JOB IS A FRONT.
WHAT'S HE COMING INTO THE CITY FOR UNLESS THIS IS THE SECRET MEETING PLACE OF THE RENEGADE HEROES?
I COULD TAKE THEM ALL OUT AT ONCE.
THAT WOULD GET ME MY OWN SOLO BOOK. OR BETTER, MY OWN MOVIE.
FIRST PERSON CAPTIONS ARE WORKING AGAIN.
Y'TALKIN' T'YOU'SELF, DUDE.
OKAY, MAYBE NOT.

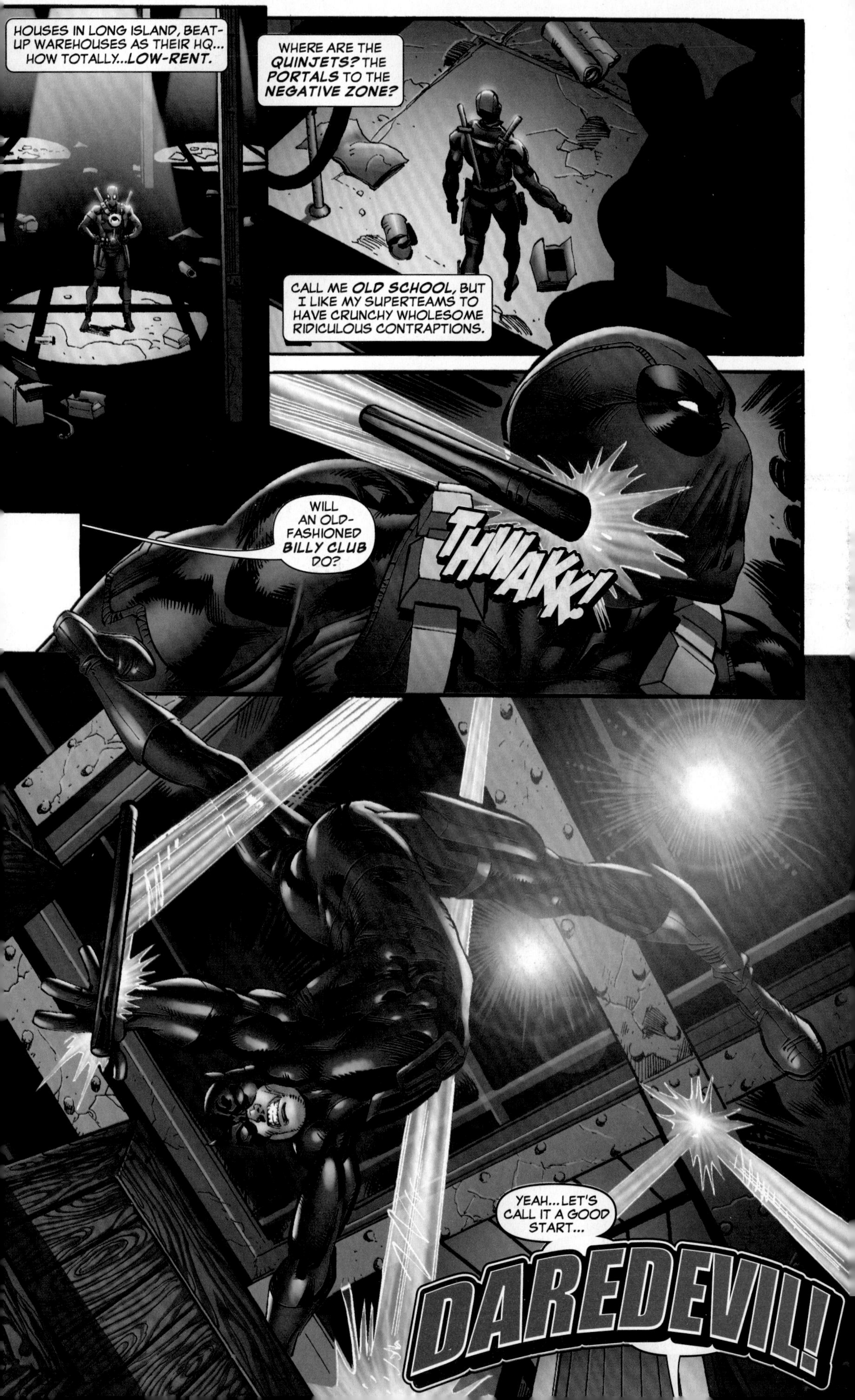
HOUSES IN LONG ISLAND, BEAT-UP WAREHOUSES AS THEIR HQ... HOW TOTALLY...LOW-RENT.
WHERE ARE THE QUINJETS? THE PORTALS TO THE NEGATIVE ZONE?
CALL ME OLD SCHOOL, BUT I LIKE MY SUPERTEAMS TO HAVE CRUNCHY WHOLESOME RIDICULOUS CONTRAPTIONS.
WILL AN OLD-FASHIONED BILLY CLUB DO?
THWAKK!
YEAH...LET'S CALL IT A GOOD START...
DAREDEVIL!

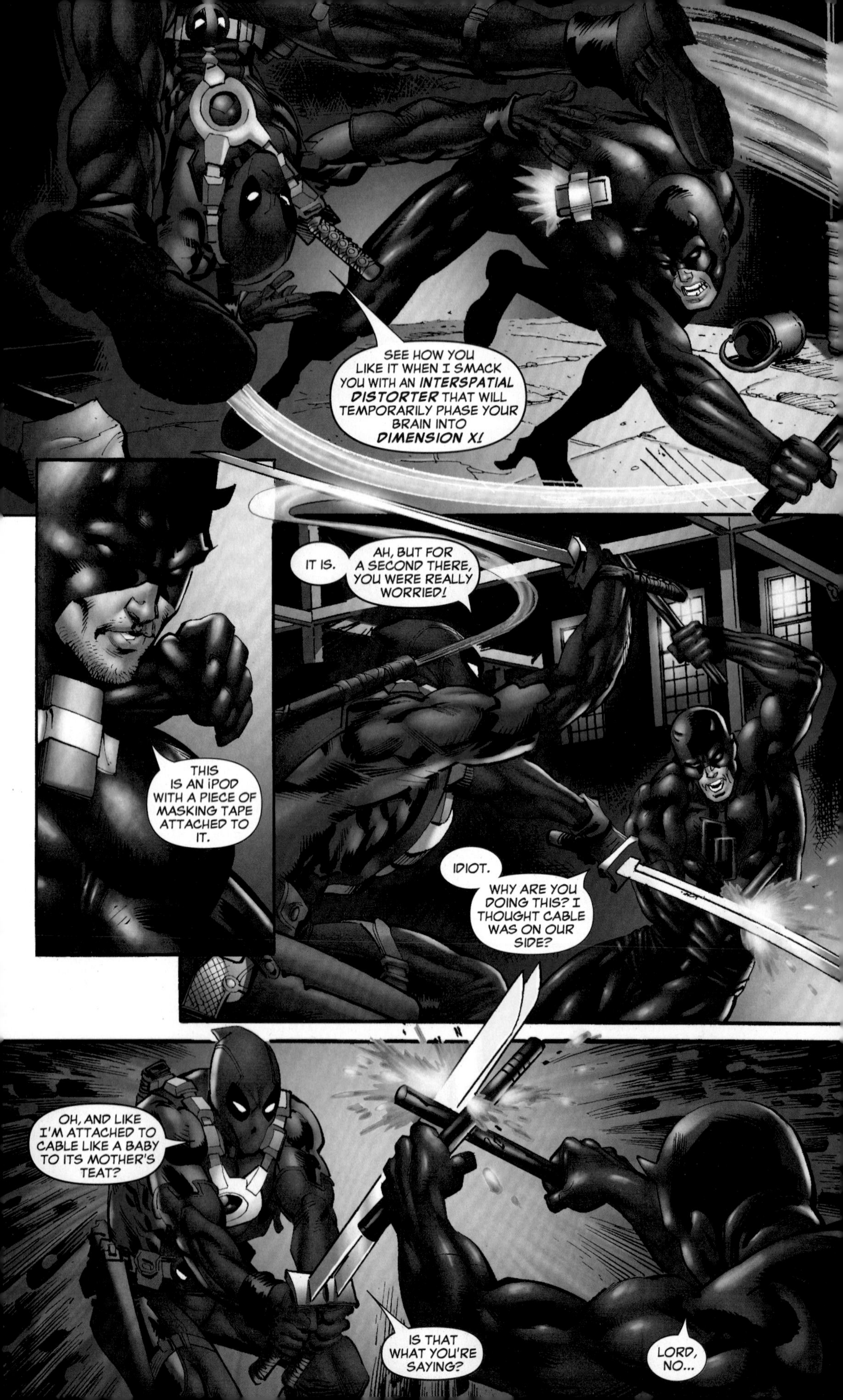

SEE HOW YOU LIKE IT WHEN I SMACK YOU WITH AN INTERSPATIAL DISTORTER THAT WILL TEMPORARILY PHASE YOUR BRAIN INTO DIMENSION X!
THIS IS AN iPOD WITH A PIECE OF MASKING TAPE ATTACHED TO IT.
IT IS.
AH, BUT FOR A SECOND THERE, YOU WERE REALLY WORRIED!
IDIOT.
WHY ARE YOU DOING THIS? I THOUGHT CABLE WAS ON OUR SIDE?
OH, AND LIKE I'M ATTACHED TO CABLE LIKE A BABY TO ITS MOTHER'S TEAT?
IS THAT WHAT YOU'RE SAYING?
LORD, NO...

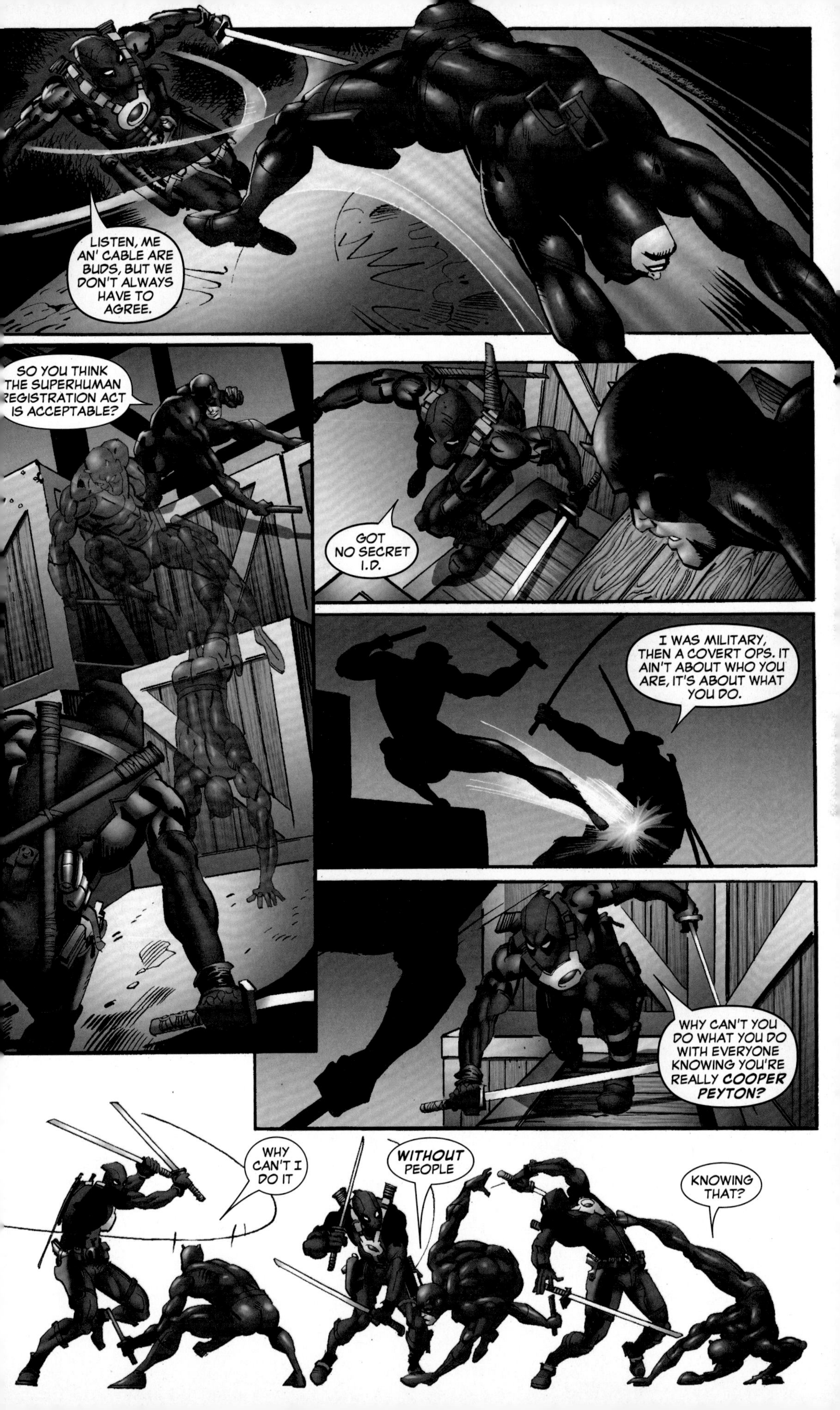

LISTEN, ME AN' CABLE ARE BUDS, BUT WE DON'T ALWAYS HAVE TO AGREE.
SO YOU THINK THE SUPERHUMAN REGISTRATION ACT IS ACCEPTABLE?
GOT NO SECRET I.D.
I WAS MILITARY, THEN A COVERT OPS. IT AIN'T ABOUT WHO YOU ARE, IT'S ABOUT WHAT YOU DO.
WHY CAN'T YOU DO WHAT YOU DO WITH EVERYONE KNOWING YOU'RE REALLY COOPER PEYTON?
WHY CAN'T I DO IT
WITHOUT PEOPLE
KNOWING THAT?

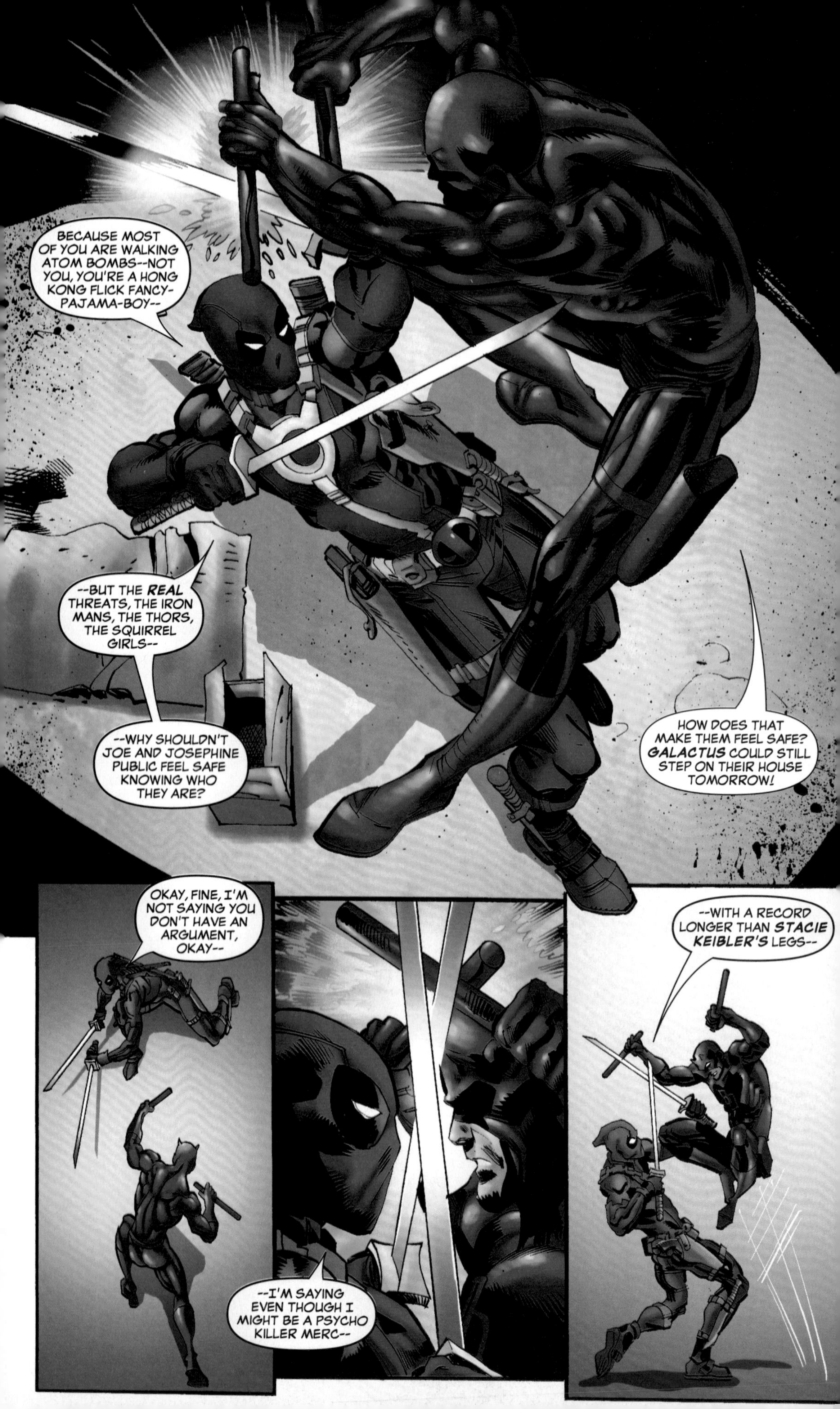
BECAUSE MOST OF YOU ARE WALKING ATOM BOMBS--NOT YOU, YOU'RE A HONG KONG FLICK FANCY-PAJAMA-BOY--
--BUT THE REAL THREATS, THE IRON MANS, THE THORS, THE SQUIRREL GIRLS--
--WHY SHOULDN'T JOE AND JOSEPHINE PUBLIC FEEL SAFE KNOWING WHO THEY ARE?
HOW DOES THAT MAKE THEM FEEL SAFE? GALACTUS COULD STILL STEP ON THEIR HOUSE TOMORROW!
OKAY, FINE, I'M NOT SAYING YOU DON'T HAVE AN ARGUMENT, OKAY--
--I'M SAYING EVEN THOUGH I MIGHT BE A PSYCHO KILLER MERC--
--WITH A RECORD LONGER THAN STACIE KEIBLER'S LEGS--

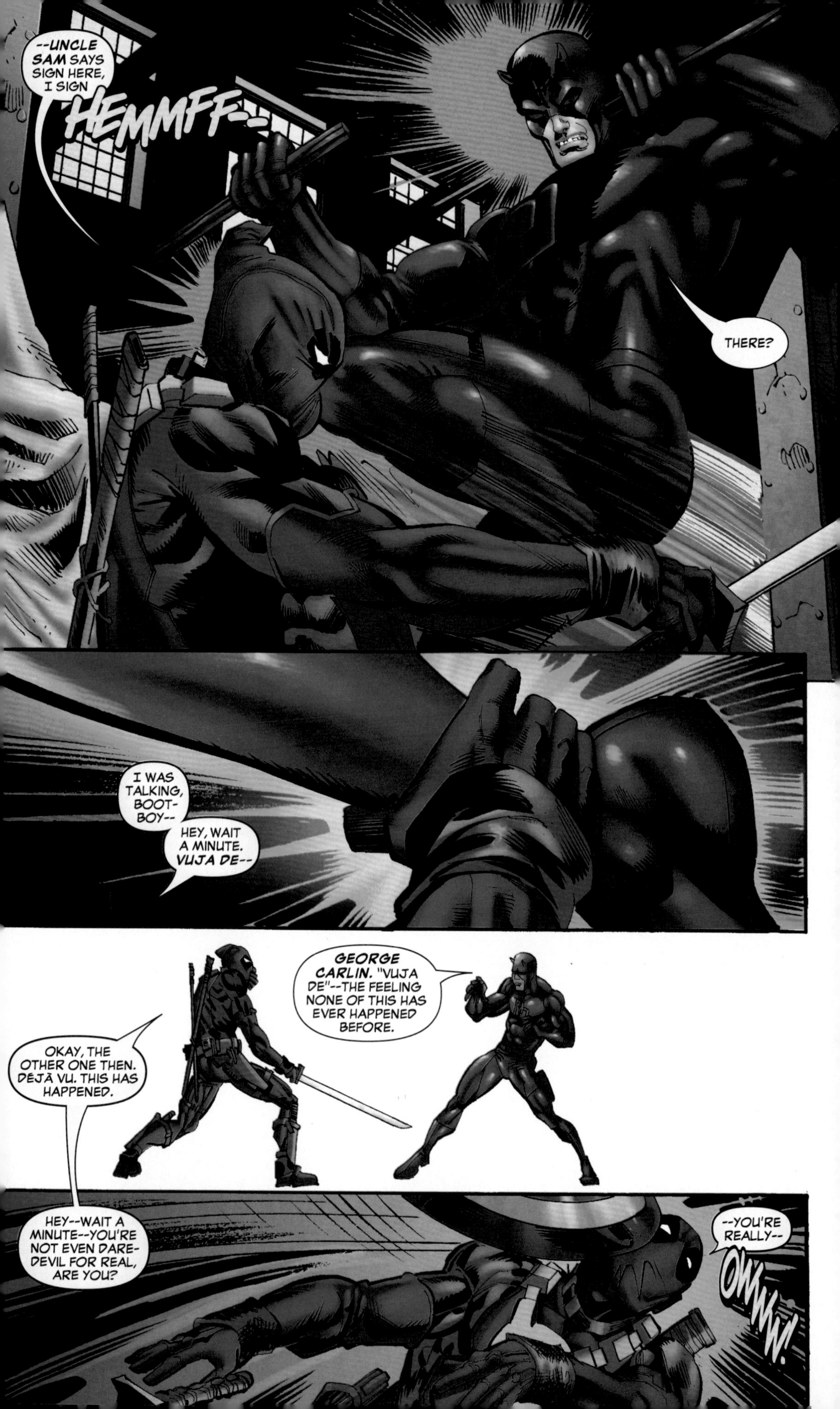
--UNCLE SAM SAYS SIGN HERE, I SIGN
HEMMFF--
THERE?
I WAS TALKING, BOOT-BOY--
HEY, WAIT A MINUTE. VUJA DE--
GEORGE CARLIN. "VUJA DE"--THE FEELING NONE OF THIS HAS EVER HAPPENED BEFORE.
OKAY, THE OTHER ONE THEN. DÉJÀ VU. THIS HAS HAPPENED.
HEY--WAIT A MINUTE--YOU'RE NOT EVEN DARE-DEVIL FOR REAL, ARE YOU?
--YOU'RE REALLY--
OWWW!

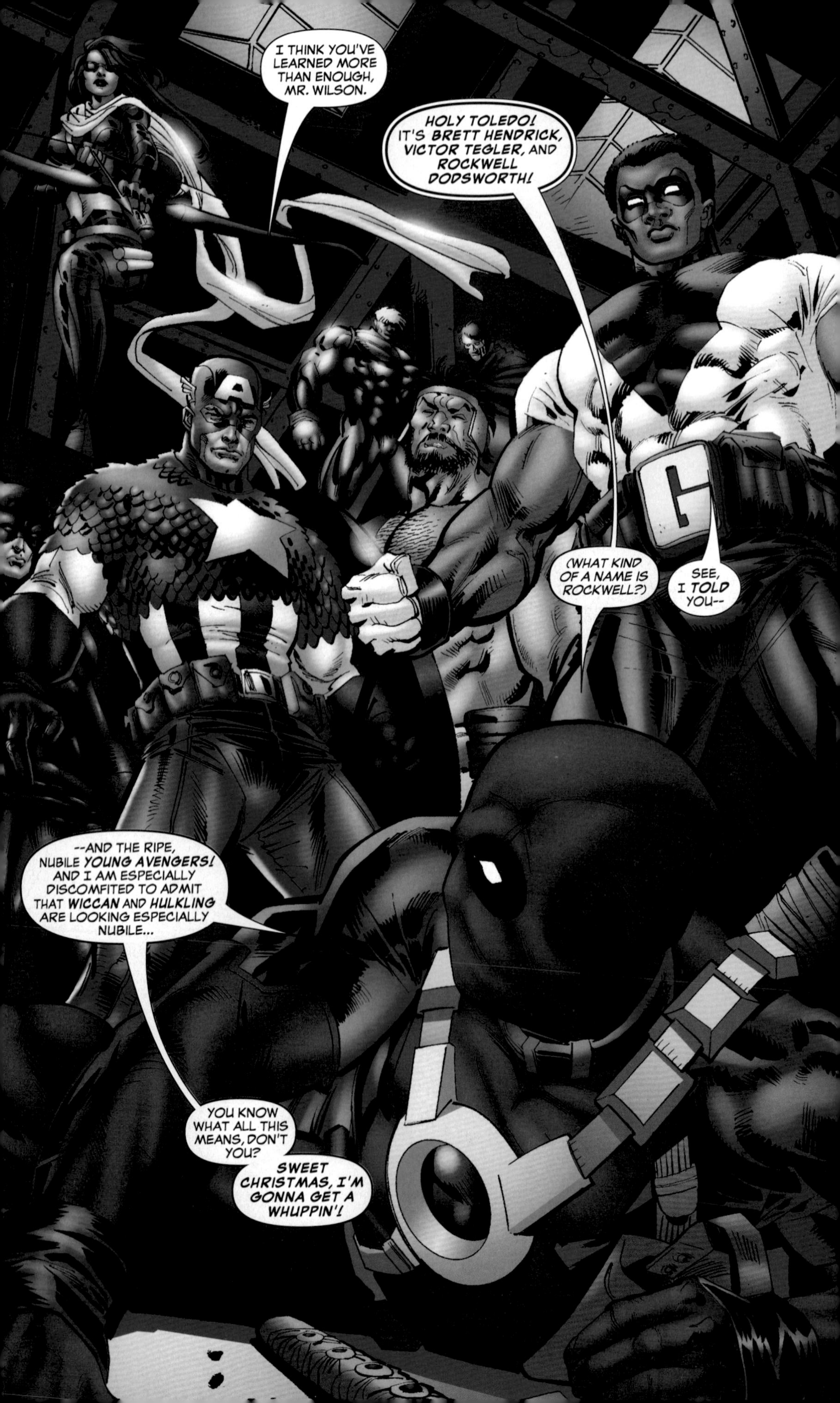
I THINK YOU'VE LEARNED MORE THAN ENOUGH, MR. WILSON.
HOLY TOLEDO! IT'S BRETT HENDRICK, VICTOR TEGLER, AND ROCKWELL DODSWORTH!
(WHAT KIND OF A NAME IS ROCKWELL?)
SEE, I TOLD YOU--
--AND THE RIPE, NUBILE YOUNG AVENGERS! AND I AM ESPECIALLY DISCOMFITED TO ADMIT THAT WICCAN AND HULKLING ARE LOOKING ESPECIALLY NUBILE...
YOU KNOW WHAT ALL THIS MEANS, DON'T YOU?
SWEET CHRISTMAS, I'M GONNA GET A WHUPPIN'!

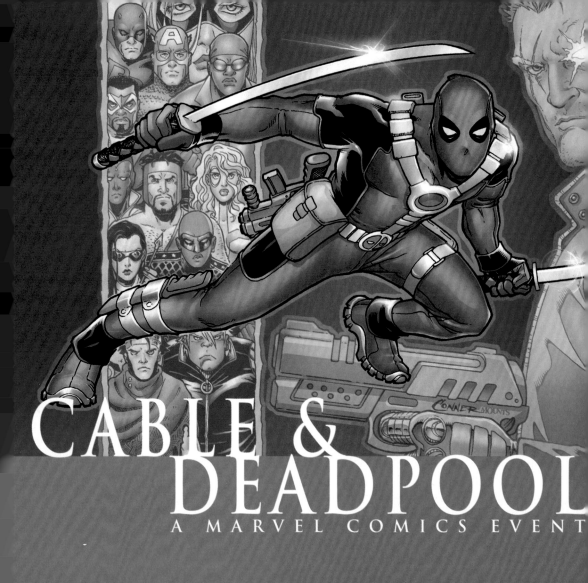

CABLE & DEADPOOL

A MARVEL COMICS EVENT

CIVIL WAR

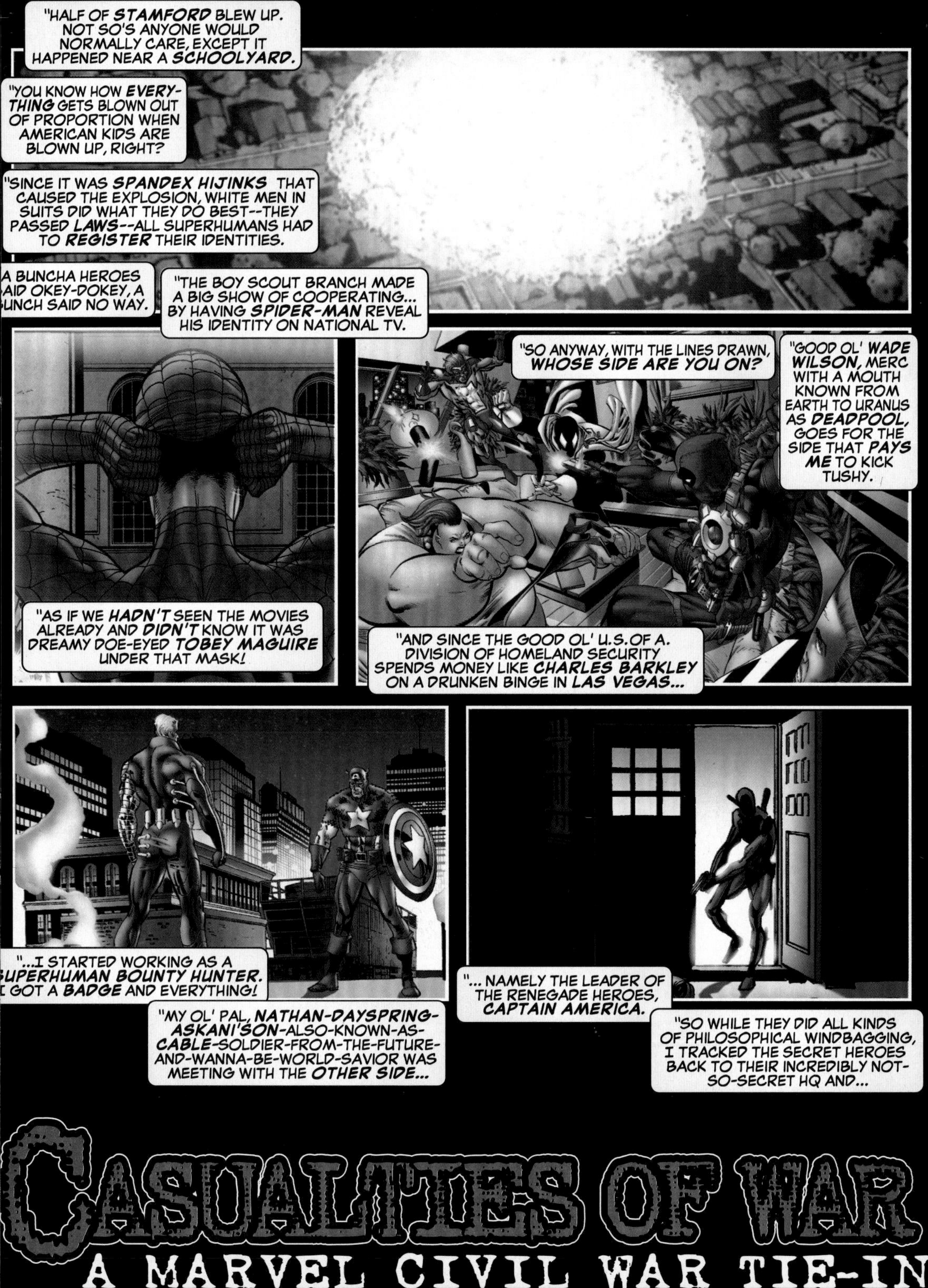
"HALF OF STAMFORD BLEW UP. NOT SO'S ANYONE WOULD NORMALLY CARE, EXCEPT IT HAPPENED NEAR A SCHOOLYARD.
"YOU KNOW HOW EVERYTHING GETS BLOWN OUT OF PROPORTION WHEN AMERICAN KIDS ARE BLOWN UP, RIGHT?
"SINCE IT WAS SPANDEX HIJINKS THAT CAUSED THE EXPLOSION, WHITE MEN IN SUITS DID WHAT THEY DO BEST--THEY PASSED LAWS--ALL SUPERHUMANS HAD TO REGISTER THEIR IDENTITIES.
A BUNCHA HEROES SAID OKEY-DOKEY, A BUNCH SAID NO WAY.
"THE BOY SCOUT BRANCH MADE A BIG SHOW OF COOPERATING... BY HAVING SPIDER-MAN REVEAL HIS IDENTITY ON NATIONAL TV.
"AS IF WE HADN'T SEEN THE MOVIES ALREADY AND DIDN'T KNOW IT WAS DREAMY DOE-EYED TOBEY MAGUIRE UNDER THAT MASK!
"SO ANYWAY, WITH THE LINES DRAWN, WHOSE SIDE ARE YOU ON?
"GOOD OL' WADE WILSON, MERC WITH A MOUTH KNOWN FROM EARTH TO URANUS AS DEADPOOL, GOES FOR THE SIDE THAT PAYS ME TO KICK TUSHY.
"AND SINCE THE GOOD OL' U.S. OF A. DIVISION OF HOMELAND SECURITY SPENDS MONEY LIKE CHARLES BARKLEY ON A DRUNKEN BINGE IN LAS VEGAS...
"...I STARTED WORKING AS A SUPERHUMAN BOUNTY HUNTER. I GOT A BADGE AND EVERYTHING!
"MY OL' PAL, NATHAN-DAYSPRING-ASKANI'SON-ALSO-KNOWN-AS-CABLE-SOLDIER-FROM-THE-FUTURE-AND-WANNA-BE-WORLD-SAVIOR WAS MEETING WITH THE OTHER SIDE...
"... NAMELY THE LEADER OF THE RENEGADE HEROES, CAPTAIN AMERICA.
"SO WHILE THEY DID ALL KINDS OF PHILOSOPHICAL WINDBAGGING, I TRACKED THE SECRET HEROES BACK TO THEIR INCREDIBLY NOT-SO-SECRET HQ AND...
CASUALTIES OF WAR
A MARVEL CIVIL WAR TIE-IN

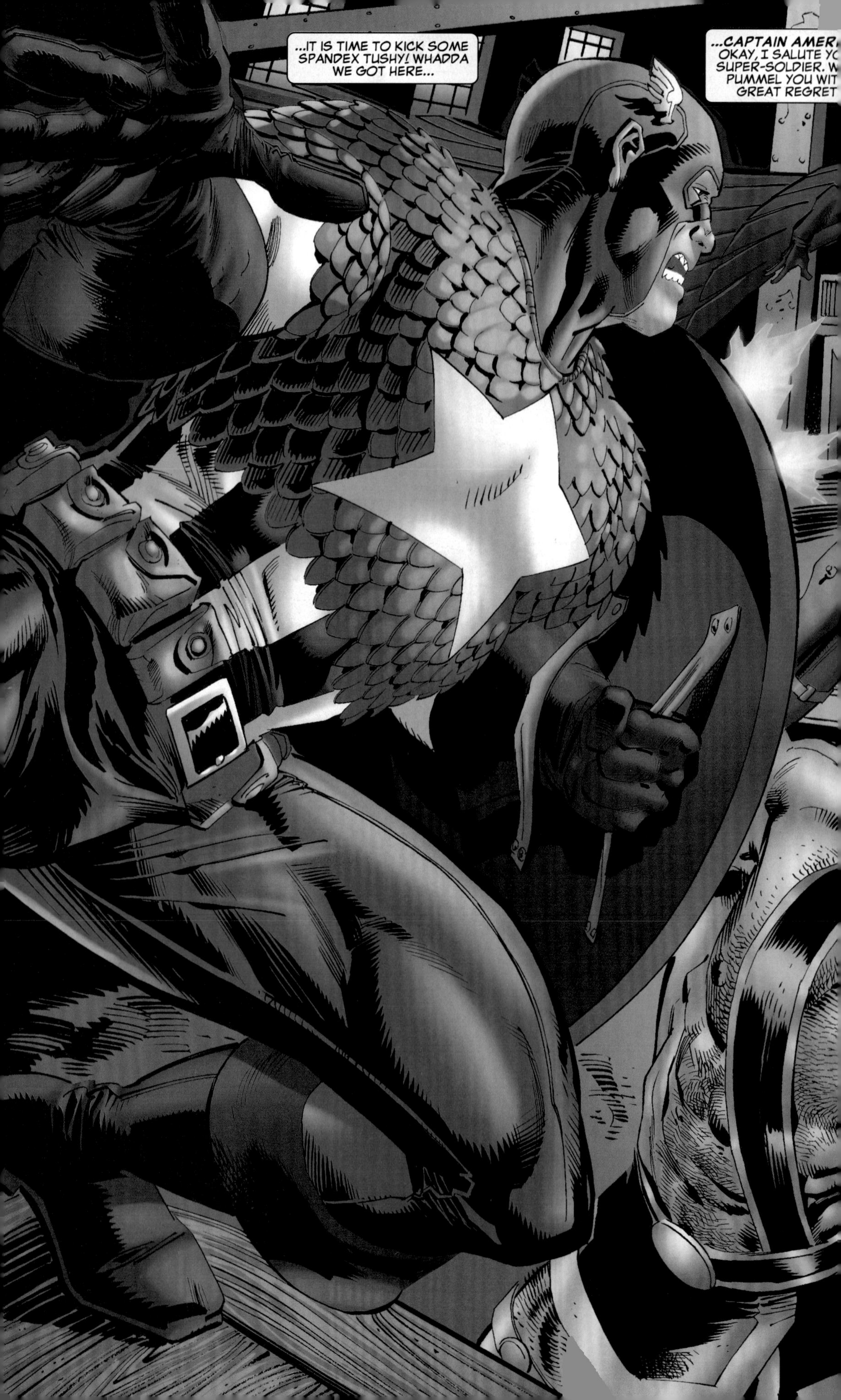

...IT IS TIME TO KICK SOME SPANDEX TUSHY! WHADDA WE GOT HERE...
...CAPTAIN AMER
OKAY, I SALUTE YO
SUPER-SOLDIER. W
PUMMEL YOU WIT
GREAT REGRET

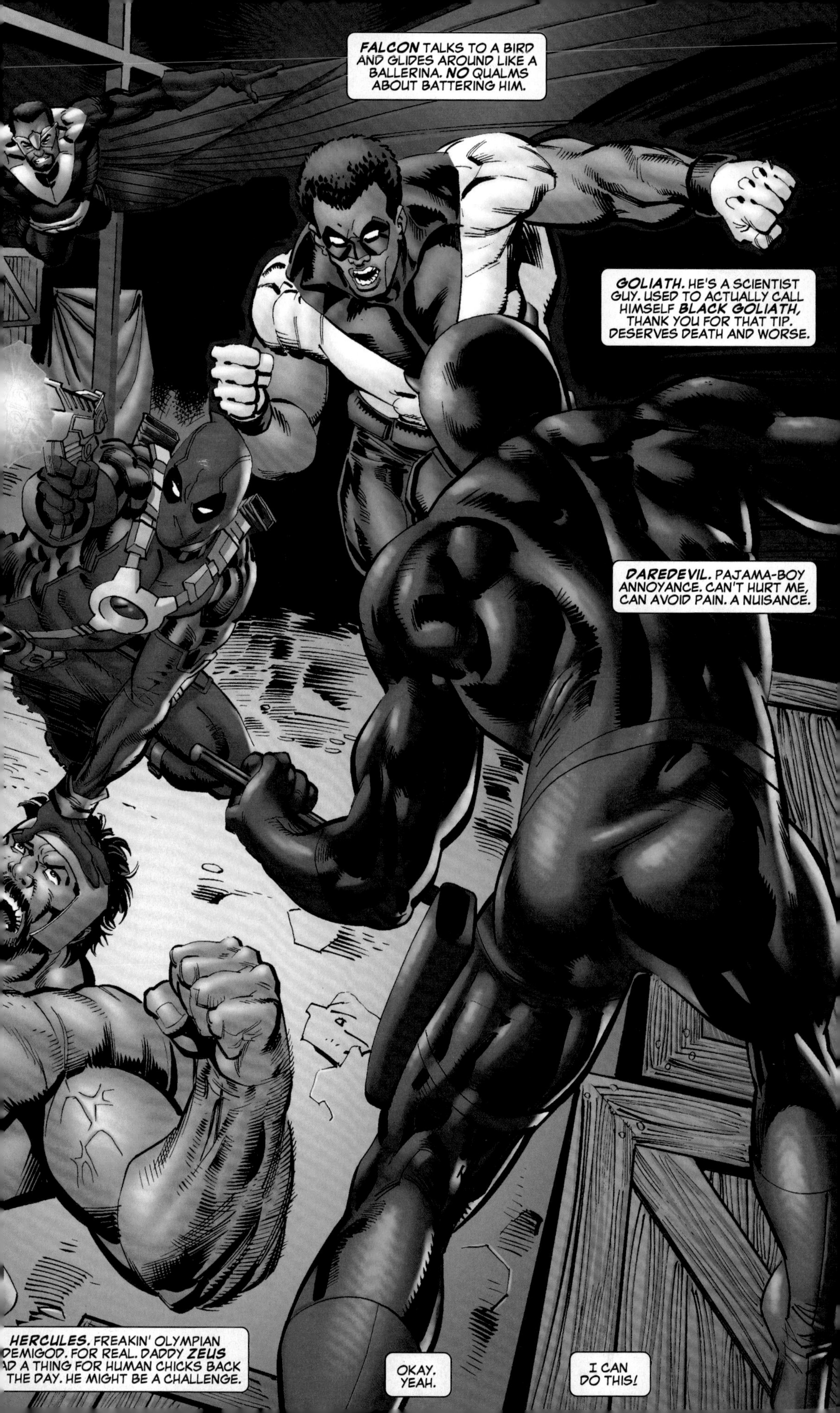
FALCON TALKS TO A BIRD AND GLIDES AROUND LIKE A BALLERINA. NO QUALMS ABOUT BATTERING HIM.
GOLIATH. HE'S A SCIENTIST GUY. USED TO ACTUALLY CALL HIMSELF BLACK GOLIATH, THANK YOU FOR THAT TIP. DESERVES DEATH AND WORSE.
DAREDEVIL. PAJAMA-BOY ANNOYANCE. CAN'T HURT ME, CAN AVOID PAIN. A NUISANCE.
HERCULES. FREAKIN' OLYMPIAN DEMIGOD. FOR REAL. DADDY ZEUS AD A THING FOR HUMAN CHICKS BACK THE DAY. HE MIGHT BE A CHALLENGE.
OKAY. YEAH.
I CAN DO THIS!

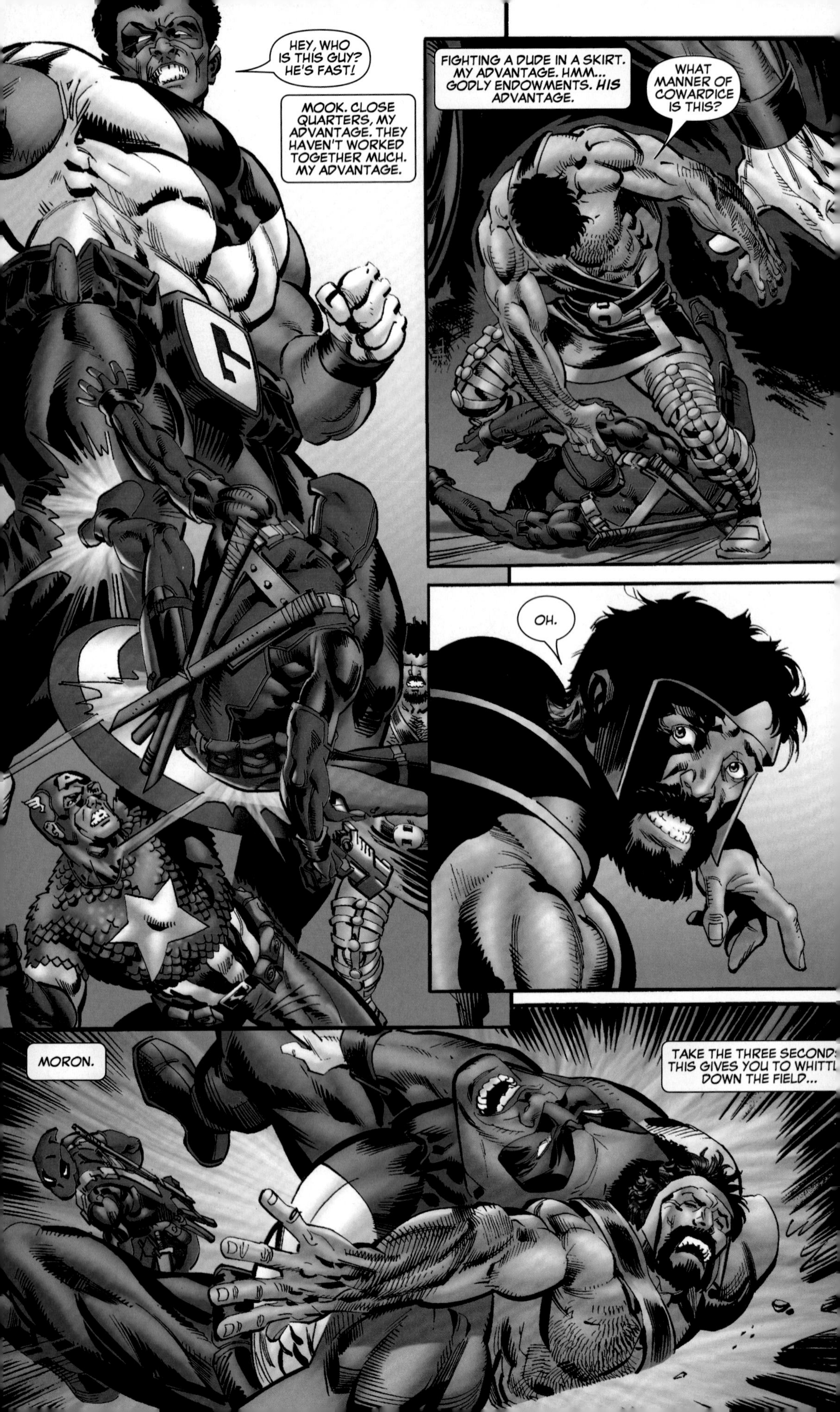
HEY, WHO IS THIS GUY? HE'S FAST!
MOOK. CLOSE QUARTERS, MY ADVANTAGE. THEY HAVEN'T WORKED TOGETHER MUCH. MY ADVANTAGE.
FIGHTING A DUDE IN A SKIRT. MY ADVANTAGE. HMM... GODLY ENDOWMENTS. *HIS* ADVANTAGE.
WHAT MANNER OF COWARDICE IS THIS?
OH.
MORON.
TAKE THE THREE SECOND THIS GIVES YOU TO WHITTL DOWN THE FIELD...

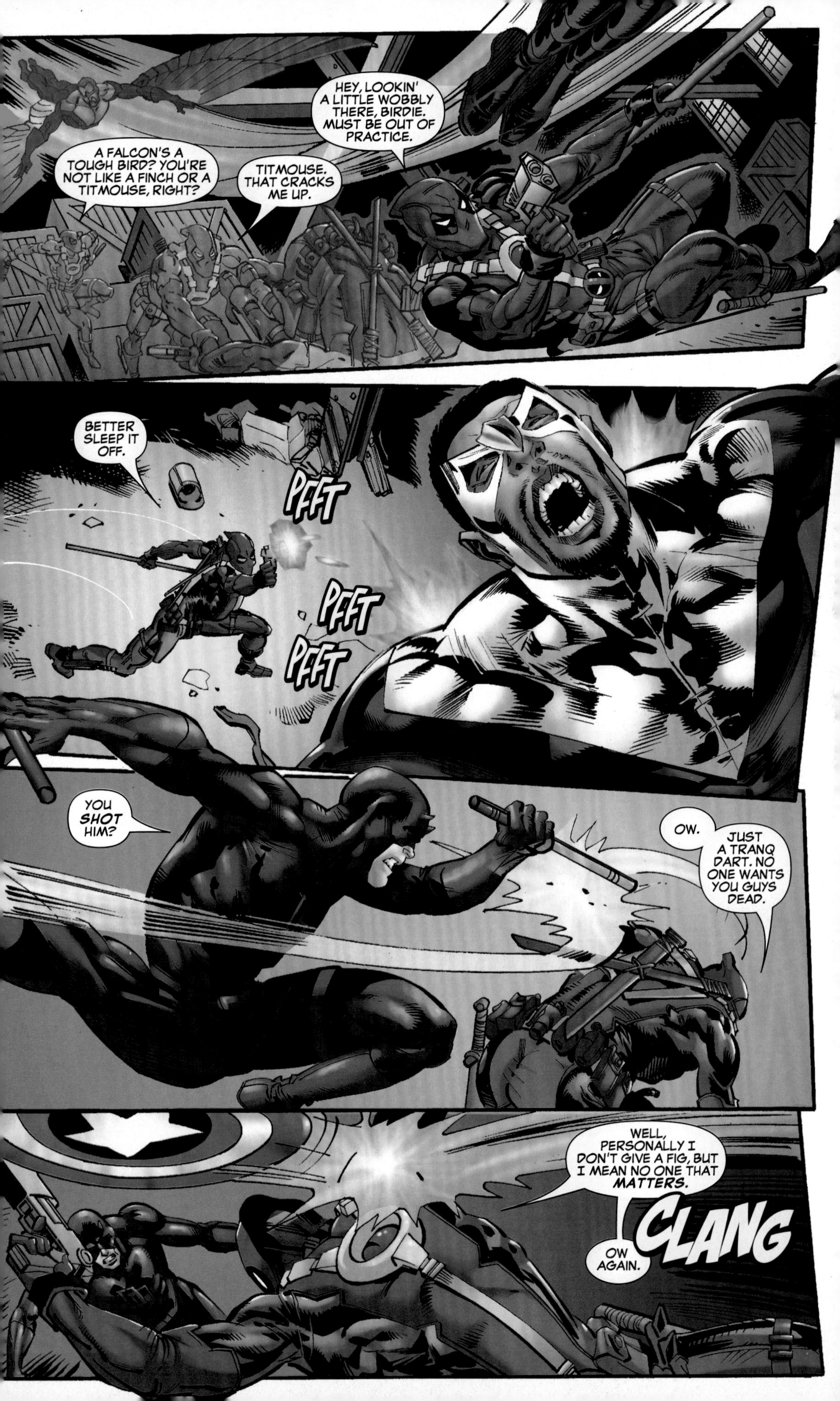
A FALCON'S A TOUGH BIRD? YOU'RE NOT LIKE A FINCH OR A TITMOUSE, RIGHT?
TITMOUSE. THAT CRACKS ME UP.
HEY, LOOKIN' A LITTLE WOBBLY THERE, BIRDIE. MUST BE OUT OF PRACTICE.
BETTER SLEEP IT OFF.
PFFT
PFFT
PFFT
YOU SHOT HIM?
OW.
JUST A TRANQ DART. NO ONE WANTS YOU GUYS DEAD.
WELL, PERSONALLY I DON'T GIVE A FIG, BUT I MEAN NO ONE THAT MATTERS.
CLANG
OW AGAIN.

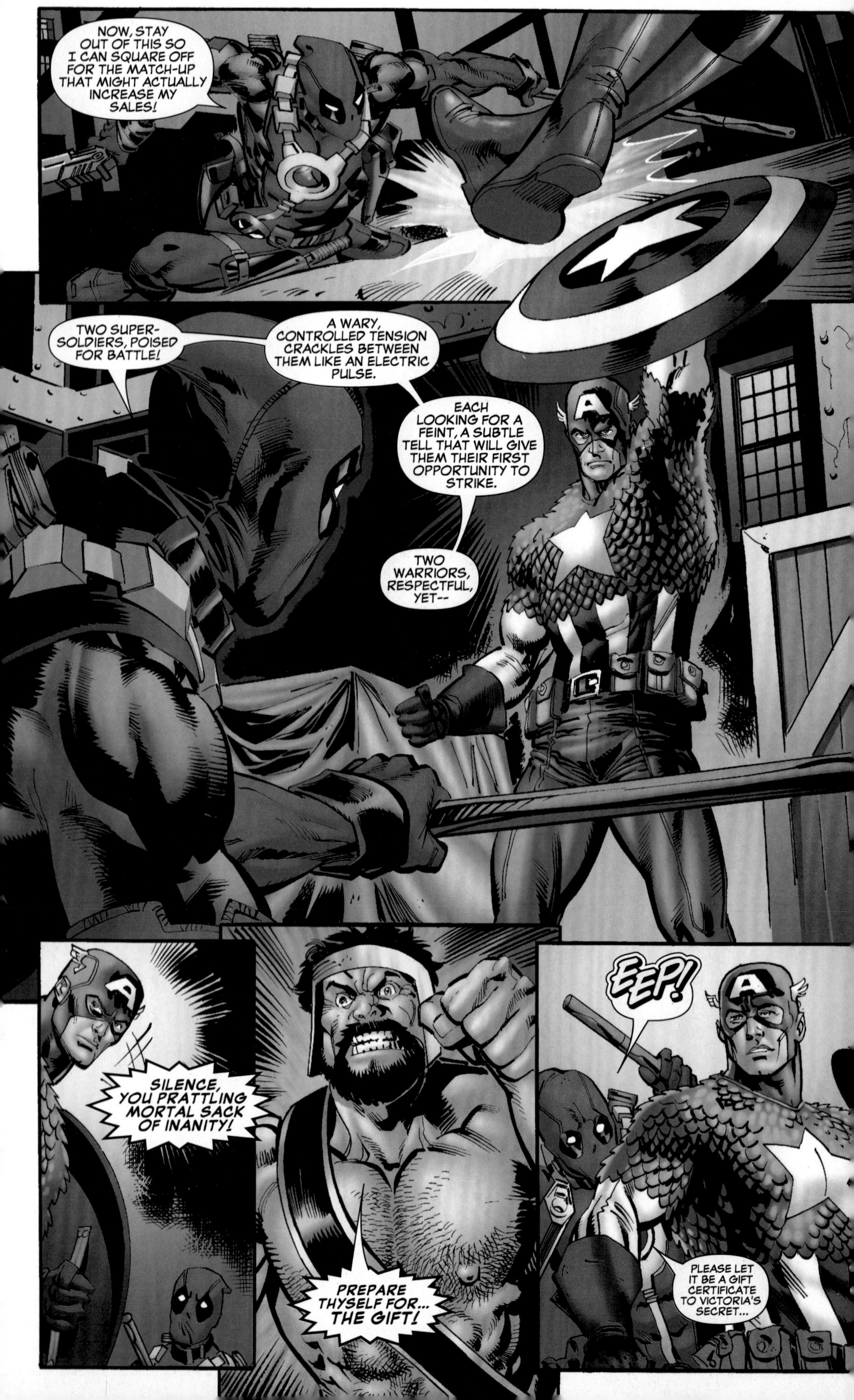

NOW, STAY OUT OF THIS SO I CAN SQUARE OFF FOR THE MATCH-UP THAT MIGHT ACTUALLY INCREASE MY SALES!
TWO SUPER-SOLDIERS, POISED FOR BATTLE!
A WARY, CONTROLLED TENSION CRACKLES BETWEEN THEM LIKE AN ELECTRIC PULSE.
EACH LOOKING FOR A FEINT, A SUBTLE TELL THAT WILL GIVE THEM THEIR FIRST OPPORTUNITY TO STRIKE.
TWO WARRIORS, RESPECTFUL, YET--
SILENCE, YOU PRATTLING MORTAL SACK OF INANITY!
PREPARE THYSELF FOR... THE GIFT!
EEP!
PLEASE LET IT BE A GIFT CERTIFICATE TO VICTORIA'S SECRET...

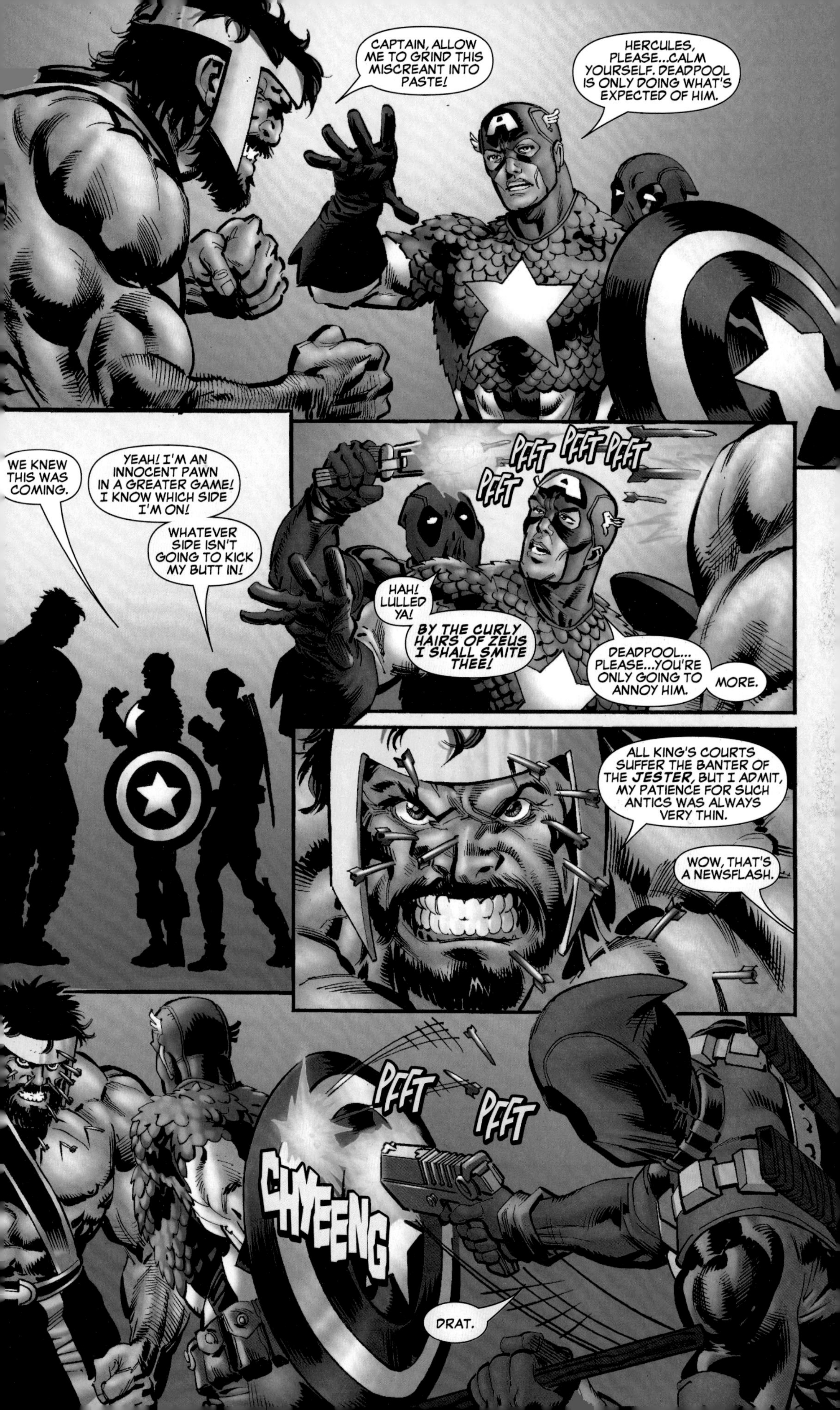
CAPTAIN, ALLOW ME TO GRIND THIS MISCREANT INTO PASTE!
HERCULES, PLEASE...CALM YOURSELF. DEADPOOL IS ONLY DOING WHAT'S EXPECTED OF HIM.
WE KNEW THIS WAS COMING.
YEAH! I'M AN INNOCENT PAWN IN A GREATER GAME! I KNOW WHICH SIDE I'M ON!
WHATEVER SIDE ISN'T GOING TO KICK MY BUTT IN!
PFFT PFFT PFFT PFFT
HAH! LULLED YA!
BY THE CURLY HAIRS OF ZEUS I SHALL SMITE THEE!
DEADPOOL... PLEASE...YOU'RE ONLY GOING TO ANNOY HIM.
MORE.
ALL KING'S COURTS SUFFER THE BANTER OF THE JESTER, BUT I ADMIT, MY PATIENCE FOR SUCH ANTICS WAS ALWAYS VERY THIN.
WOW, THAT'S A NEWSFLASH.
PFFT
PFFT
CHYEENG
DRAT.

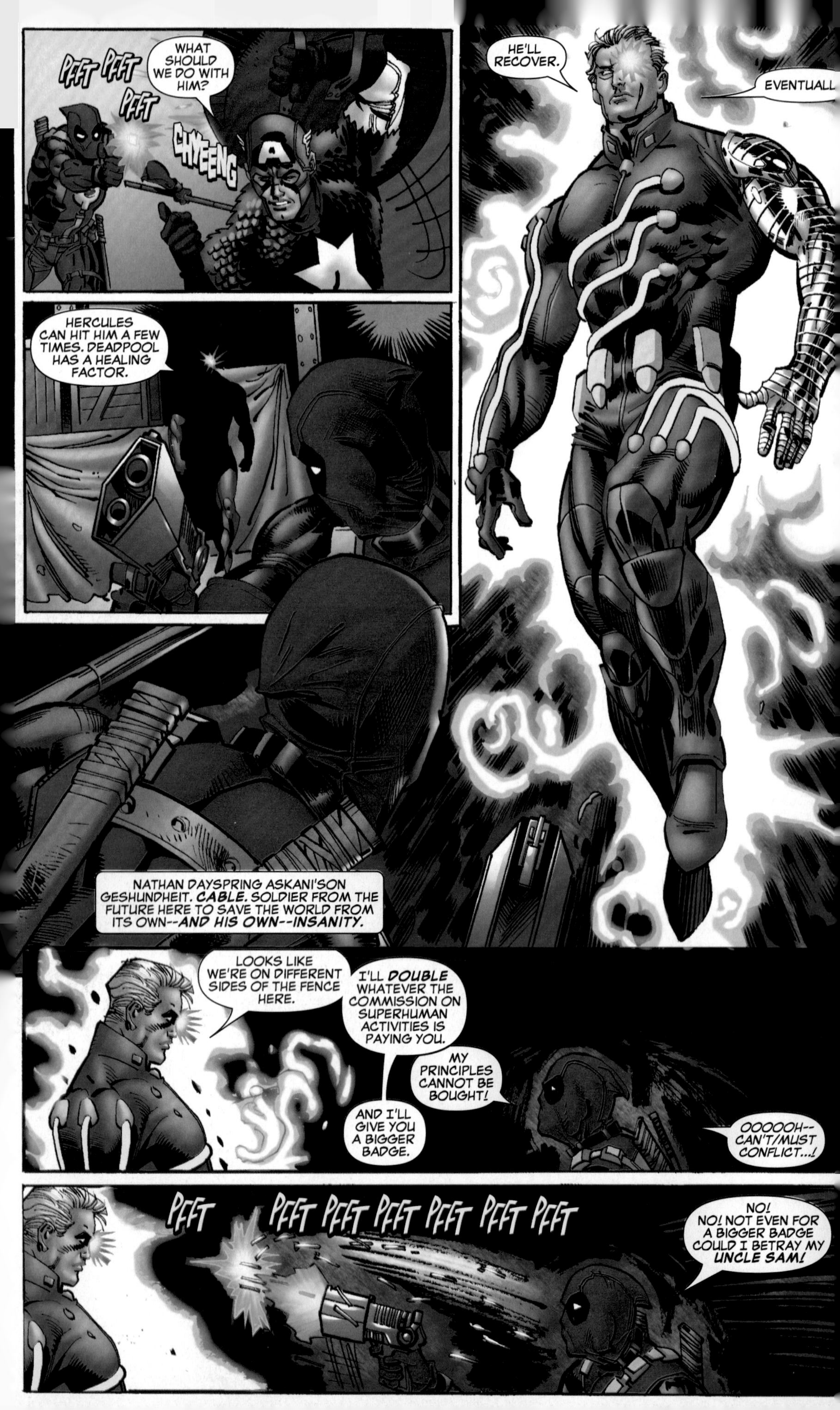
PFFT PFFT
PFFT
WHAT SHOULD WE DO WITH HIM?
CHYEENG
HE'LL RECOVER.
EVENTUALL
HERCULES CAN HIT HIM A FEW TIMES. DEADPOOL HAS A HEALING FACTOR.
NATHAN DAYSPRING ASKANI'SON GESHUNDHEIT. CABLE. SOLDIER FROM THE FUTURE HERE TO SAVE THE WORLD FROM ITS OWN--AND HIS OWN--INSANITY.
LOOKS LIKE WE'RE ON DIFFERENT SIDES OF THE FENCE HERE.
I'LL DOUBLE WHATEVER THE COMMISSION ON SUPERHUMAN ACTIVITIES IS PAYING YOU.
MY PRINCIPLES CANNOT BE BOUGHT!
AND I'LL GIVE YOU A BIGGER BADGE.
OOOOOH--CAN'T/MUST CONFLICT...!
PFFT PFFT PFFT PFFT PFFT PFFT PFFT
NO! NO! NOT EVEN FOR A BIGGER BADGE COULD I BETRAY MY UNCLE SAM!

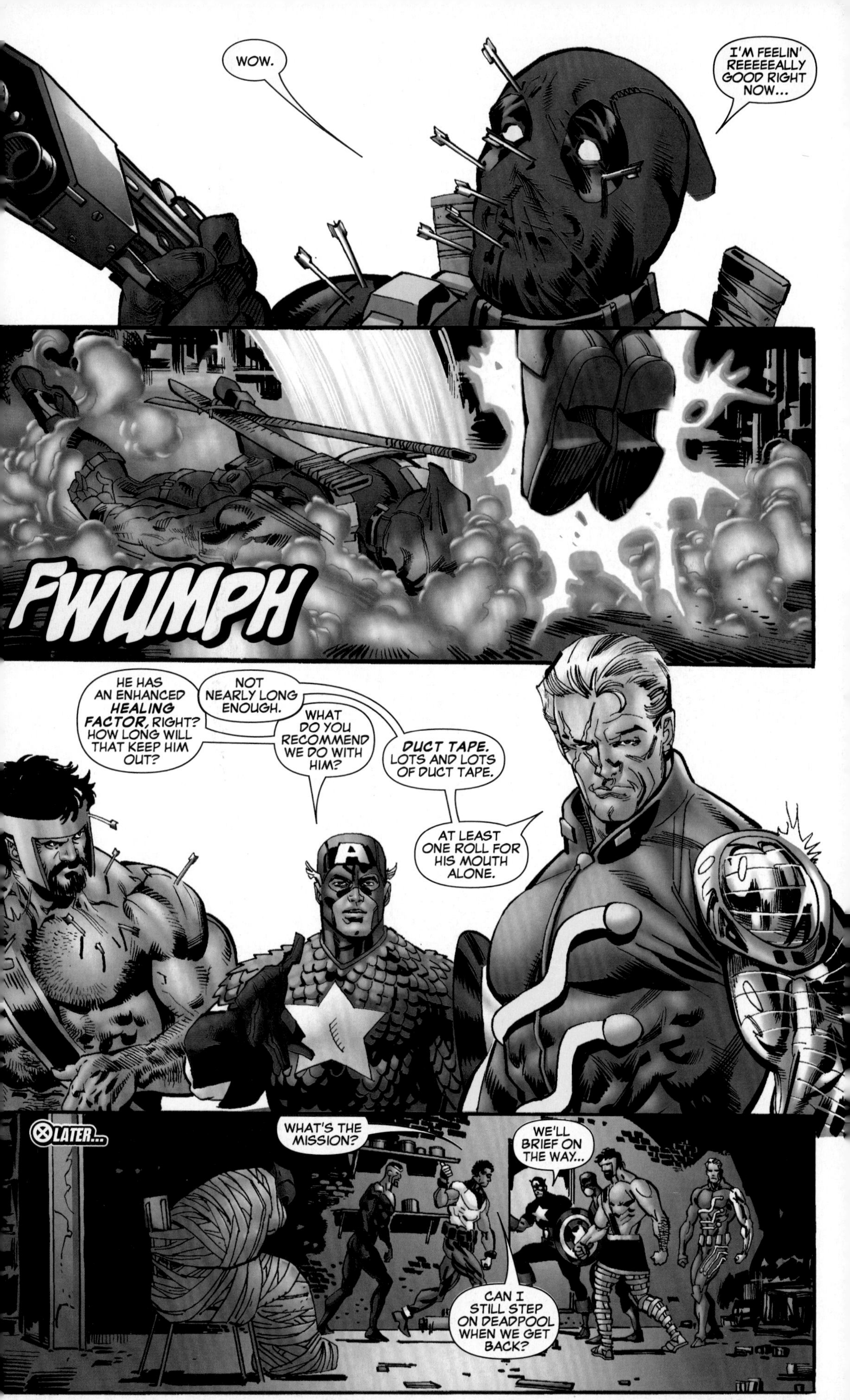

WOW.
I'M FEELIN' REEEEEALLY GOOD RIGHT NOW...
FWUMPH
HE HAS AN ENHANCED **HEALING FACTOR**, RIGHT? HOW LONG WILL THAT KEEP HIM OUT?
NOT NEARLY LONG ENOUGH.
WHAT DO YOU RECOMMEND WE DO WITH HIM?
DUCT TAPE. LOTS AND LOTS OF DUCT TAPE.
AT LEAST ONE ROLL FOR HIS MOUTH ALONE.
LATER...
WHAT'S THE MISSION?
WE'LL BRIEF ON THE WAY...
CAN I STILL STEP ON DEADPOOL WHEN WE GET BACK?

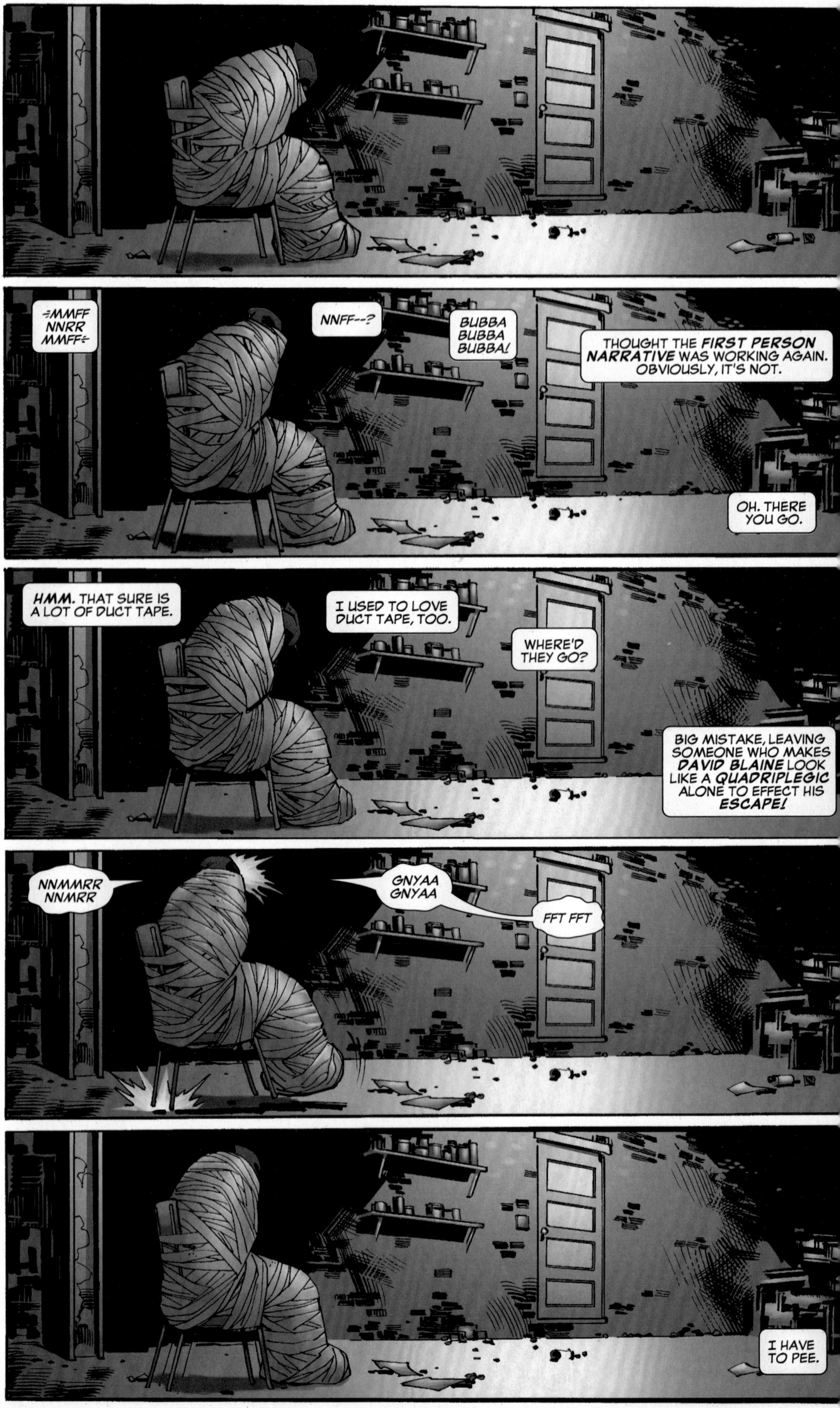

=MMFF NNRR MMFF=
NNFF--?
BUBBA BUBBA BUBBA!
THOUGHT THE FIRST PERSON NARRATIVE WAS WORKING AGAIN. OBVIOUSLY, IT'S NOT.
OH. THERE YOU GO.
HMM. THAT SURE IS A LOT OF DUCT TAPE.
I USED TO LOVE DUCT TAPE, TOO.
WHERE'D THEY GO?
BIG MISTAKE, LEAVING SOMEONE WHO MAKES DAVID BLAINE LOOK LIKE A QUADRIPLEGIC ALONE TO EFFECT HIS ESCAPE!
NNMMRR NNMRR
GNYAA GNYAA
FFT FFT
I HAVE TO PEE.

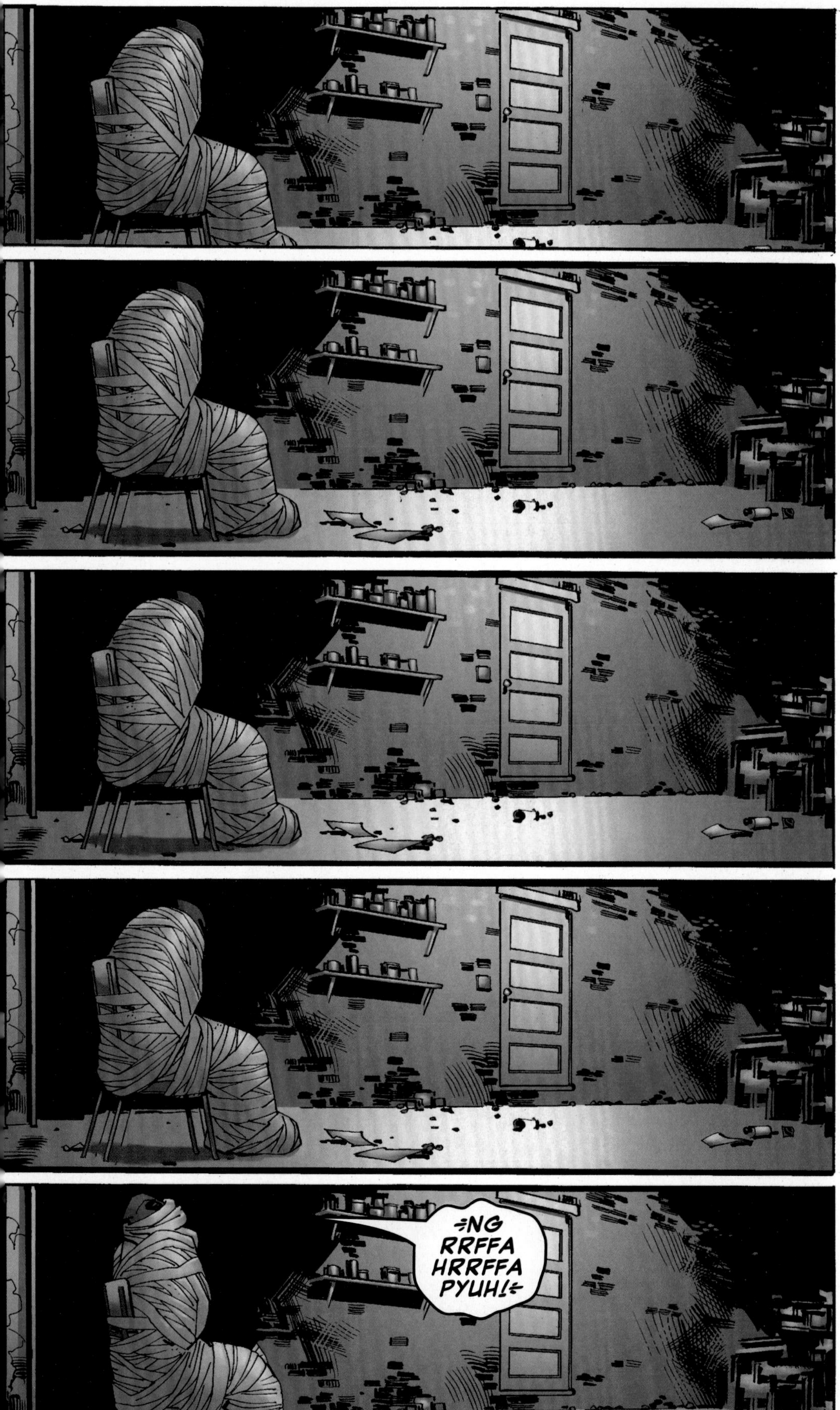

NG RRFFA HRRFFA PYUH!
I REALLY HAVE TO PEE!

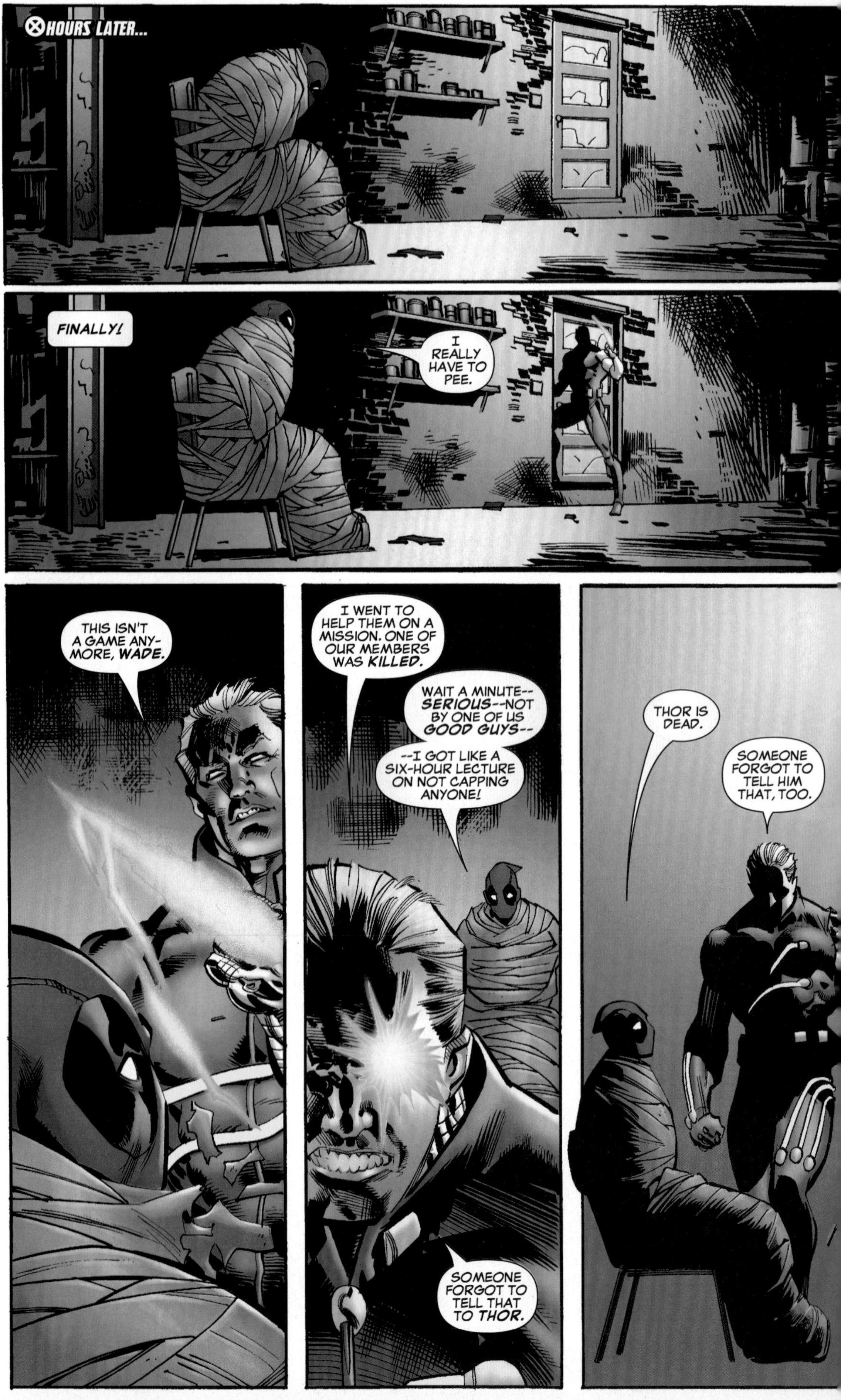
HOURS LATER...
FINALLY!
I REALLY HAVE TO PEE.
THIS ISN'T A GAME ANY-MORE, WADE.
I WENT TO HELP THEM ON A MISSION. ONE OF OUR MEMBERS WAS KILLED.
WAIT A MINUTE-- SERIOUS--NOT BY ONE OF US GOOD GUYS--
--I GOT LIKE A SIX-HOUR LECTURE ON NOT CAPPING ANYONE!
SOMEONE FORGOT TO TELL THAT TO THOR.
THOR IS DEAD.
SOMEONE FORGOT TO TELL HIM THAT, TOO.

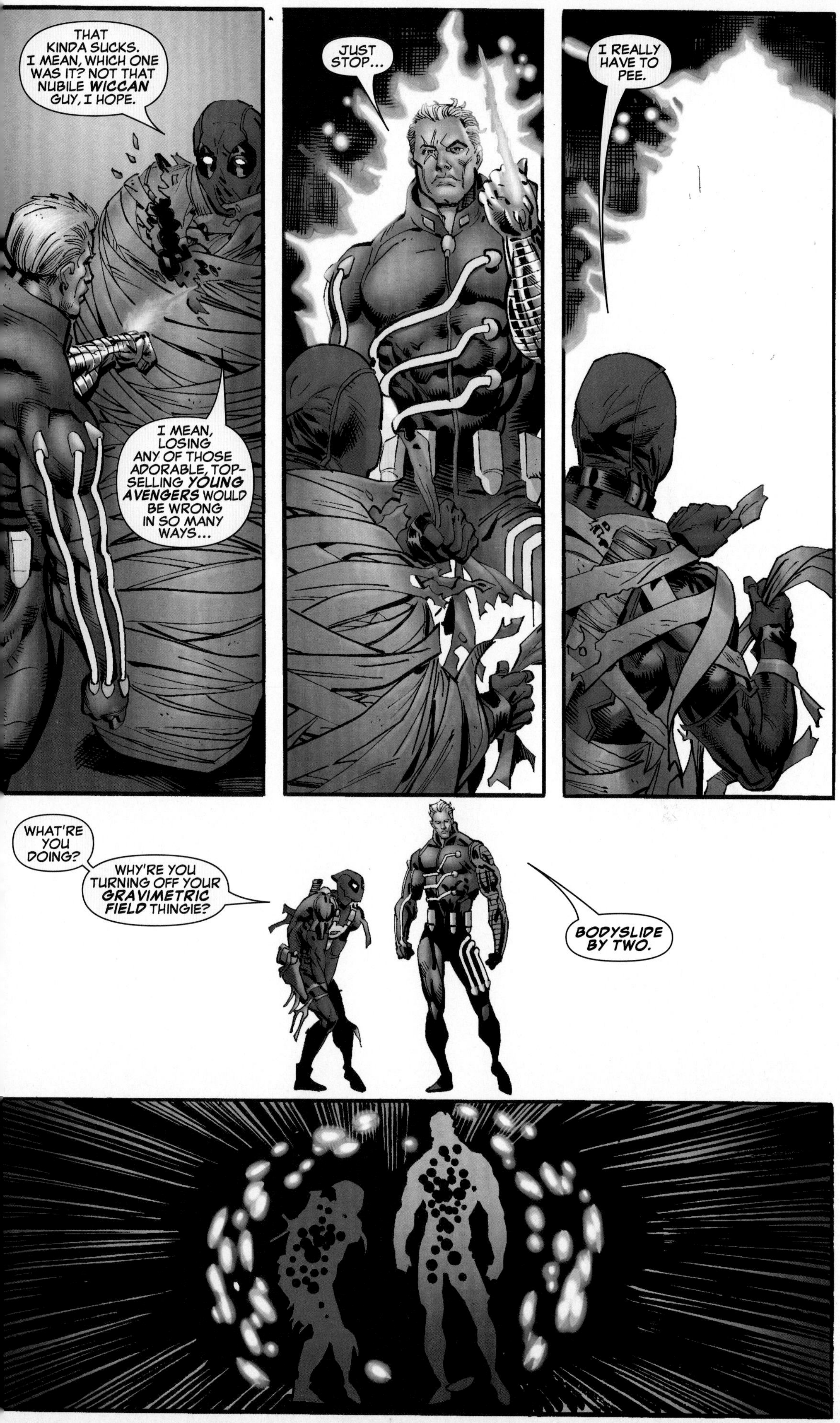
THAT KINDA SUCKS. I MEAN, WHICH ONE WAS IT? NOT THAT NUBILE WICCAN GUY, I HOPE.
I MEAN, LOSING ANY OF THOSE ADORABLE, TOP-SELLING YOUNG AVENGERS WOULD BE WRONG IN SO MANY WAYS...
JUST STOP...
I REALLY HAVE TO PEE.
WHAT'RE YOU DOING?
WHY'RE YOU TURNING OFF YOUR GRAVIMETRIC FIELD THINGIE?
BODYSLIDE BY TWO.

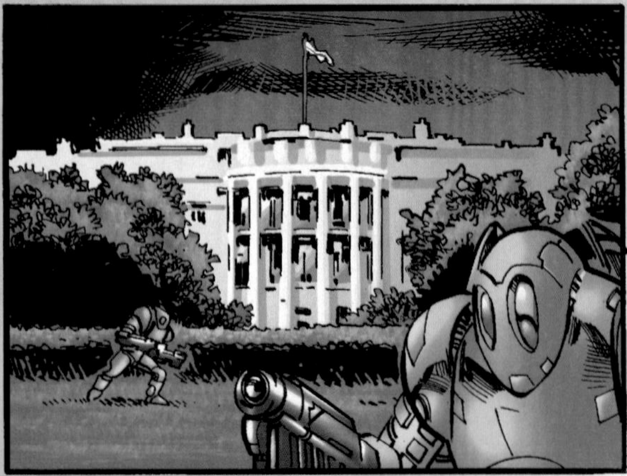

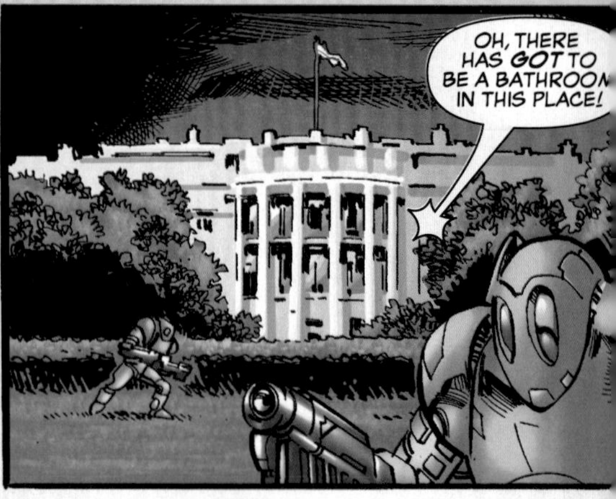
OH, THERE HAS GOT TO BE A BATHROOM IN THIS PLACE!

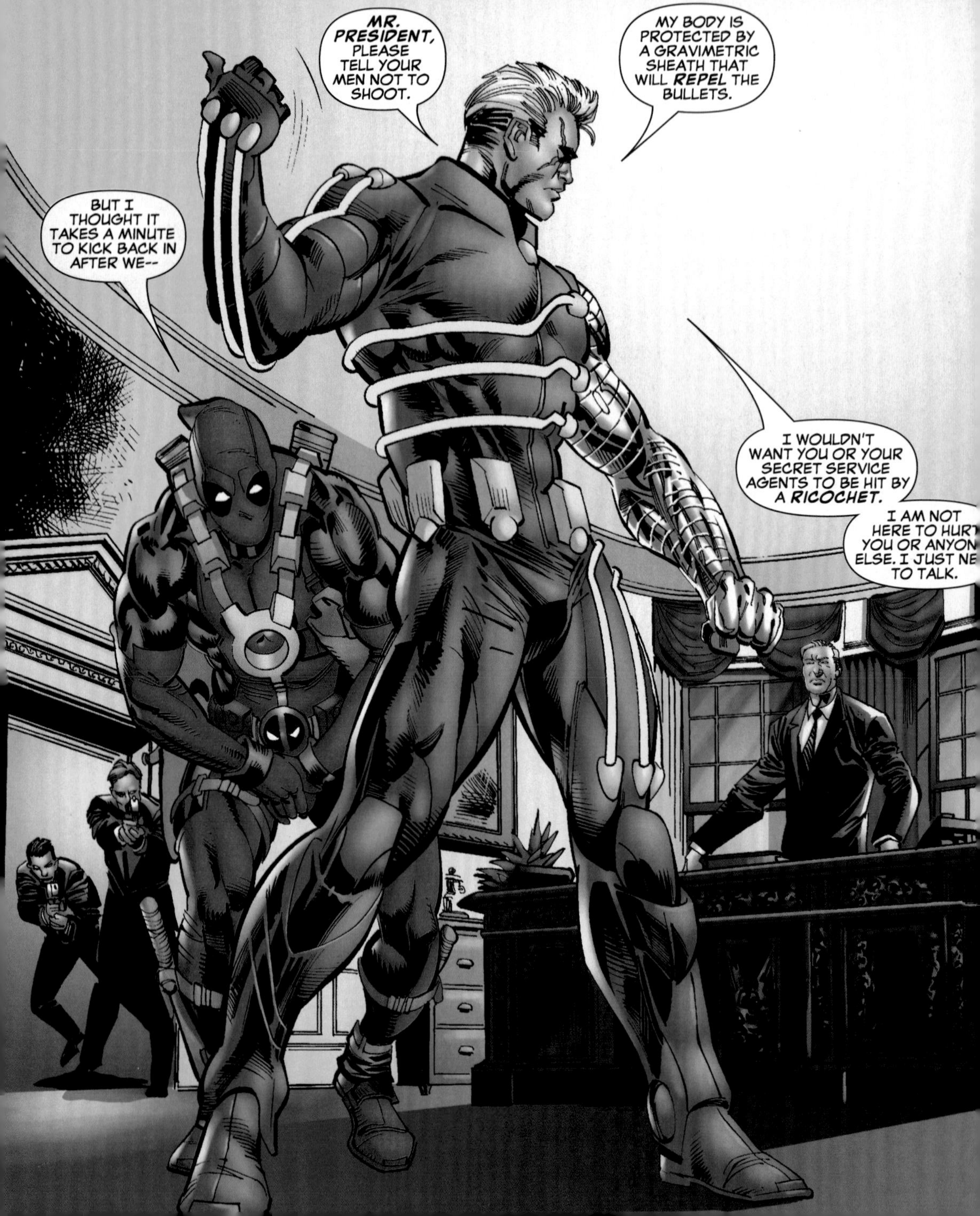
MR. PRESIDENT, PLEASE TELL YOUR MEN NOT TO SHOOT.
MY BODY IS PROTECTED BY A GRAVIMETRIC SHEATH THAT WILL REPEL THE BULLETS.
BUT I THOUGHT IT TAKES A MINUTE TO KICK BACK IN AFTER WE--
I WOULDN'T WANT YOU OR YOUR SECRET SERVICE AGENTS TO BE HIT BY A RICOCHET.
I AM NOT HERE TO HURT YOU OR ANYONE ELSE. I JUST NEED TO TALK.

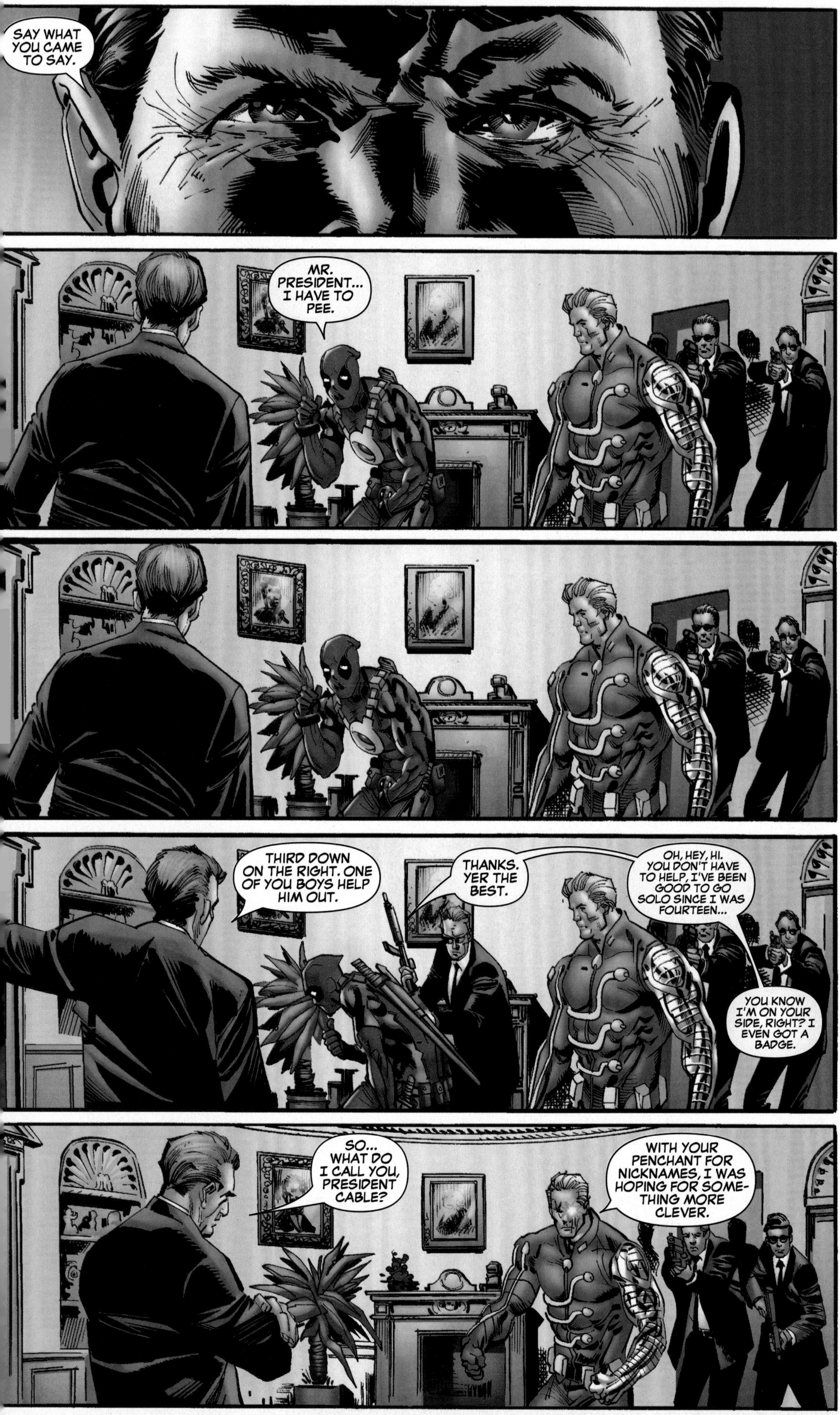
SAY WHAT YOU CAME TO SAY.
MR. PRESIDENT... I HAVE TO PEE.
THIRD DOWN ON THE RIGHT. ONE OF YOU BOYS HELP HIM OUT.
THANKS. YER THE BEST.
OH, HEY, HI. YOU DON'T HAVE TO HELP, I'VE BEEN GOOD TO GO SOLO SINCE I WAS FOURTEEN...
YOU KNOW I'M ON YOUR SIDE, RIGHT? I EVEN GOT A BADGE.
SO... WHAT DO I CALL YOU, PRESIDENT CABLE?
WITH YOUR PENCHANT FOR NICKNAMES, I WAS HOPING FOR SOME-THING MORE CLEVER.

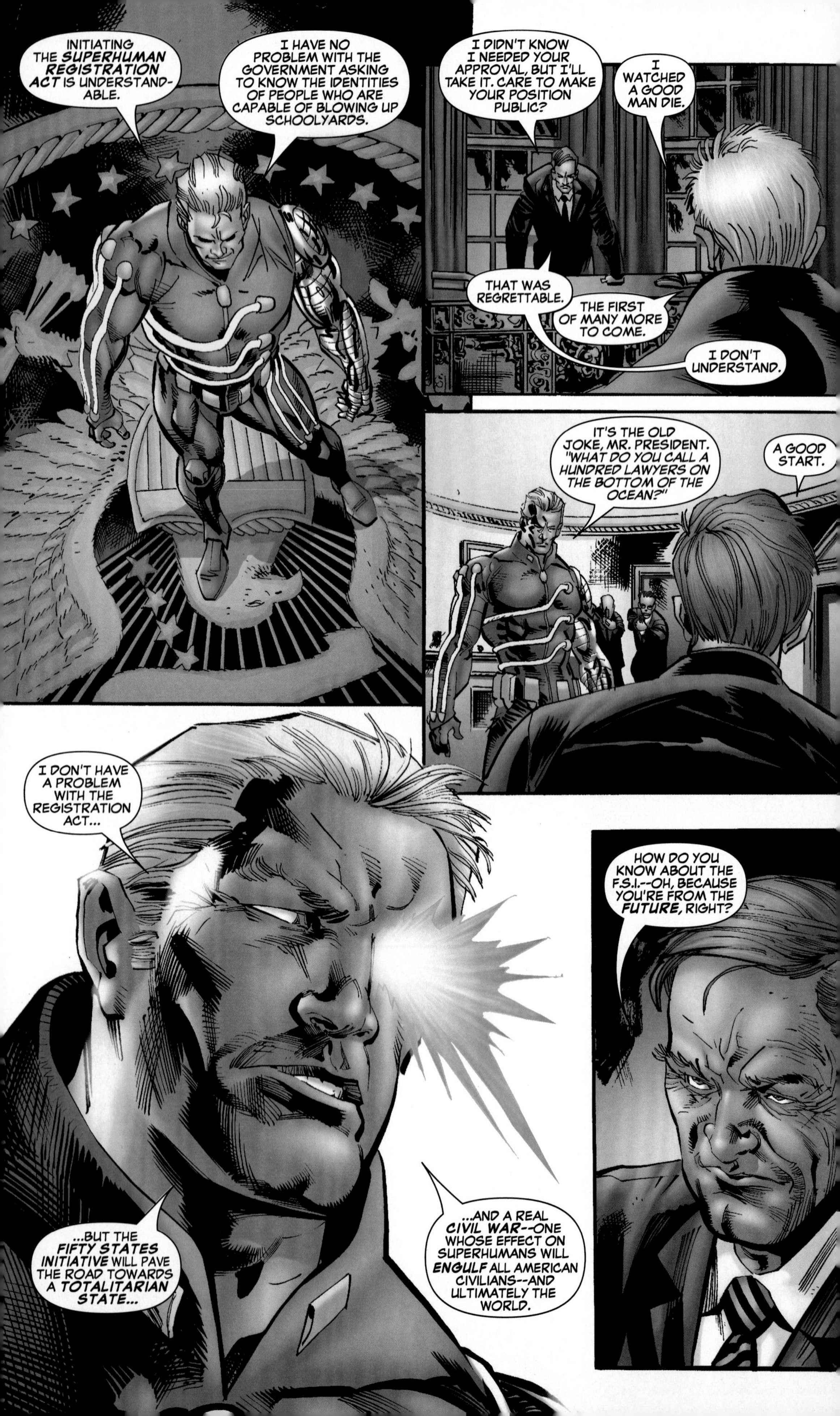

INITIATING THE SUPERHUMAN REGISTRATION ACT IS UNDERSTAND-ABLE.
I HAVE NO PROBLEM WITH THE GOVERNMENT ASKING TO KNOW THE IDENTITIES OF PEOPLE WHO ARE CAPABLE OF BLOWING UP SCHOOLYARDS.
I DIDN'T KNOW I NEEDED YOUR APPROVAL, BUT I'LL TAKE IT. CARE TO MAKE YOUR POSITION PUBLIC?
I WATCHED A GOOD MAN DIE.
THAT WAS REGRETTABLE.
THE FIRST OF MANY MORE TO COME.
I DON'T UNDERSTAND.
IT'S THE OLD JOKE, MR. PRESIDENT. "WHAT DO YOU CALL A HUNDRED LAWYERS ON THE BOTTOM OF THE OCEAN?"
A GOOD START.
I DON'T HAVE A PROBLEM WITH THE REGISTRATION ACT...
...BUT THE FIFTY STATES INITIATIVE WILL PAVE THE ROAD TOWARDS A TOTALITARIAN STATE...
...AND A REAL CIVIL WAR--ONE WHOSE EFFECT ON SUPERHUMANS WILL ENGULF ALL AMERICAN CIVILIANS--AND ULTIMATELY THE WORLD.
HOW DO YOU KNOW ABOUT THE F.S.I.--OH, BECAUSE YOU'RE FROM THE FUTURE, RIGHT?

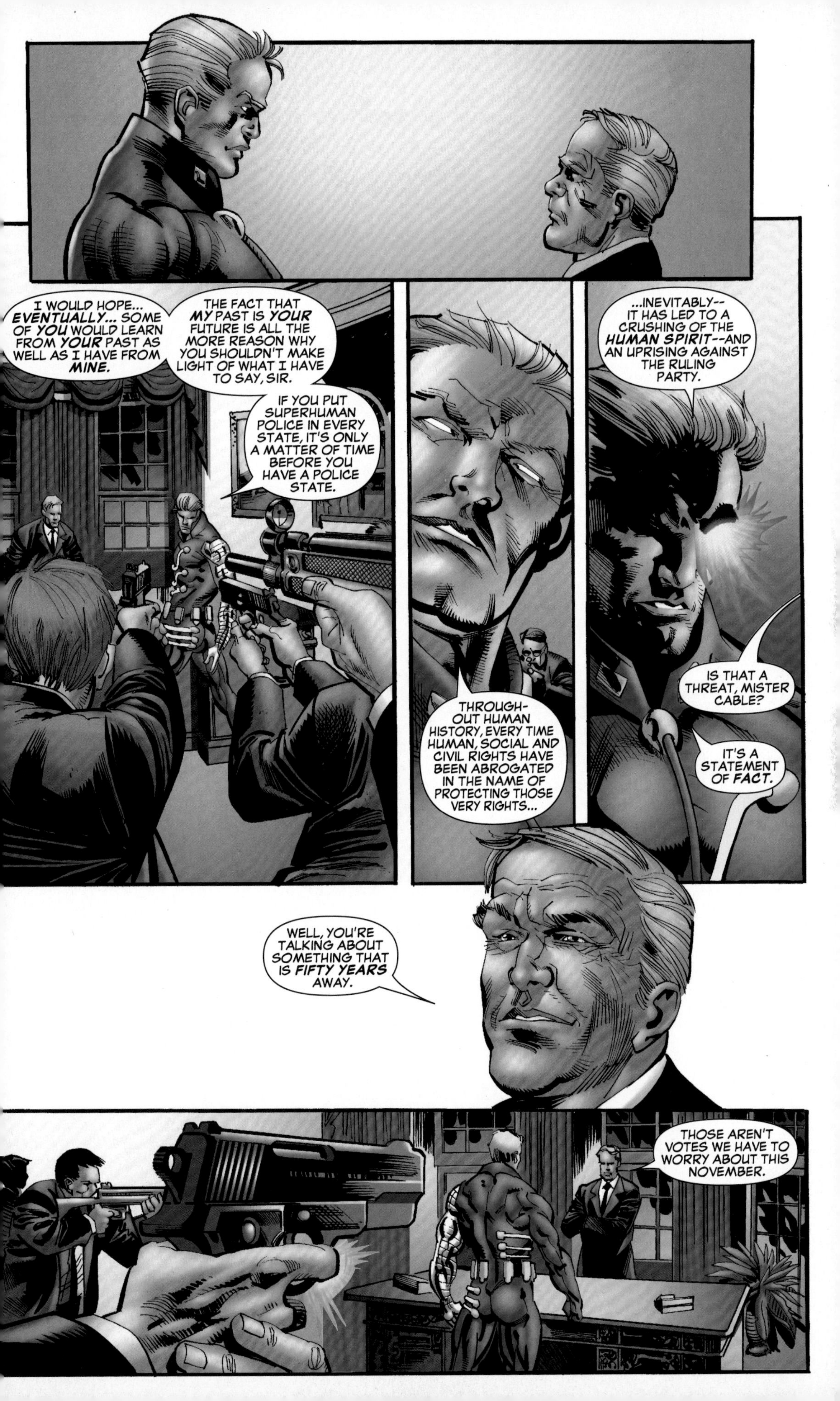
I WOULD HOPE... EVENTUALLY... SOME OF YOU WOULD LEARN FROM YOUR PAST AS WELL AS I HAVE FROM MINE.
THE FACT THAT MY PAST IS YOUR FUTURE IS ALL THE MORE REASON WHY YOU SHOULDN'T MAKE LIGHT OF WHAT I HAVE TO SAY, SIR.
IF YOU PUT SUPERHUMAN POLICE IN EVERY STATE, IT'S ONLY A MATTER OF TIME BEFORE YOU HAVE A POLICE STATE.
THROUGH-OUT HUMAN HISTORY, EVERY TIME HUMAN, SOCIAL AND CIVIL RIGHTS HAVE BEEN ABROGATED IN THE NAME OF PROTECTING THOSE VERY RIGHTS...
...INEVITABLY-- IT HAS LED TO A CRUSHING OF THE HUMAN SPIRIT--AND AN UPRISING AGAINST THE RULING PARTY.
IS THAT A THREAT, MISTER CABLE?
IT'S A STATEMENT OF FACT.
WELL, YOU'RE TALKING ABOUT SOMETHING THAT IS FIFTY YEARS AWAY.
THOSE AREN'T VOTES WE HAVE TO WORRY ABOUT THIS NOVEMBER.

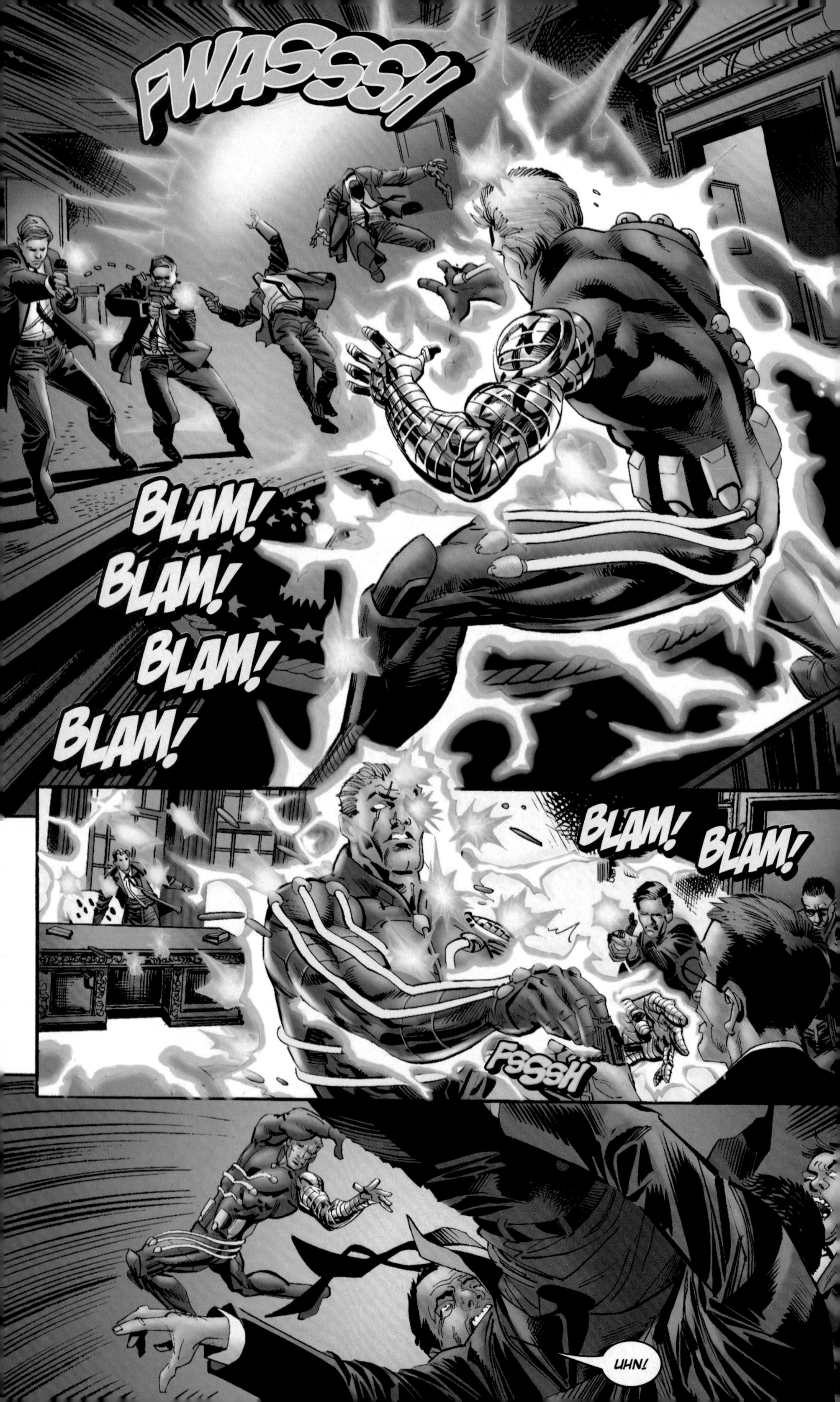
FWASSSH
BLAM!
BLAM!
BLAM!
BLAM!
BLAM!
BLAM!
FSSSH
UHN!

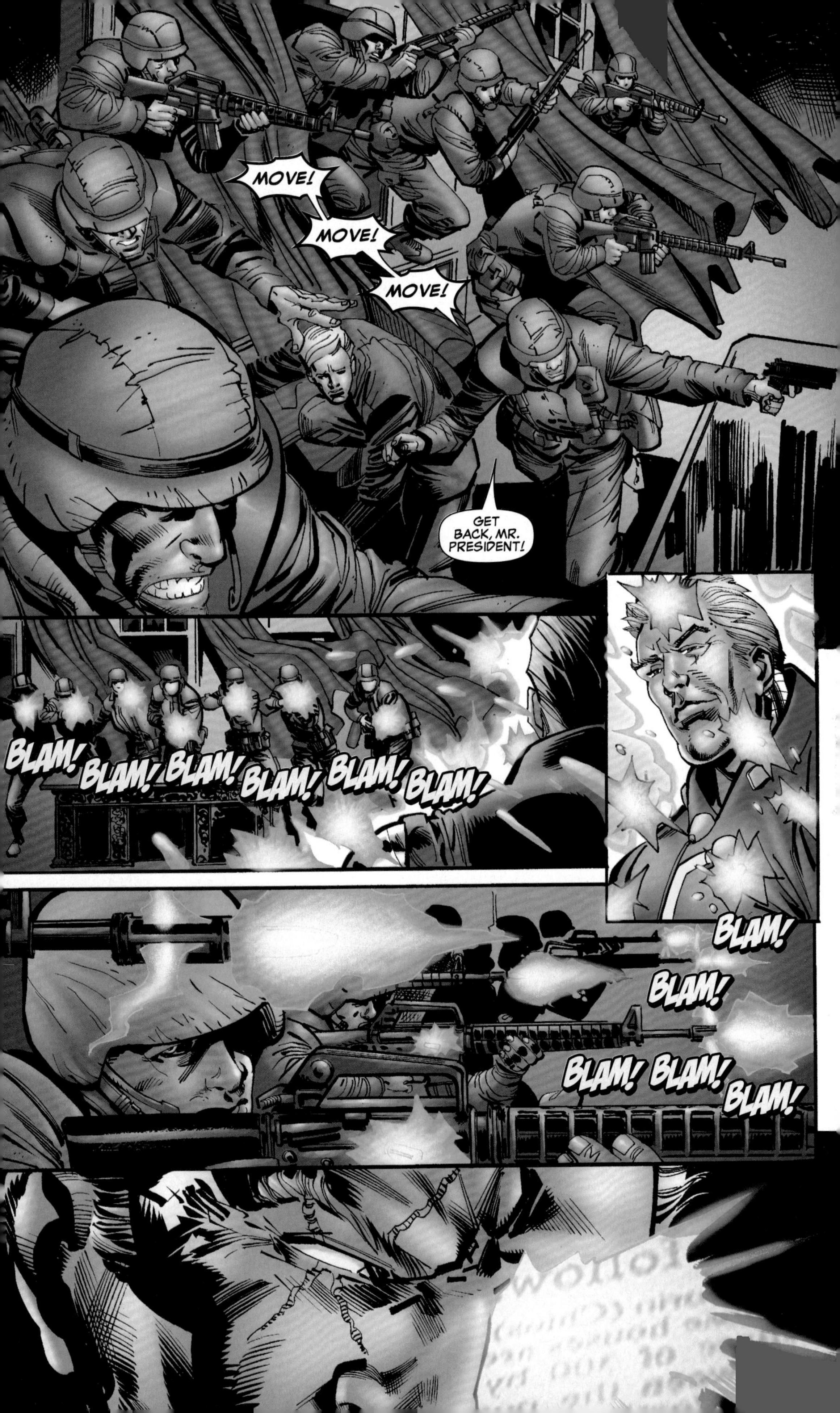
MOVE!
MOVE!
MOVE!
GET BACK, MR. PRESIDENT!
BLAM! BLAM! BLAM! BLAM! BLAM! BLAM!
BLAM!
BLAM!
BLAM! BLAM! BLAM!

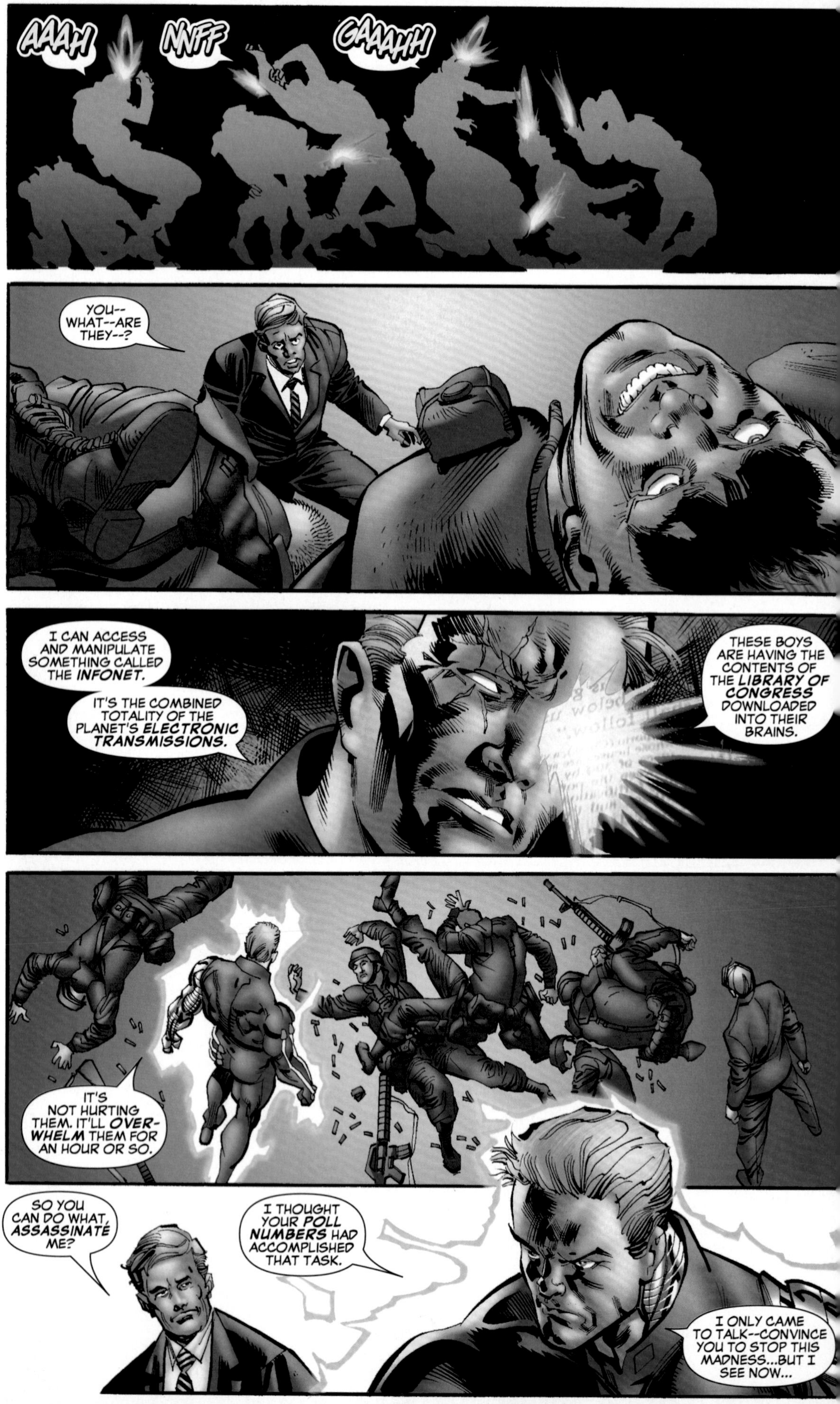
AAAH
NNFF
GAAAHH
YOU-- WHAT--ARE THEY--?
I CAN ACCESS AND MANIPULATE SOMETHING CALLED THE INFONET.
IT'S THE COMBINED TOTALITY OF THE PLANET'S ELECTRONIC TRANSMISSIONS.
THESE BOYS ARE HAVING THE CONTENTS OF THE LIBRARY OF CONGRESS DOWNLOADED INTO THEIR BRAINS.
IT'S NOT HURTING THEM. IT'LL OVER-WHELM THEM FOR AN HOUR OR SO.
SO YOU CAN DO WHAT, ASSASSINATE ME?
I THOUGHT YOUR POLL NUMBERS HAD ACCOMPLISHED THAT TASK.
I ONLY CAME TO TALK--CONVINCE YOU TO STOP THIS MADNESS...BUT I SEE NOW...

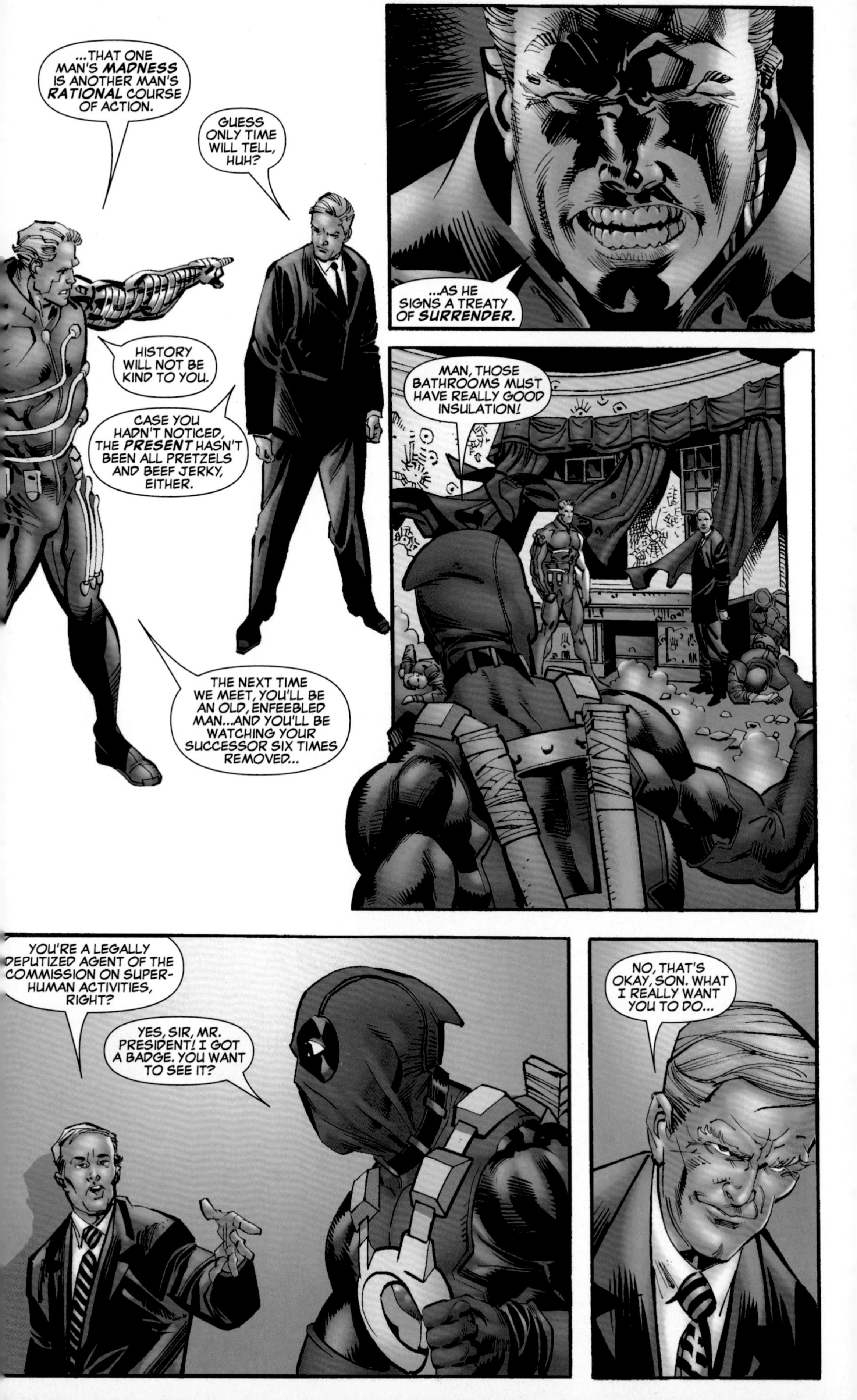
...THAT ONE MAN'S MADNESS IS ANOTHER MAN'S RATIONAL COURSE OF ACTION.
GUESS ONLY TIME WILL TELL, HUH?
HISTORY WILL NOT BE KIND TO YOU.
CASE YOU HADN'T NOTICED, THE PRESENT HASN'T BEEN ALL PRETZELS AND BEEF JERKY, EITHER.
THE NEXT TIME WE MEET, YOU'LL BE AN OLD, ENFEEBLED MAN...AND YOU'LL BE WATCHING YOUR SUCCESSOR SIX TIMES REMOVED...
...AS HE SIGNS A TREATY OF SURRENDER.
MAN, THOSE BATHROOMS MUST HAVE REALLY GOOD INSULATION!
YOU'RE A LEGALLY DEPUTIZED AGENT OF THE COMMISSION ON SUPER-HUMAN ACTIVITIES, RIGHT?
YES, SIR, MR. PRESIDENT! I GOT A BADGE. YOU WANT TO SEE IT?
NO, THAT'S OKAY, SON. WHAT I REALLY WANT YOU TO DO...

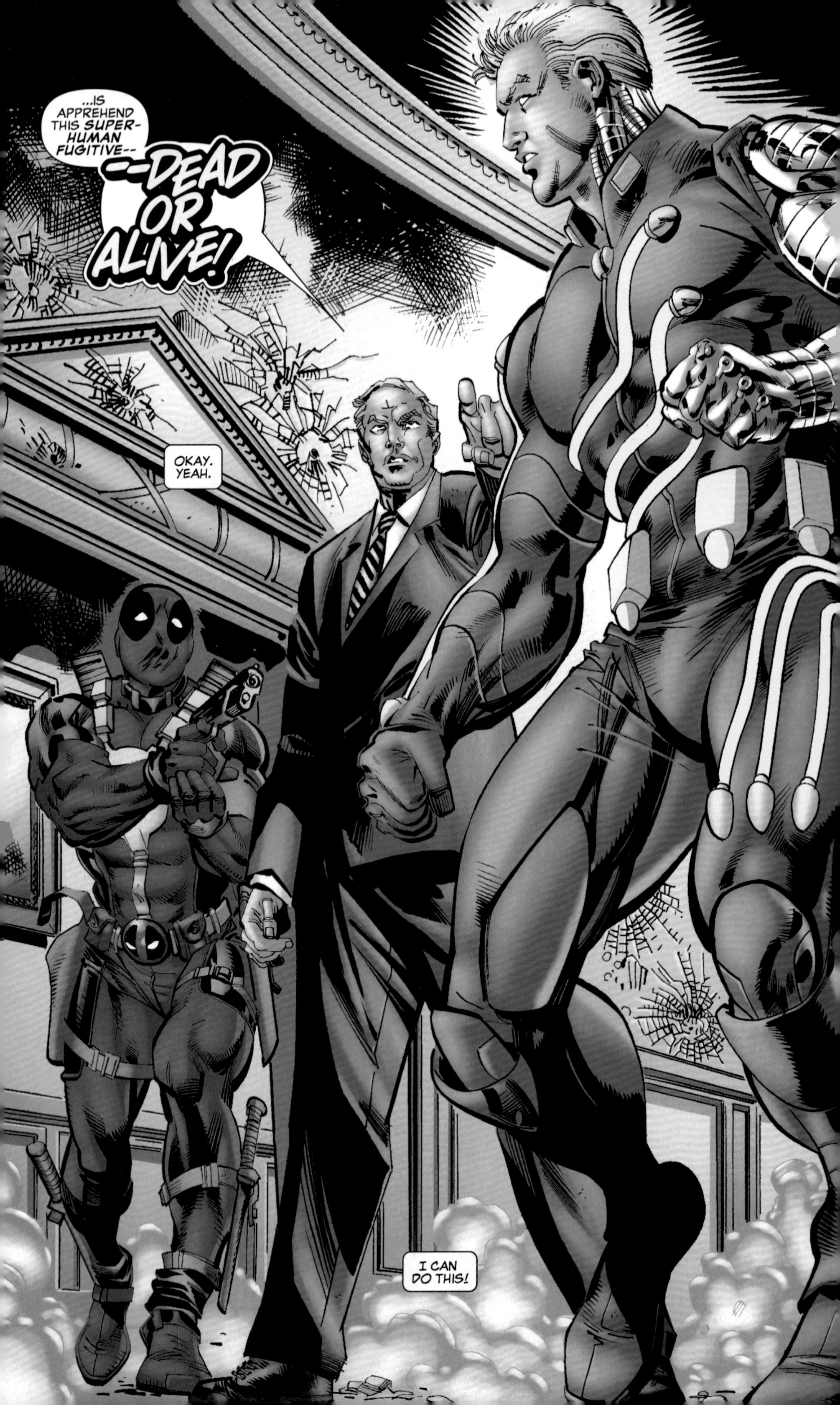
...IS APPREHEND THIS SUPER-HUMAN FUGITIVE--
--DEAD OR ALIVE!
OKAY. YEAH.
I CAN DO THIS!

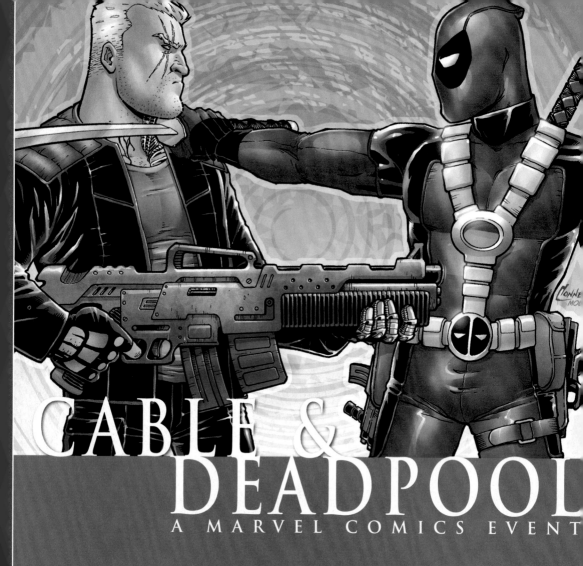

CABLE & DEADPOOL

A MARVEL COMICS EVENT

CIVIL WAR

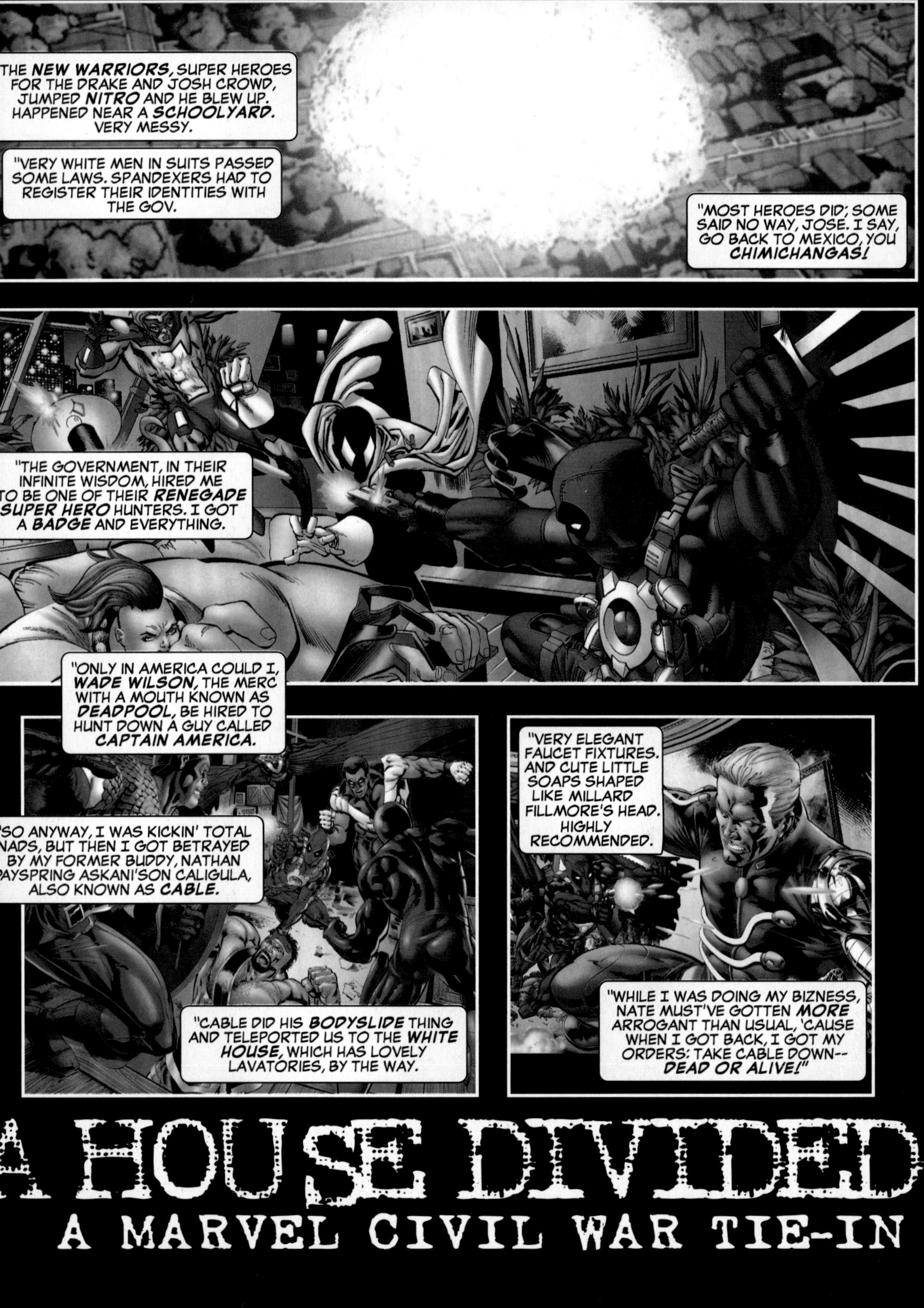
THE NEW WARRIORS, SUPER HEROES FOR THE DRAKE AND JOSH CROWD, JUMPED NITRO AND HE BLEW UP. HAPPENED NEAR A SCHOOLYARD. VERY MESSY.
"VERY WHITE MEN IN SUITS PASSED SOME LAWS. SPANDEXERS HAD TO REGISTER THEIR IDENTITIES WITH THE GOV.
"MOST HEROES DID; SOME SAID NO WAY, JOSE. I SAY, GO BACK TO MEXICO, YOU CHIMICHANGAS!
"THE GOVERNMENT, IN THEIR INFINITE WISDOM, HIRED ME TO BE ONE OF THEIR RENEGADE SUPER HERO HUNTERS. I GOT A BADGE AND EVERYTHING.
"ONLY IN AMERICA COULD I, WADE WILSON, THE MERC WITH A MOUTH KNOWN AS DEADPOOL, BE HIRED TO HUNT DOWN A GUY CALLED CAPTAIN AMERICA.
"SO ANYWAY, I WAS KICKIN' TOTAL NADS, BUT THEN I GOT BETRAYED BY MY FORMER BUDDY, NATHAN DAYSPRING ASKANI'SON CALIGULA, ALSO KNOWN AS CABLE.
"CABLE DID HIS BODYSLIDE THING AND TELEPORTED US TO THE WHITE HOUSE, WHICH HAS LOVELY LAVATORIES, BY THE WAY.
"VERY ELEGANT FAUCET FIXTURES. AND CUTE LITTLE SOAPS SHAPED LIKE MILLARD FILLMORE'S HEAD. HIGHLY RECOMMENDED.
"WHILE I WAS DOING MY BIZNESS, NATE MUST'VE GOTTEN MORE ARROGANT THAN USUAL, 'CAUSE WHEN I GOT BACK, I GOT MY ORDERS: TAKE CABLE DOWN--DEAD OR ALIVE!"

A HOUSE DIVIDED

A MARVEL CIVIL WAR TIE-IN

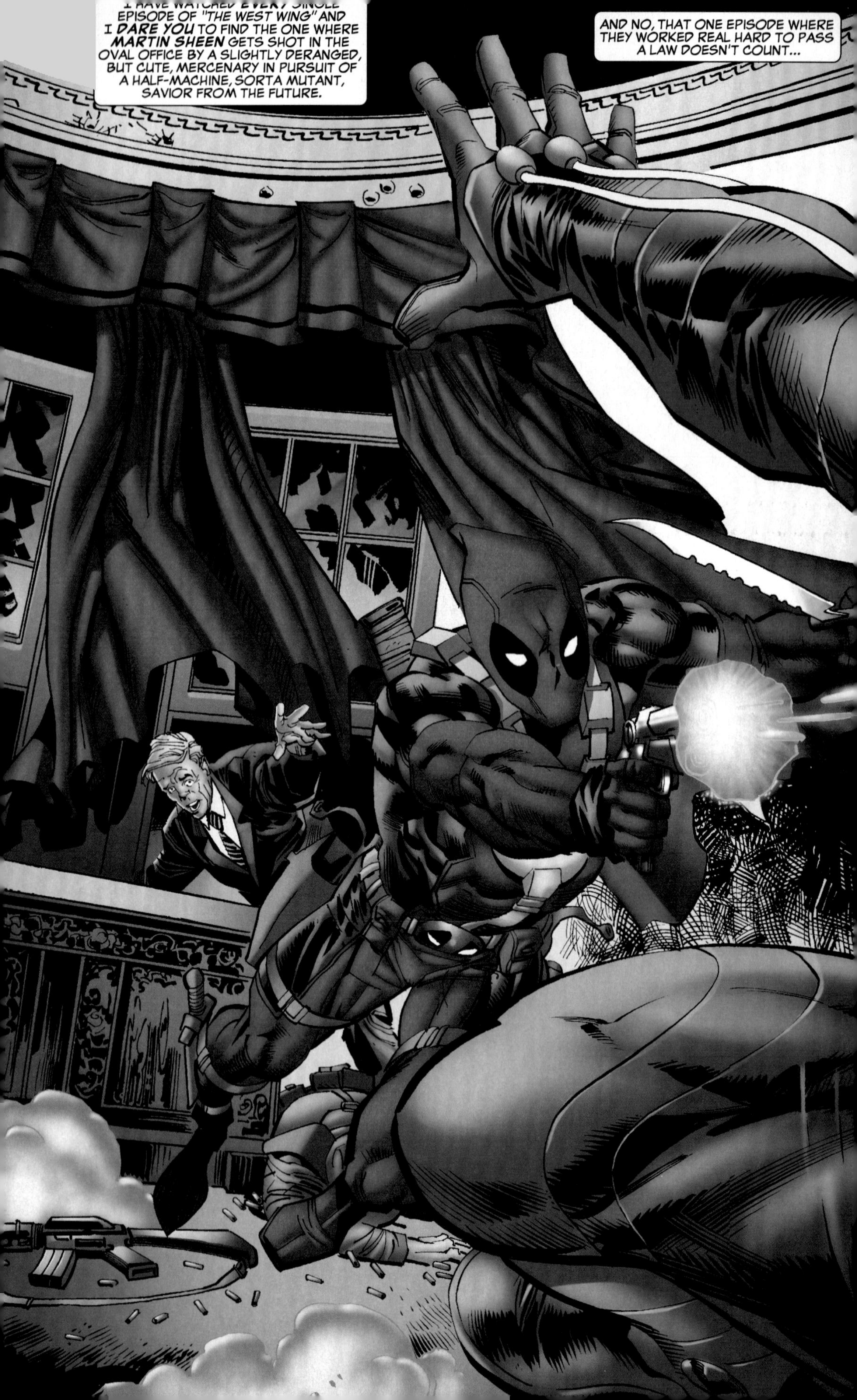
EPISODE OF "THE WEST WING" AND I DARE YOU TO FIND THE ONE WHERE MARTIN SHEEN GETS SHOT IN THE OVAL OFFICE BY A SLIGHTLY DERANGED, BUT CUTE, MERCENARY IN PURSUIT OF A HALF-MACHINE, SORTA MUTANT, SAVIOR FROM THE FUTURE.
AND NO, THAT ONE EPISODE WHERE THEY WORKED REAL HARD TO PASS A LAW DOESN'T COUNT...

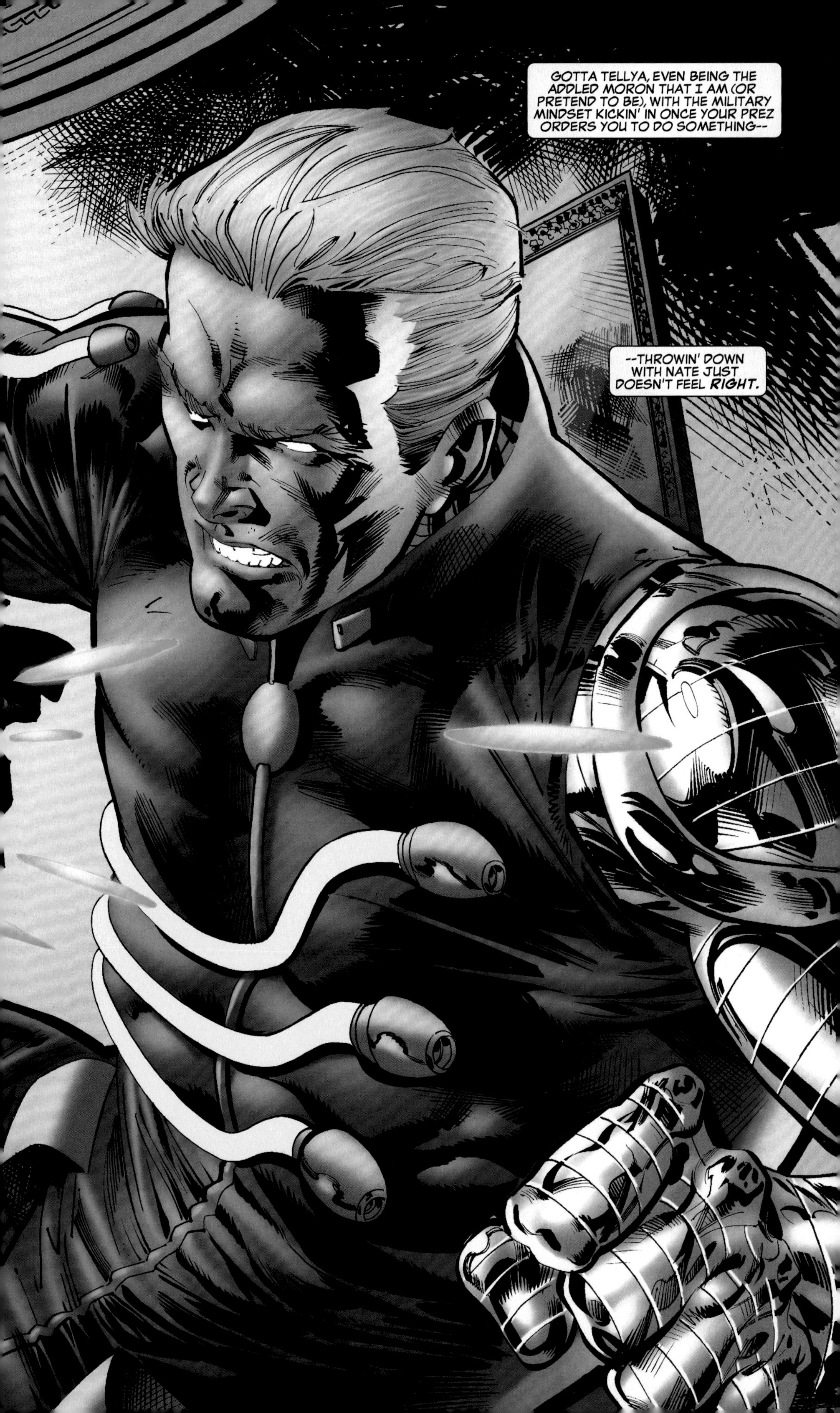
GOTTA TELLYA, EVEN BEING THE ADDLED MORON THAT I AM (OR PRETEND TO BE), WITH THE MILITARY MINDSET KICKIN' IN ONCE YOUR PREZ ORDERS YOU TO DO SOMETHING--
--THROWIN' DOWN WITH NATE JUST DOESN'T FEEL RIGHT.

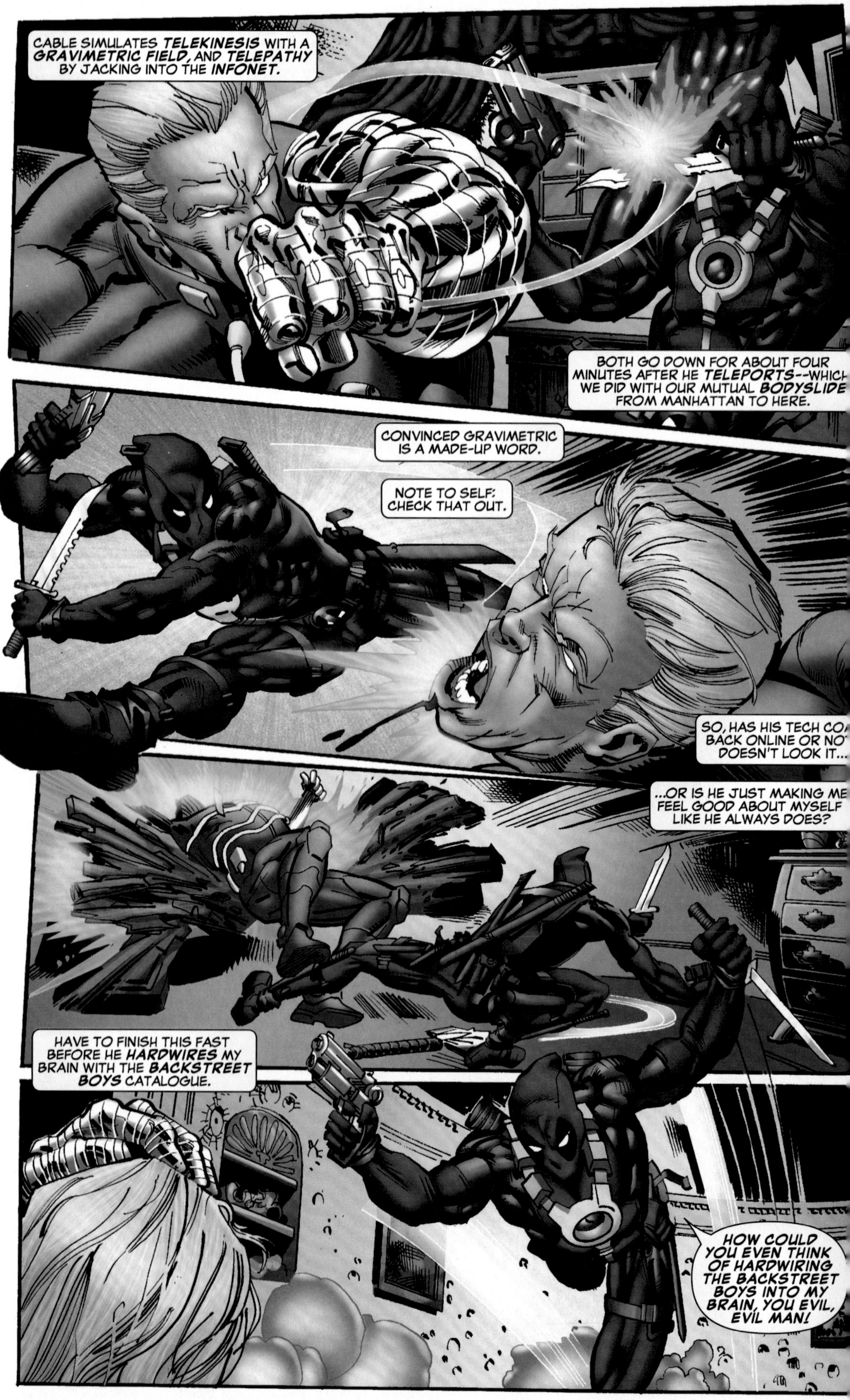
CABLE SIMULATES TELEKINESIS WITH A GRAVIMETRIC FIELD, AND TELEPATHY BY JACKING INTO THE INFONET.
BOTH GO DOWN FOR ABOUT FOUR MINUTES AFTER HE TELEPORTS--WHICH WE DID WITH OUR MUTUAL BODYSLIDE FROM MANHATTAN TO HERE.
CONVINCED GRAVIMETRIC IS A MADE-UP WORD.
NOTE TO SELF: CHECK THAT OUT.
SO, HAS HIS TECH CO BACK ONLINE OR NO DOESN'T LOOK IT...
...OR IS HE JUST MAKING ME FEEL GOOD ABOUT MYSELF LIKE HE ALWAYS DOES?
HAVE TO FINISH THIS FAST BEFORE HE HARDWIRES MY BRAIN WITH THE BACKSTREET BOYS CATALOGUE.
HOW COULD YOU EVEN THINK OF HARDWIRING THE BACKSTREET BOYS INTO MY BRAIN, YOU EVIL, EVIL MAN!

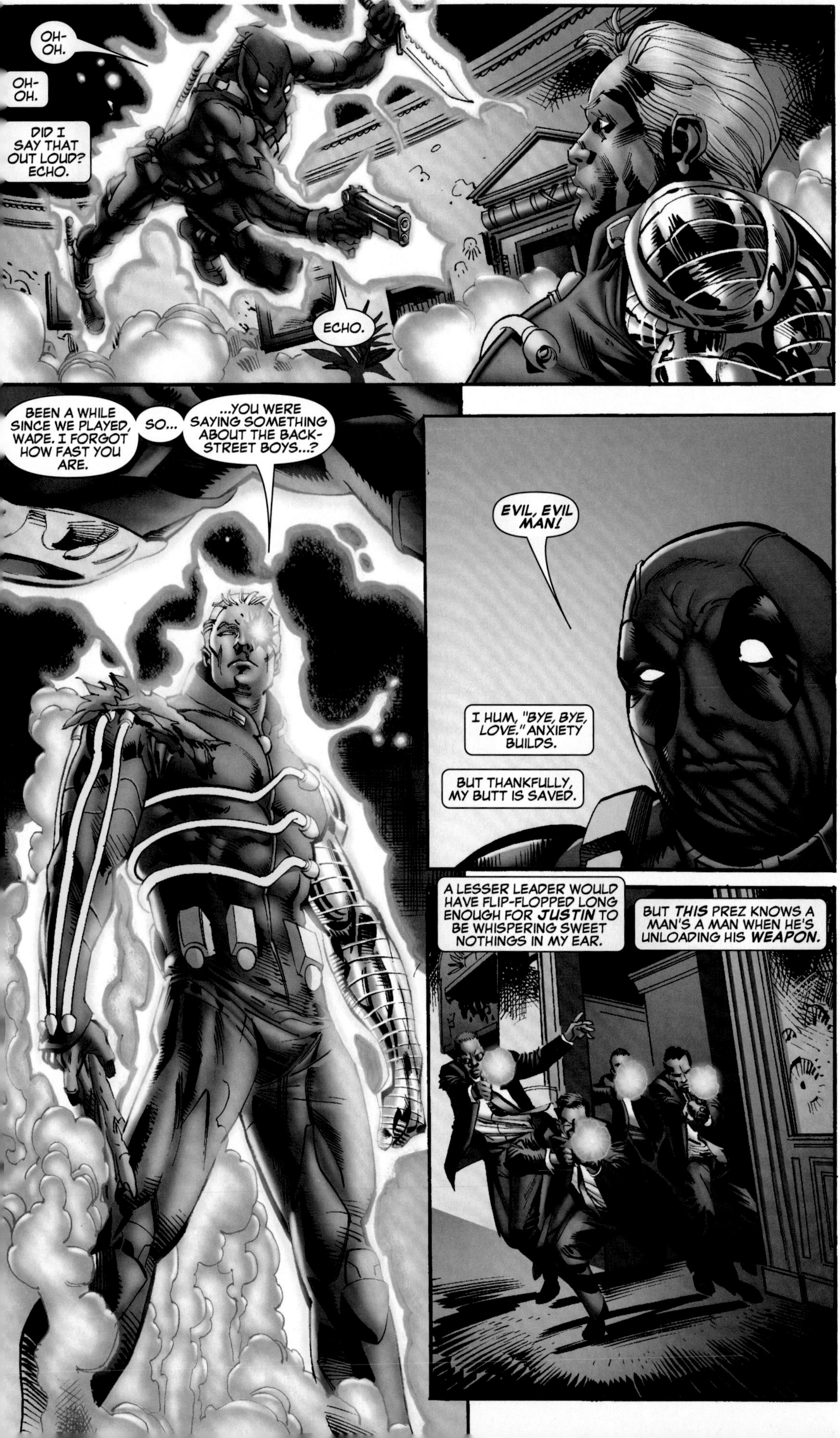
OH-OH.
OH-OH.
DID I SAY THAT OUT LOUD? ECHO.
ECHO.
BEEN A WHILE SINCE WE PLAYED, WADE. I FORGOT HOW FAST YOU ARE.
SO...
...YOU WERE SAYING SOMETHING ABOUT THE BACK-STREET BOYS...?
EVIL, EVIL MAN!
I HUM, "BYE, BYE, LOVE." ANXIETY BUILDS.
BUT THANKFULLY, MY BUTT IS SAVED.
A LESSER LEADER WOULD HAVE FLIP-FLOPPED LONG ENOUGH FOR JUSTIN TO BE WHISPERING SWEET NOTHINGS IN MY EAR.
BUT THIS PREZ KNOWS A MAN'S A MAN WHEN HE'S UNLOADING HIS WEAPON.

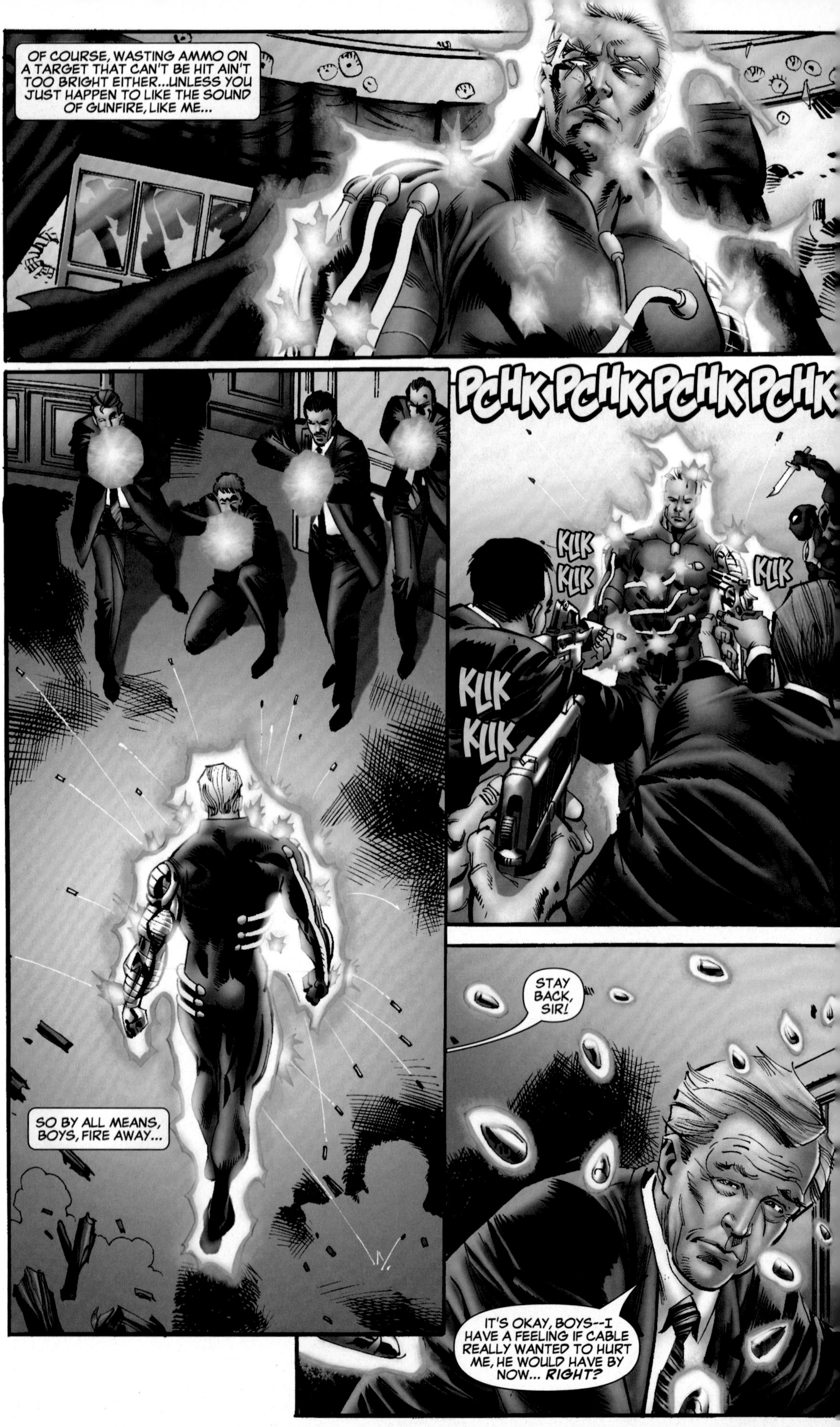
OF COURSE, WASTING AMMO ON A TARGET THAT CAN'T BE HIT AIN'T TOO BRIGHT EITHER...UNLESS YOU JUST HAPPEN TO LIKE THE SOUND OF GUNFIRE, LIKE ME...
SO BY ALL MEANS, BOYS, FIRE AWAY...
PCHK PCHK PCHK PCHK
KLIK
KLIK
KLIK
KLIK
KLIK
STAY BACK, SIR!
IT'S OKAY, BOYS--I HAVE A FEELING IF CABLE REALLY WANTED TO HURT ME, HE WOULD HAVE BY NOW... RIGHT?

FIRST THING I SAID WAS THAT I ONLY CAME TO TALK.

MY STAFF MUST'VE MISSED THE APPOINTMENT YOU MADE THROUGH PROPER DIPLOMATIC CHANNELS.

BUT SINCE THE GOVERNMENT DOESN'T RECOGNIZE MY PRESIDENCY IN RUMEKISTAN, WOULD THEY HAVE TAKEN MY CALL?

SEE, THAT'S THE TICKET, MR. PREZ-- KEEP NATE BUSY.

LONG AS HE'S BUSY TRYING TO CONVINCE YOU OF HOW SMART HE IS, THEN HE'S NOT SHOWING YOU HOW TOUGH HE IS.

MARINES'RE SCRAMBLED. WHITE HOUSE IS SURROUNDED. THERE IS NO WAY THIS ENDS WELL FOR YOU.

DEPENDS ON YOUR DEFINITION OF "WELL."

THEY CAN'T GET THROUGH THE GRAVITY SHIELD CABLE SET UP.

OKAY, NATE, GUESS YOU WIN--IF YOU CALL A COMPLETE STALEMATED WASTE OF TIME A VICTORY...

...BUT WHAT THE HECK HAVE YOU "WON"--?

NATE'S JAW UNCLENCHES JUST A BIT. NOW LET'S SEE IF THAT'S A GOOD THING OR NOT...

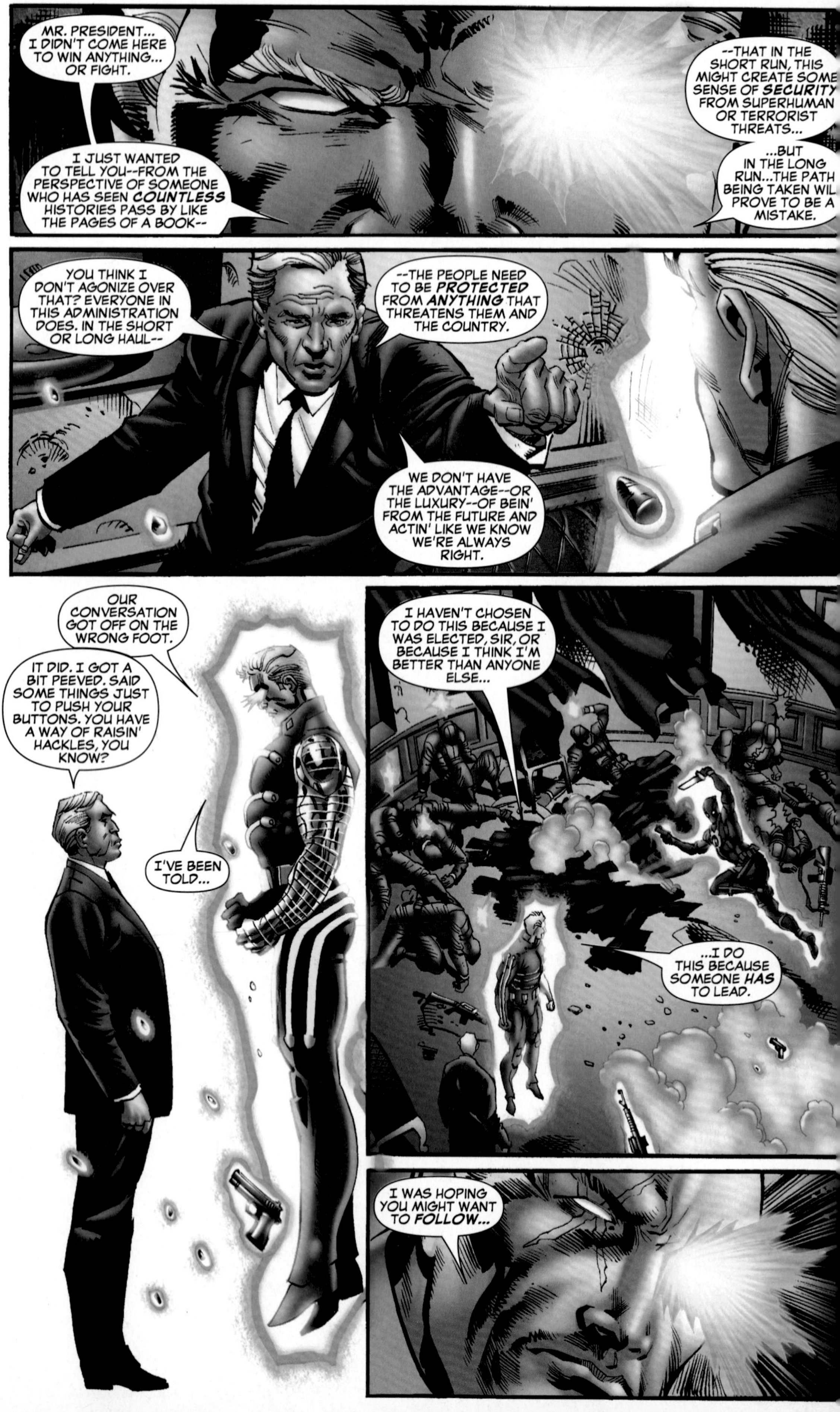
MR. PRESIDENT... I DIDN'T COME HERE TO WIN ANYTHING... OR FIGHT.
I JUST WANTED TO TELL YOU--FROM THE PERSPECTIVE OF SOMEONE WHO HAS SEEN COUNTLESS HISTORIES PASS BY LIKE THE PAGES OF A BOOK--
--THAT IN THE SHORT RUN, THIS MIGHT CREATE SOME SENSE OF SECURITY FROM SUPERHUMAN OR TERRORIST THREATS...
...BUT IN THE LONG RUN...THE PATH BEING TAKEN WIL PROVE TO BE A MISTAKE.
YOU THINK I DON'T AGONIZE OVER THAT? EVERYONE IN THIS ADMINISTRATION DOES. IN THE SHORT OR LONG HAUL--
--THE PEOPLE NEED TO BE PROTECTED FROM ANYTHING THAT THREATENS THEM AND THE COUNTRY.
WE DON'T HAVE THE ADVANTAGE--OR THE LUXURY--OF BEIN' FROM THE FUTURE AND ACTIN' LIKE WE KNOW WE'RE ALWAYS RIGHT.
OUR CONVERSATION GOT OFF ON THE WRONG FOOT.
IT DID. I GOT A BIT PEEVED. SAID SOME THINGS JUST TO PUSH YOUR BUTTONS. YOU HAVE A WAY OF RAISIN' HACKLES, YOU KNOW?
I'VE BEEN TOLD...
I HAVEN'T CHOSEN TO DO THIS BECAUSE I WAS ELECTED, SIR, OR BECAUSE I THINK I'M BETTER THAN ANYONE ELSE...
...I DO THIS BECAUSE SOMEONE HAS TO LEAD.
I WAS HOPING YOU MIGHT WANT TO FOLLOW...

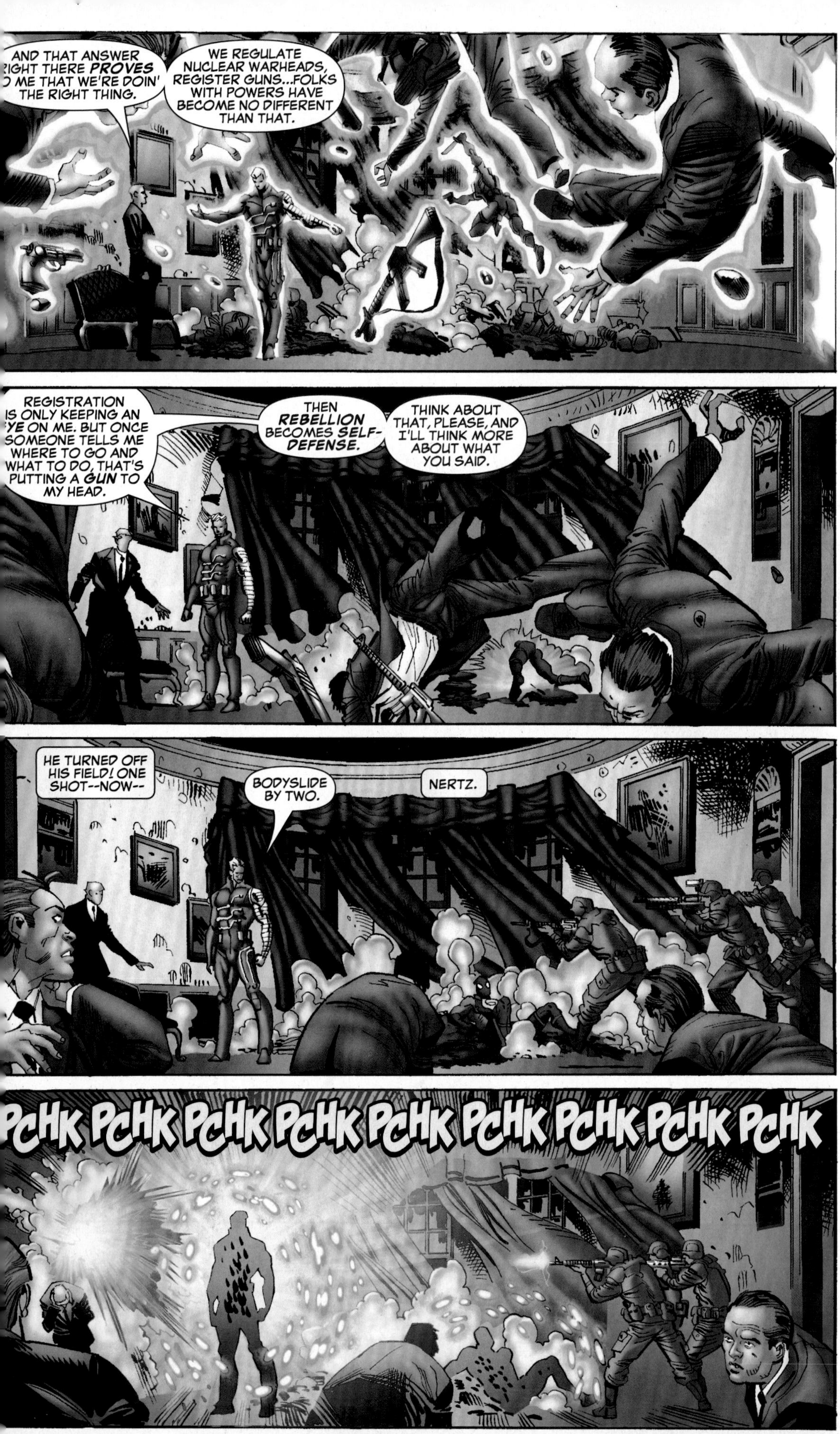

AND THAT ANSWER RIGHT THERE PROVES TO ME THAT WE'RE DOIN' THE RIGHT THING.
WE REGULATE NUCLEAR WARHEADS, REGISTER GUNS...FOLKS WITH POWERS HAVE BECOME NO DIFFERENT THAN THAT.
REGISTRATION IS ONLY KEEPING AN EYE ON ME. BUT ONCE SOMEONE TELLS ME WHERE TO GO AND WHAT TO DO, THAT'S PUTTING A GUN TO MY HEAD.
THEN REBELLION BECOMES SELF-DEFENSE.
THINK ABOUT THAT, PLEASE, AND I'LL THINK MORE ABOUT WHAT YOU SAID.
HE TURNED OFF HIS FIELD! ONE SHOT--NOW--
BODYSLIDE BY TWO.
NERTZ.
PCHK PCHK PCHK PCHK PCHK PCHK PCHK PCHK PCHK

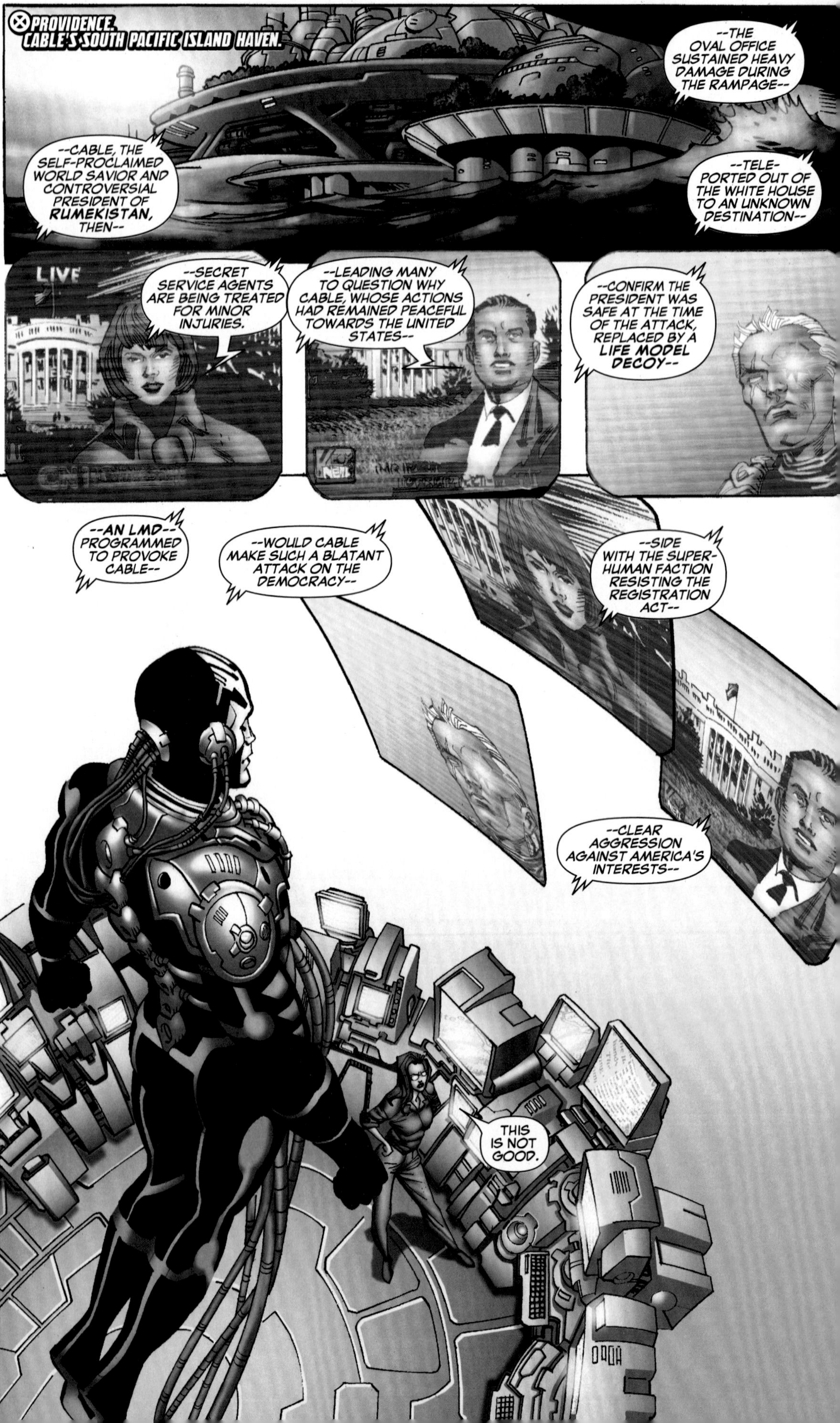
PROVIDENCE. CABLE'S SOUTH PACIFIC ISLAND HAVEN.
--CABLE, THE SELF-PROCLAIMED WORLD SAVIOR AND CONTROVERSIAL PRESIDENT OF RUMEKISTAN, THEN--
--THE OVAL OFFICE SUSTAINED HEAVY DAMAGE DURING THE RAMPAGE--
--TELE-PORTED OUT OF THE WHITE HOUSE TO AN UNKNOWN DESTINATION--
LIVE
--SECRET SERVICE AGENTS ARE BEING TREATED FOR MINOR INJURIES.
--LEADING MANY TO QUESTION WHY CABLE, WHOSE ACTIONS HAD REMAINED PEACEFUL TOWARDS THE UNITED STATES--
--CONFIRM THE PRESIDENT WAS SAFE AT THE TIME OF THE ATTACK, REPLACED BY A LIFE MODEL DECOY--
--AN LMD-- PROGRAMMED TO PROVOKE CABLE--
--WOULD CABLE MAKE SUCH A BLATANT ATTACK ON THE DEMOCRACY--
--SIDE WITH THE SUPER-HUMAN FACTION RESISTING THE REGISTRATION ACT--
--CLEAR AGGRESSION AGAINST AMERICA'S INTERESTS--
THIS IS NOT GOOD.

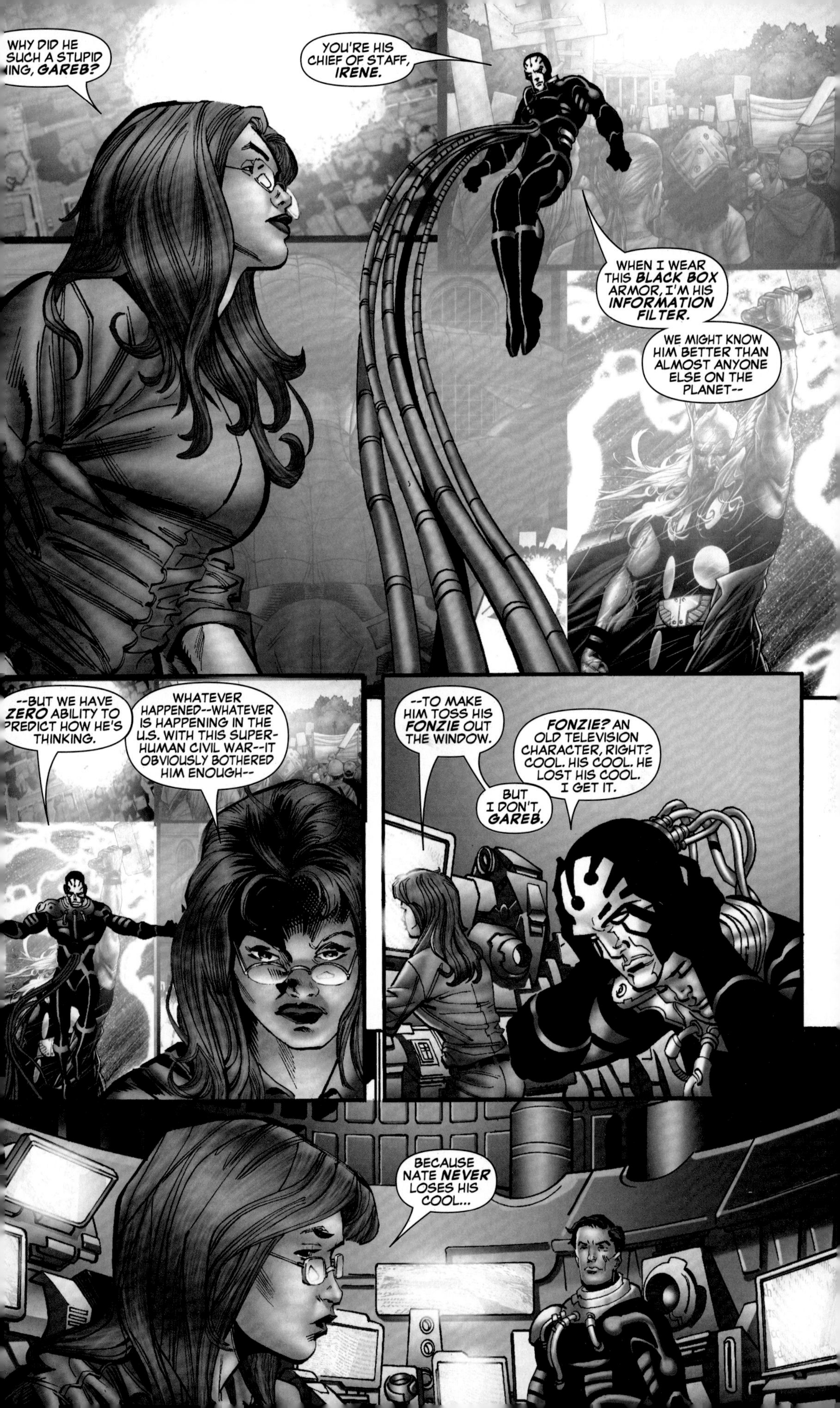

WHY DID HE SUCH A STUPID ING, GAREB?
YOU'RE HIS CHIEF OF STAFF, IRENE.
WHEN I WEAR THIS BLACK BOX ARMOR, I'M HIS INFORMATION FILTER.
WE MIGHT KNOW HIM BETTER THAN ALMOST ANYONE ELSE ON THE PLANET--
--BUT WE HAVE ZERO ABILITY TO PREDICT HOW HE'S THINKING.
WHATEVER HAPPENED--WHATEVER IS HAPPENING IN THE U.S. WITH THIS SUPER-HUMAN CIVIL WAR--IT OBVIOUSLY BOTHERED HIM ENOUGH--
--TO MAKE HIM TOSS HIS FONZIE OUT THE WINDOW.
FONZIE? AN OLD TELEVISION CHARACTER, RIGHT? COOL. HIS COOL. HE LOST HIS COOL. I GET IT.
BUT I DON'T, GAREB.
BECAUSE NATE NEVER LOSES HIS COOL...

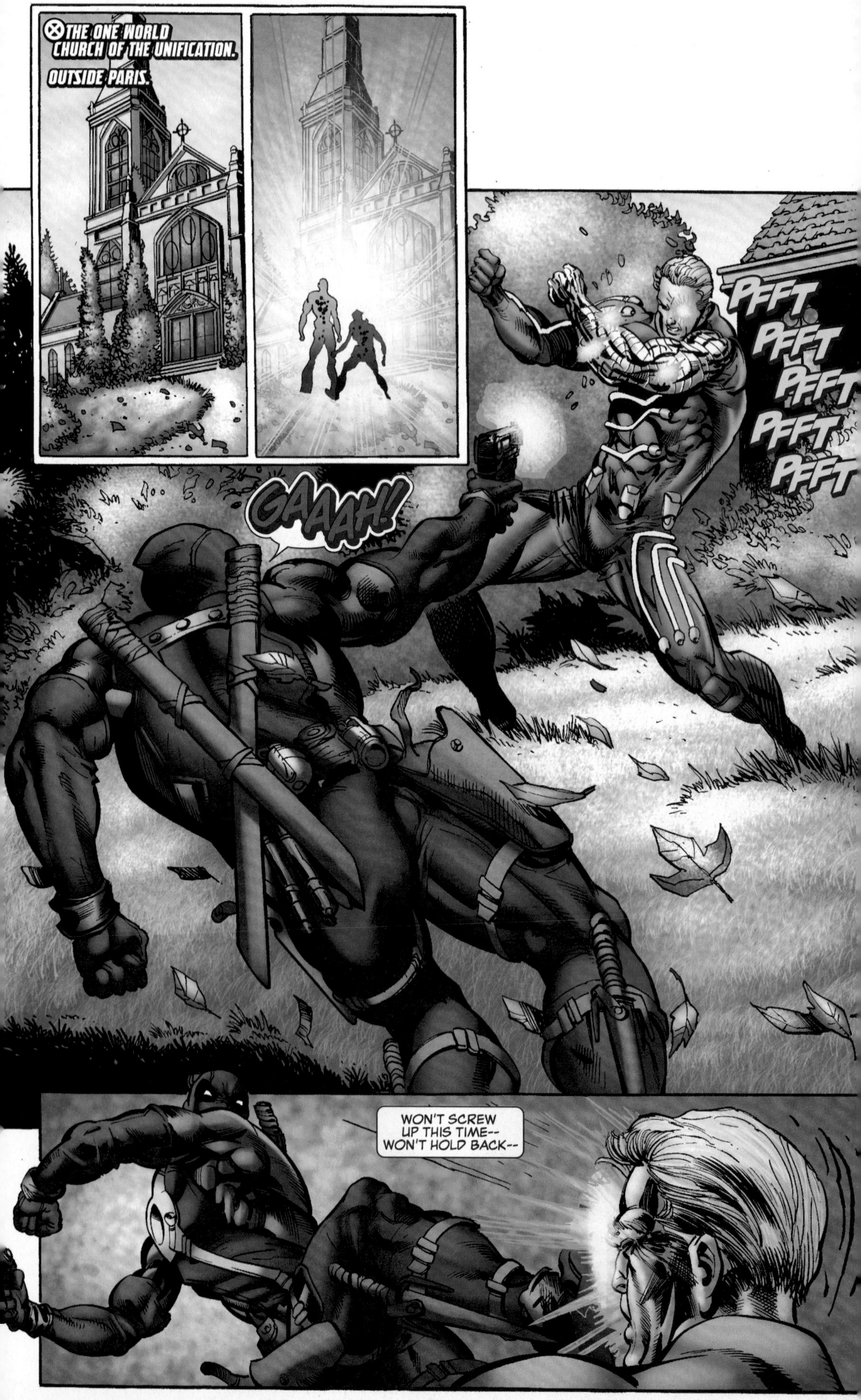
THE ONE WORLD CHURCH OF THE UNIFICATION.
OUTSIDE PARIS.
PFFT
PFFT
PFFT
PFFT
PFFT
GAAAH!
WON'T SCREW UP THIS TIME-- WON'T HOLD BACK--

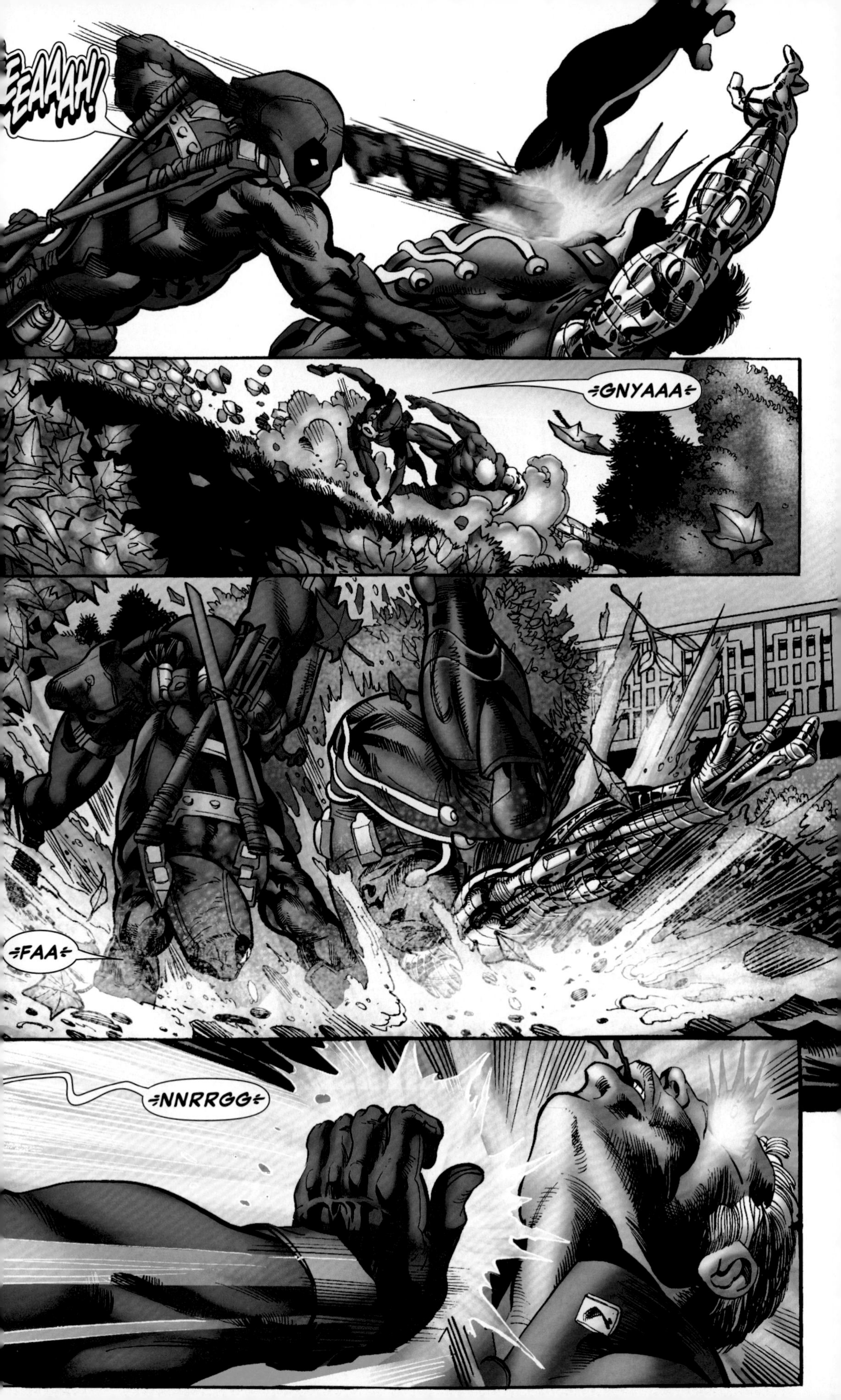
EEAAAH!
GNYAAA
FAA
NNRRGG

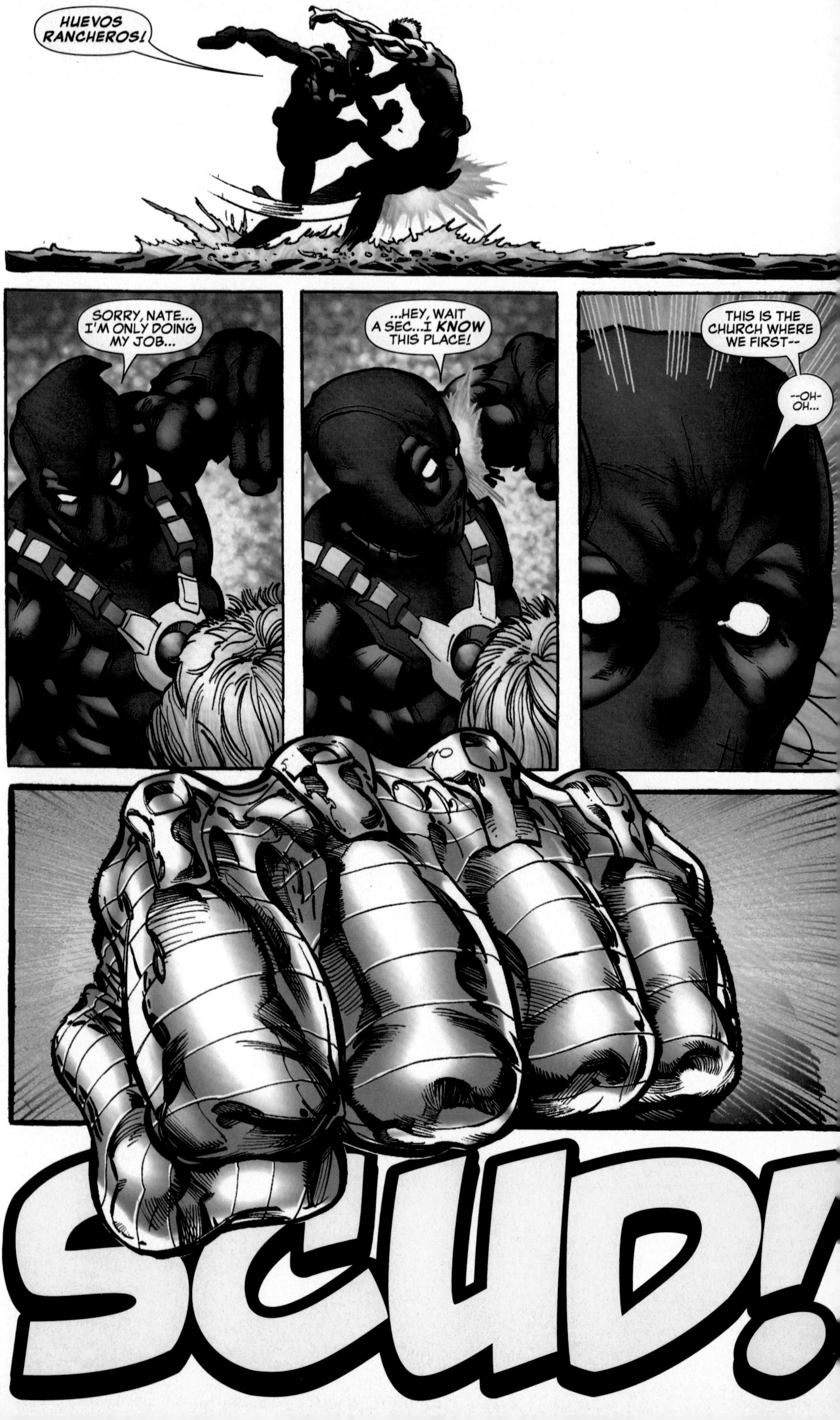
HUEVOS RANCHEROS!
SORRY, NATE... I'M ONLY DOING MY JOB...
...HEY, WAIT A SEC...I KNOW THIS PLACE!
THIS IS THE CHURCH WHERE WE FIRST--
--OH-OH...
SCUD!

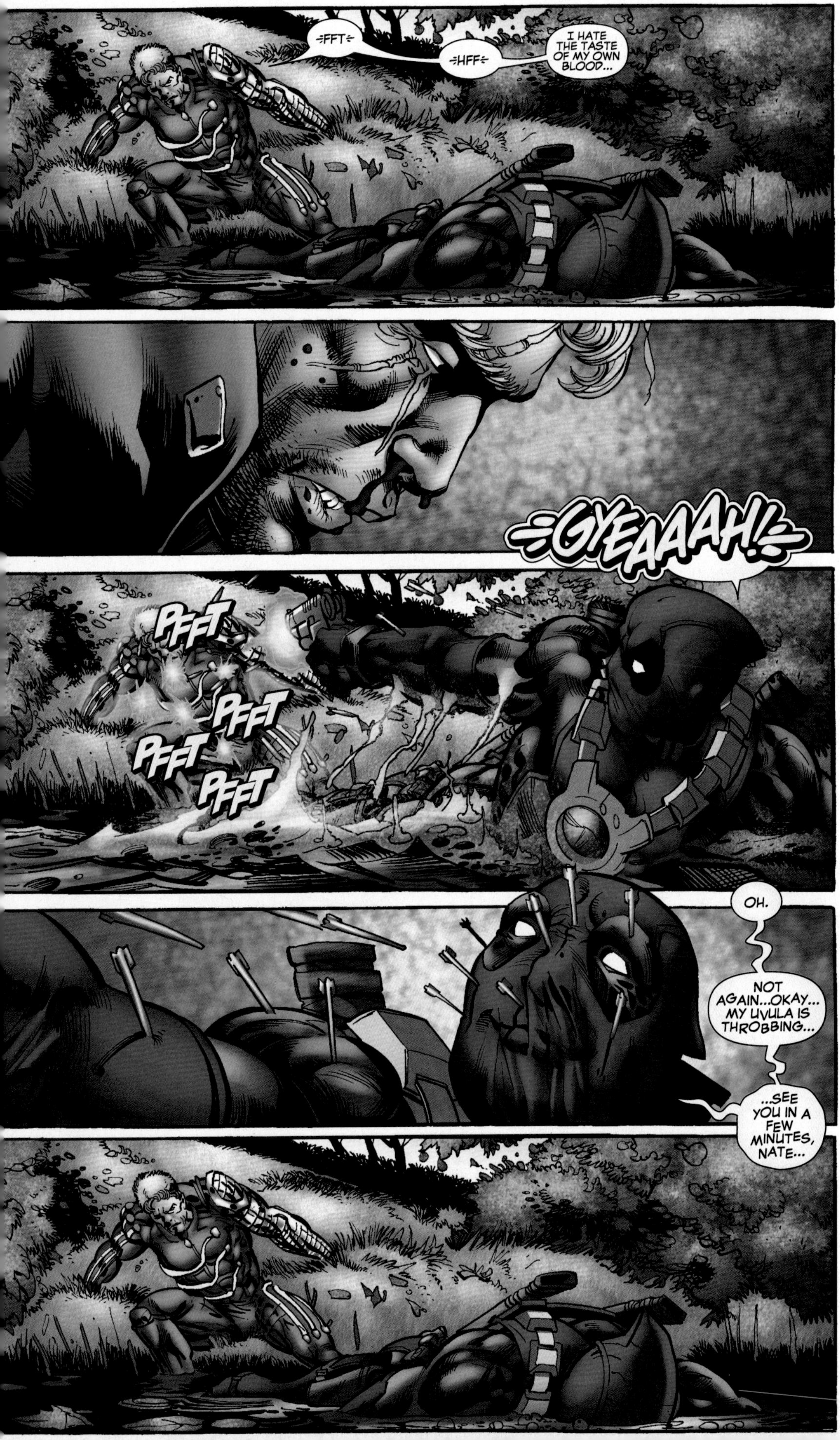

FFT
HFF
I HATE THE TASTE OF MY OWN BLOOD...
GYEAAAH!
PFFT
PFFT
PFFT
PFFT
OH.
NOT AGAIN...OKAY... MY UVULA IS THROBBING...
...SEE YOU IN A FEW MINUTES, NATE...

...NO, DON'T TICKLE ME THERE... YOU NAUGHTY, NAUGHTY...

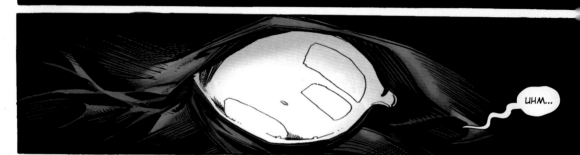

UHM...

THE USUAL DREAM, HUH?

PRETTY MUCH.

I BROKE YOUR NOSE, HUH? THAT'S FUNNY.

I DUCT TAPED YOU AGAIN. THAT'S FUNNY, TOO.

SHOULD WE JUST WAIT UNTIL NATURE CALLS AGAIN?

EVIL, EVIL MAN!

HEY, HOW COME WE HAVE AN AUDIENCE?

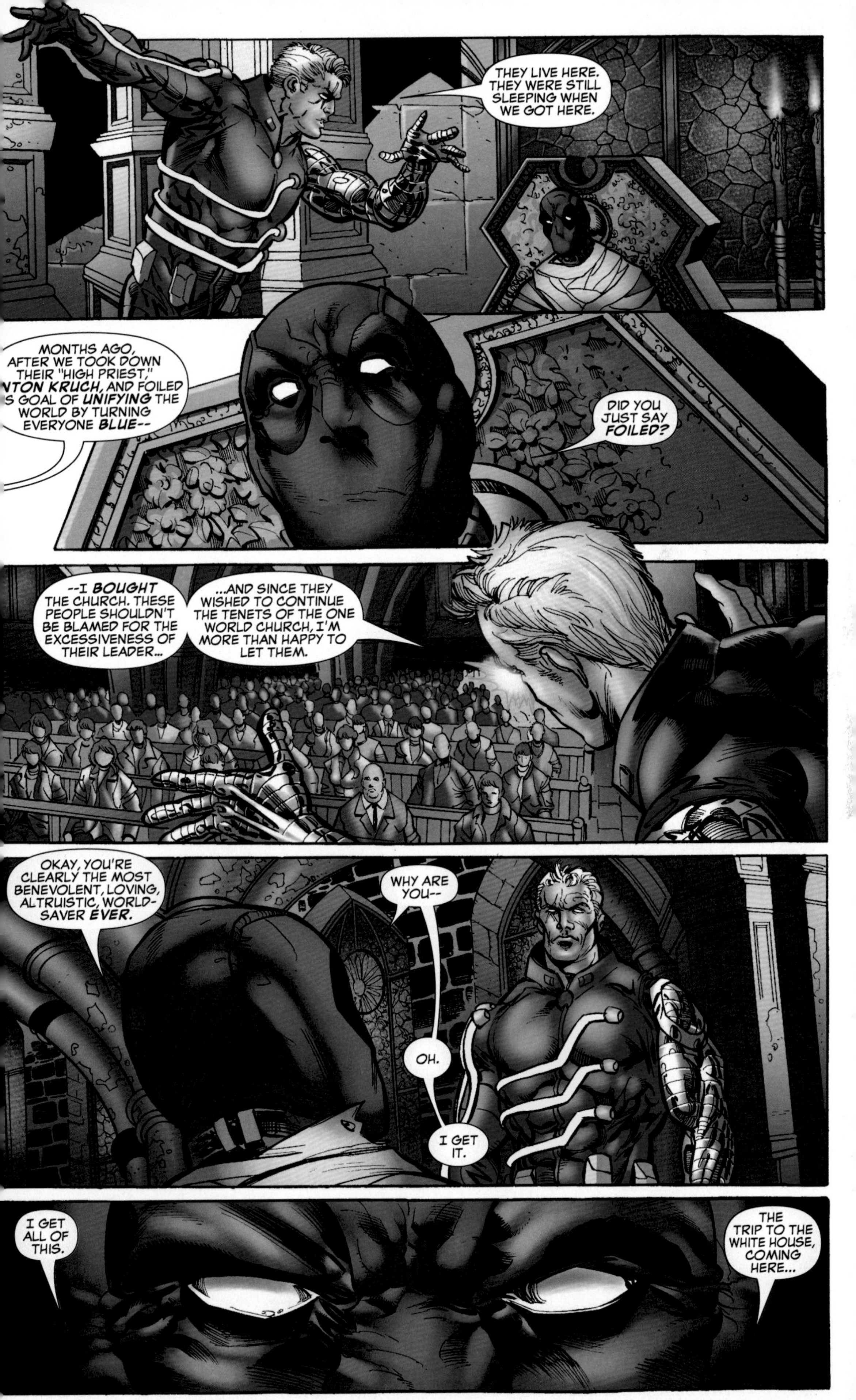

THEY LIVE HERE. THEY WERE STILL SLEEPING WHEN WE GOT HERE.
MONTHS AGO, AFTER WE TOOK DOWN THEIR "HIGH PRIEST," NTON KRUCH, AND FOILED S GOAL OF UNIFYING THE WORLD BY TURNING EVERYONE BLUE--
DID YOU JUST SAY FOILED?
--I BOUGHT THE CHURCH. THESE PEOPLE SHOULDN'T BE BLAMED FOR THE EXCESSIVENESS OF THEIR LEADER...
...AND SINCE THEY WISHED TO CONTINUE THE TENETS OF THE ONE WORLD CHURCH, I'M MORE THAN HAPPY TO LET THEM.
OKAY, YOU'RE CLEARLY THE MOST BENEVOLENT, LOVING, ALTRUISTIC, WORLD-SAVER EVER.
WHY ARE YOU--
OH.
I GET IT.
I GET ALL OF THIS.
THE TRIP TO THE WHITE HOUSE, COMING HERE...

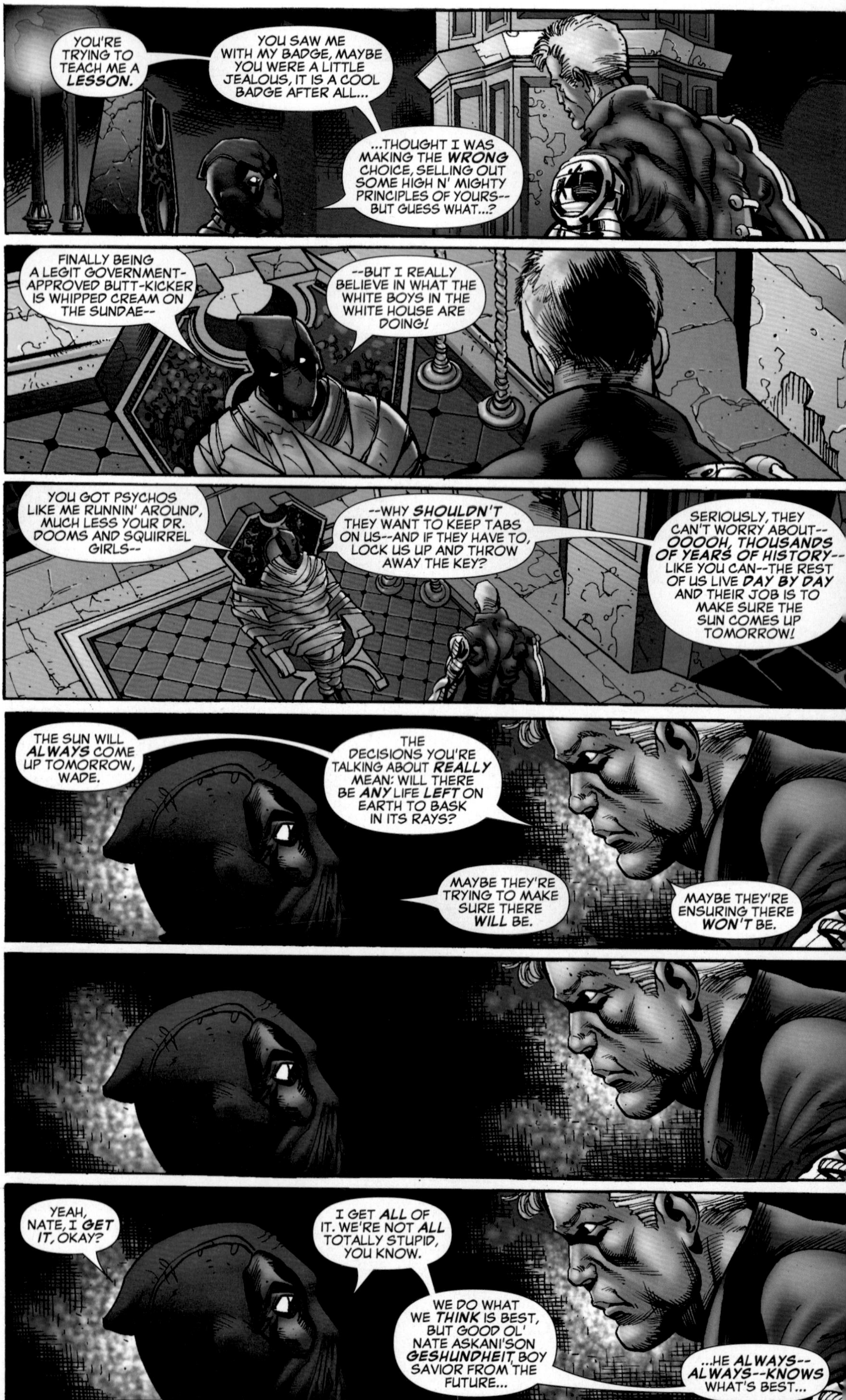

YOU'RE TRYING TO TEACH ME A **LESSON.**
YOU SAW ME WITH MY BADGE, MAYBE YOU WERE A LITTLE JEALOUS, IT IS A COOL BADGE AFTER ALL...
...THOUGHT I WAS MAKING THE **WRONG** CHOICE, SELLING OUT SOME HIGH N' MIGHTY PRINCIPLES OF YOURS-- BUT GUESS WHAT...?
FINALLY BEING A LEGIT GOVERNMENT-APPROVED BUTT-KICKER IS WHIPPED CREAM ON THE SUNDAE--
--BUT I REALLY BELIEVE IN WHAT THE WHITE BOYS IN THE WHITE HOUSE ARE DOING!
YOU GOT PSYCHOS LIKE ME RUNNIN' AROUND, MUCH LESS YOUR DR. DOOMS AND SQUIRREL GIRLS--
--WHY **SHOULDN'T** THEY WANT TO KEEP TABS ON US--AND IF THEY HAVE TO, LOCK US UP AND THROW AWAY THE KEY?
SERIOUSLY, THEY CAN'T WORRY ABOUT-- **OOOOH, THOUSANDS OF YEARS OF HISTORY**-- LIKE YOU CAN--THE REST OF US LIVE **DAY BY DAY** AND THEIR JOB IS TO MAKE SURE THE SUN COMES UP TOMORROW!
THE SUN WILL **ALWAYS** COME UP TOMORROW, WADE.
THE DECISIONS YOU'RE TALKING ABOUT **REALLY** MEAN: WILL THERE BE **ANY** LIFE **LEFT** ON EARTH TO BASK IN ITS RAYS?
MAYBE THEY'RE TRYING TO MAKE SURE THERE **WILL** BE.
MAYBE THEY'RE ENSURING THERE **WON'T** BE.
YEAH, NATE, I **GET IT**, OKAY?
I GET **ALL** OF IT. WE'RE NOT **ALL** TOTALLY STUPID, YOU KNOW.
WE DO WHAT WE **THINK** IS BEST, BUT GOOD OL' NATE ASKANI'SON **GESHUNDHEIT**, BOY SAVIOR FROM THE FUTURE...
...HE **ALWAYS**-- **ALWAYS--KNOWS** WHAT'S BEST...

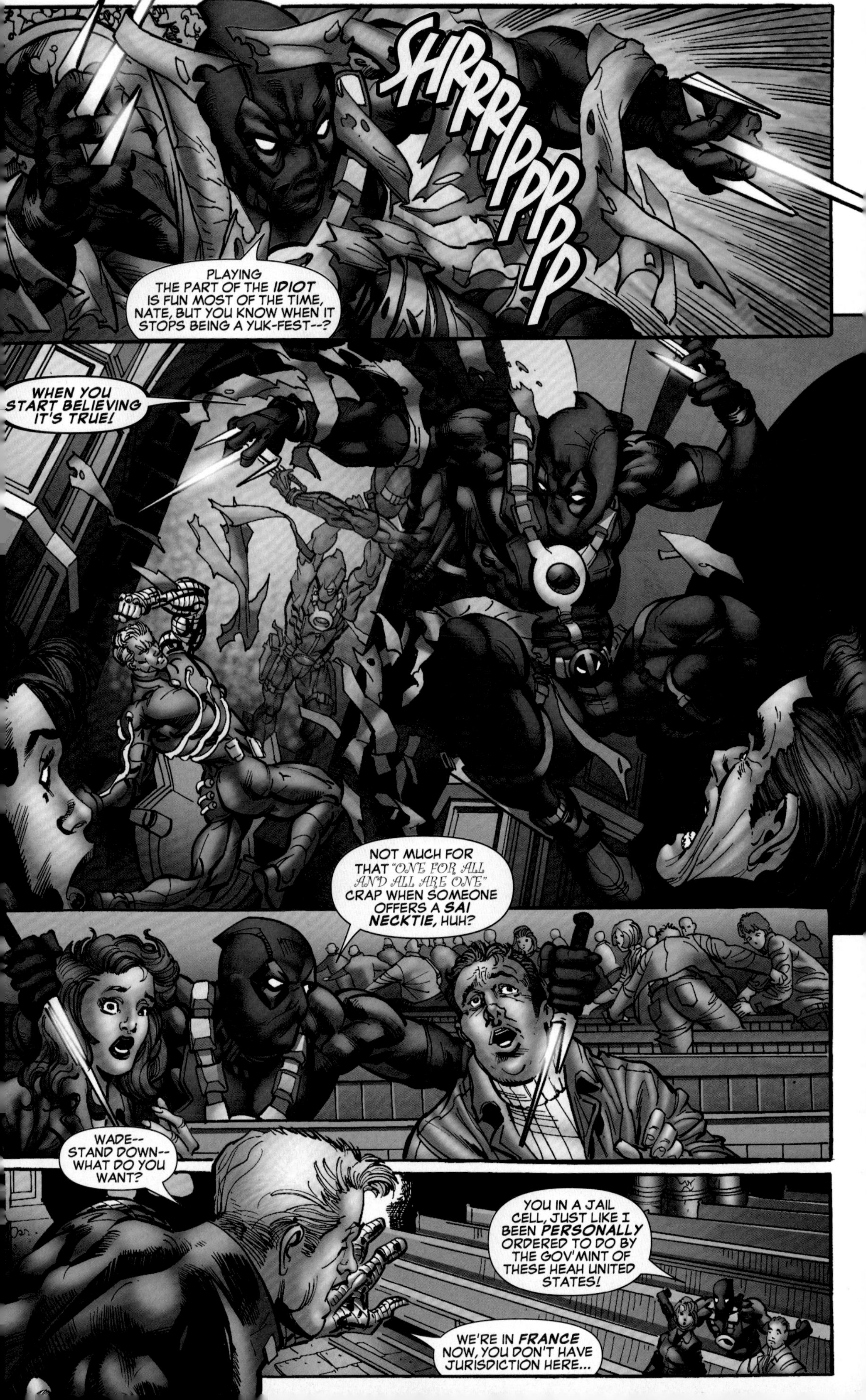
SHRRRIPPPPP
PLAYING THE PART OF THE IDIOT IS FUN MOST OF THE TIME, NATE, BUT YOU KNOW WHEN IT STOPS BEING A YUK-FEST--?
WHEN YOU START BELIEVING IT'S TRUE!
NOT MUCH FOR THAT "ONE FOR ALL AND ALL ARE ONE" CRAP WHEN SOMEONE OFFERS A SAI NECKTIE, HUH?
WADE-- STAND DOWN-- WHAT DO YOU WANT?
YOU IN A JAIL CELL, JUST LIKE I BEEN PERSONALLY ORDERED TO DO BY THE GOV'MINT OF THESE HEAH UNITED STATES!
WE'RE IN FRANCE NOW, YOU DON'T HAVE JURISDICTION HERE...

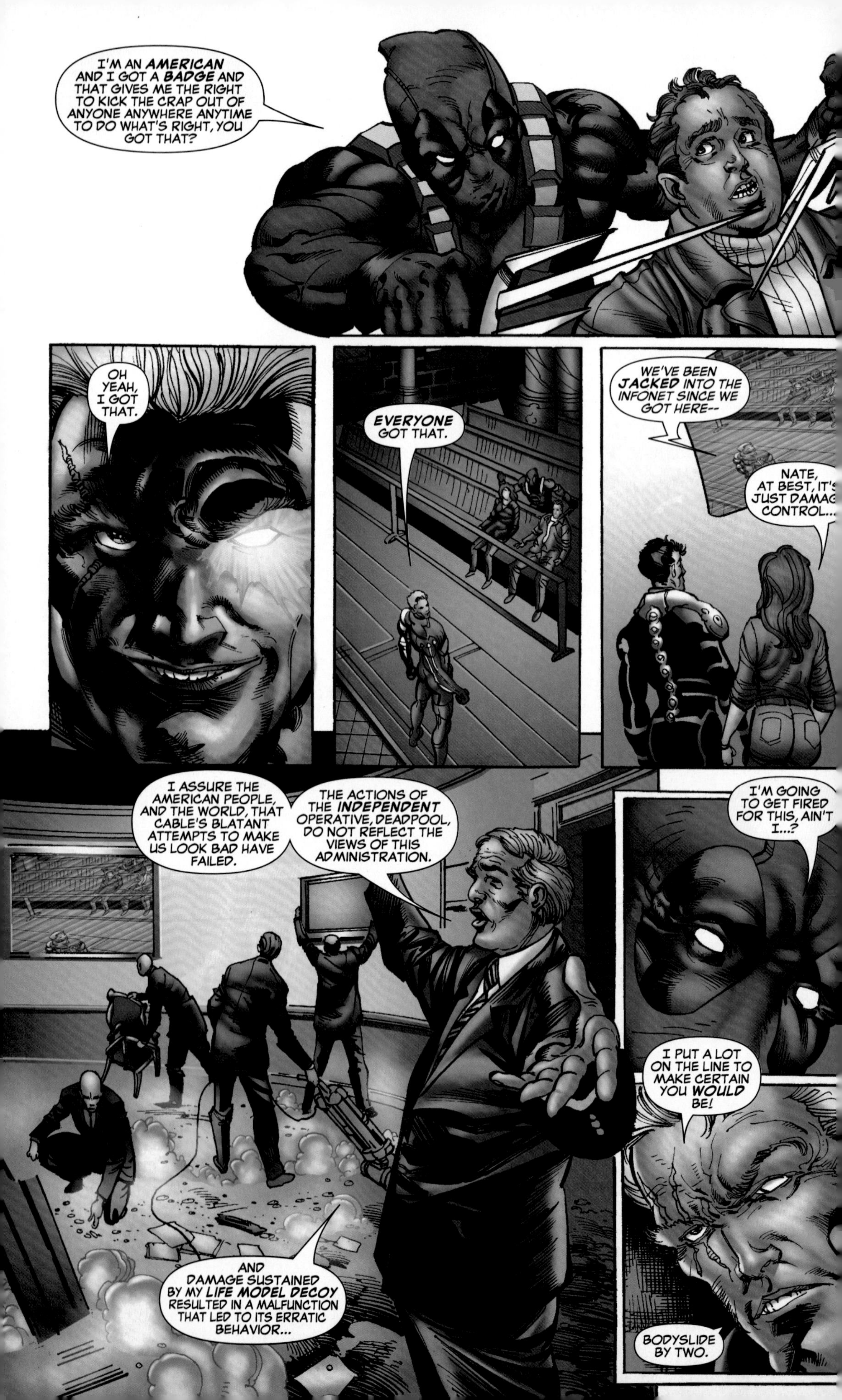

I'M AN AMERICAN AND I GOT A BADGE AND THAT GIVES ME THE RIGHT TO KICK THE CRAP OUT OF ANYONE ANYWHERE ANYTIME TO DO WHAT'S RIGHT, YOU GOT THAT?
OH YEAH, I GOT THAT.
EVERYONE GOT THAT.
WE'VE BEEN JACKED INTO THE INFONET SINCE WE GOT HERE--
NATE, AT BEST, IT'S JUST DAMAG CONTROL...
I ASSURE THE AMERICAN PEOPLE, AND THE WORLD, THAT CABLE'S BLATANT ATTEMPTS TO MAKE US LOOK BAD HAVE FAILED.
THE ACTIONS OF THE INDEPENDENT OPERATIVE, DEADPOOL, DO NOT REFLECT THE VIEWS OF THIS ADMINISTRATION.
AND DAMAGE SUSTAINED BY MY LIFE MODEL DECOY RESULTED IN A MALFUNCTION THAT LED TO ITS ERRATIC BEHAVIOR...
I'M GOING TO GET FIRED FOR THIS, AIN'T I...?
I PUT A LOT ON THE LINE TO MAKE CERTAIN YOU WOULD BE!
BODYSLIDE BY TWO.

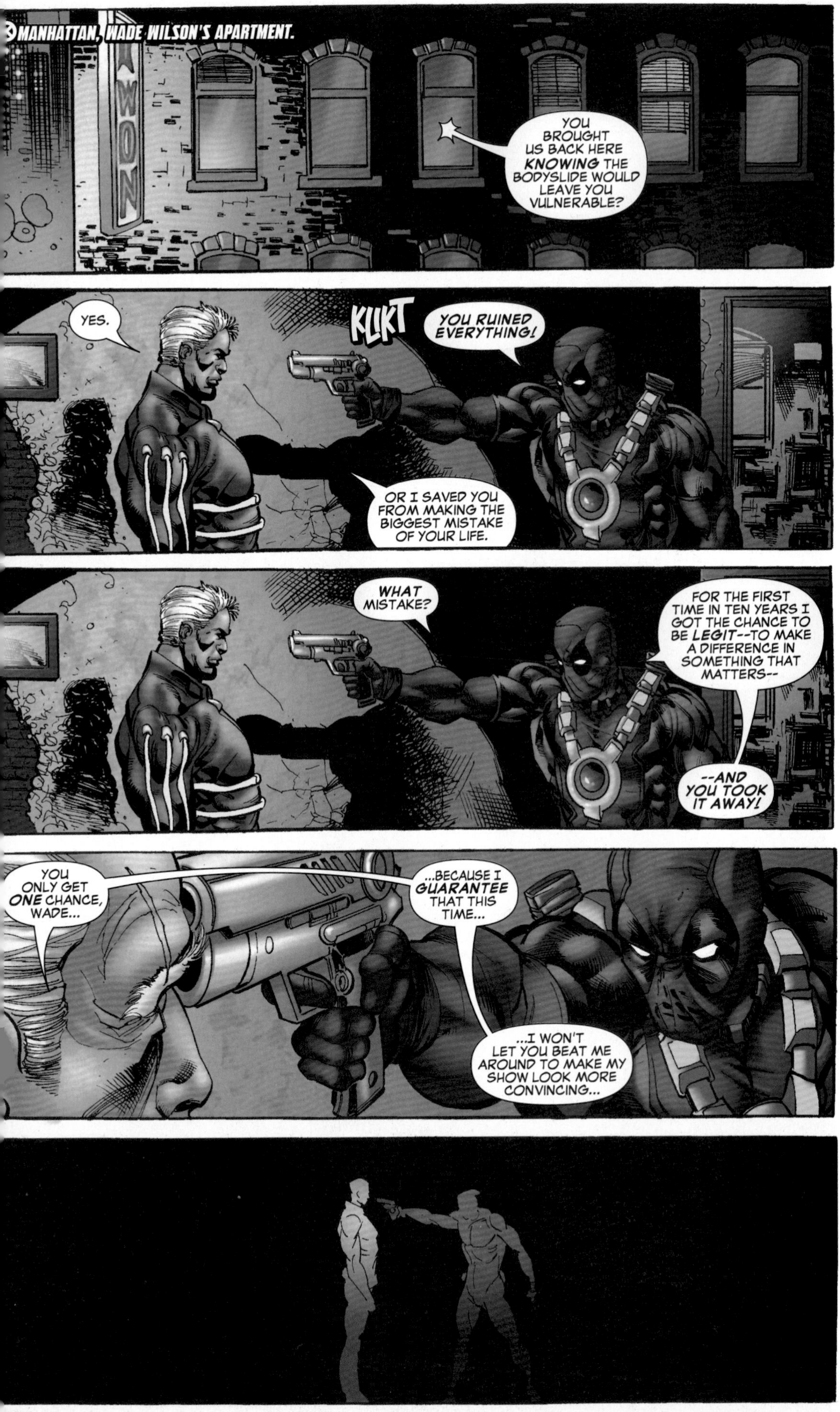
MANHATTAN, WADE WILSON'S APARTMENT.
YOU BROUGHT US BACK HERE KNOWING THE BODYSLIDE WOULD LEAVE YOU VULNERABLE?
YES.
KLIKT
YOU RUINED EVERYTHING!
OR I SAVED YOU FROM MAKING THE BIGGEST MISTAKE OF YOUR LIFE.
WHAT MISTAKE?
FOR THE FIRST TIME IN TEN YEARS I GOT THE CHANCE TO BE LEGIT--TO MAKE A DIFFERENCE IN SOMETHING THAT MATTERS--
--AND YOU TOOK IT AWAY!
YOU ONLY GET ONE CHANCE, WADE...
...BECAUSE I GUARANTEE THAT THIS TIME...
...I WON'T LET YOU BEAT ME AROUND TO MAKE MY SHOW LOOK MORE CONVINCING...

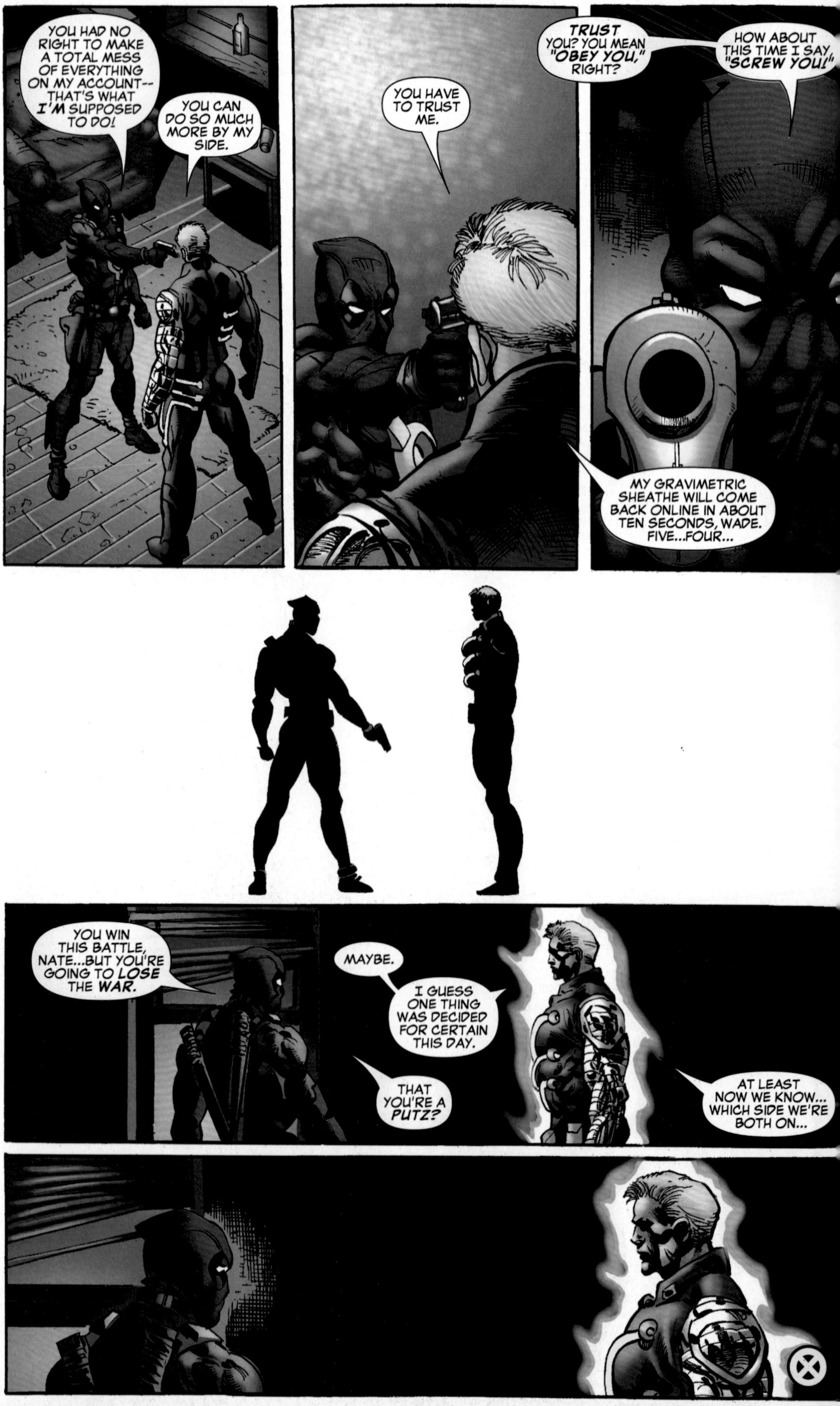
YOU HAD NO RIGHT TO MAKE A TOTAL MESS OF EVERYTHING ON MY ACCOUNT-- THAT'S WHAT I'M SUPPOSED TO DO!
YOU CAN DO SO MUCH MORE BY MY SIDE.
YOU HAVE TO TRUST ME.
TRUST YOU? YOU MEAN "OBEY YOU," RIGHT?
HOW ABOUT THIS TIME I SAY, "SCREW YOU!"
MY GRAVIMETRIC SHEATHE WILL COME BACK ONLINE IN ABOUT TEN SECONDS, WADE. FIVE...FOUR...
YOU WIN THIS BATTLE, NATE...BUT YOU'RE GOING TO LOSE THE WAR.
MAYBE.
I GUESS ONE THING WAS DECIDED FOR CERTAIN THIS DAY.
THAT YOU'RE A PUTZ?
AT LEAST NOW WE KNOW... WHICH SIDE WE'RE BOTH ON...